PRAISE FOR *HUSTLE*

"A first-class work of sound reporting and balanced, piece-by-piece evidence and inescapable conclusions. It's the baseball book we've been awaiting."

—Roger Angell, *The New Yorker*

"Theodore Dreiser would have loved this story, but he could not have written it nearly so well as Michael Y. Sokolove.... [Sokolove] is a 'natural' literary stylist, [with] the gifts of a social historian.... This is a book for all seasons, not just summer."

—*The New York Times Book Review*

"Pete Rose used to brag that the only books he read were the several variations of the 'Pete Rose Story.' He could benefit from reading this one.... [In looking] into the life and milieu of the player they called 'Charlie Hustle,' Sokolove has done us a favor—and, maybe, Rose, too."

—*The Wall Street Journal*

"*Hustle* should be required wrapping for anybody who wants to please and fascinate a sports fan for Christmas. . . . Sokolove follows [Rose's] trail with rueful discipline. . . . 'A man can belong both in the Hall of Fame and in federal prison,' Sokolove writes. But to understand why, you must read *Hustle*."

—*The Sporting News*

"*Hustle* poignantly probes the essence of Pete Rose, from his childhood days through his blatantly lewd lifestyle and his long association—often in his Riverfront Stadium office—with known drug dealers and steroid pushers and gamblers. . . . A touching but sad story. . . . It tells the facts about Rose—both the delightful and the despicable."

—*San Mateo Times*

"Mike Sokolove's riveting new book [is] *Hustle*; if you are, or ever were, a Pete Rose fan, you need to read this book."

—*Baseball America*

"Before [the let's-forgive-Pete-Rose bandwagon] happens, Michael Y. Sokolove's new book needs to be distributed free at all ballparks."

—*The Village Voice*

HUSTLE

THE MYTH, LIFE, AND LIES OF PETE ROSE

Michael Y. Sokolove

A Fireside Book
Published by Simon & Schuster
New York   London   Toronto   Sydney   Tokyo   Singapore

FIRESIDE
Simon & Schuster Building
Rockefeller Center
1230 Avenue of the Americas
New York, New York   10020

First Fireside Edition 1992

FIRESIDE and colophon are registered trademarks
of Simon & Schuster Inc.

Designed by Irving Perkins Associates
Manufactured in the United States of America

10 9 8 7 6 5 4 3 2 1
10 9 8 7 6 5 4 3 2 1 Pbk.

Library of Congress Cataloging-in-Publication Data
Sokolove, Michael Y.
    Hustle: the myth, life, and lies of Pete Rose/Michael Y. Sokolove.
        p. cm.
    Includes index.
    1. Rose, Pete, 1941– . 2. Baseball players—United States—Biography
3. Cincinnati Reds (Baseball team)—History. I. Title.
GV865.R65S66   1990
796.357′092—dc20   90-44900
[B]   CIP

ISBN: 0-671-69503-7
ISBN: 0-671-75970-1 Pbk.

FOR ANN

Acknowledgments

A great many people helped me with this book.

My agent, Michael Carlisle, was a source of support, encouragement, and sound advice at every step of the way. My editor at Simon & Schuster, Jeff Neuman, took a strong hand in shaping and sharpening the book, for which I am grateful.

Numerous friends helped in direct and indirect ways, including Bruce Martin, Carolyn Acker, Matthew Purdy, Bill Eddins, and Larry Eichel.

My parents, who gave me the love of reading, writing, and baseball—in no particular order—lent their enthusiasm to this project, as did Nancy Sokolove, Bob Sokolove, Roxane Sokolove, Jane Gerhart, and Richard Gerhart.

I'm indebted to my former employer, the *Philadelphia Daily News*, for giving me wonderful opportunities as well as valued friends and mentors.

Buzz Bissinger, Barry Forbis, Deborah Williams, Al Hasbrouck, Lou Volpe, Sheila Saidman, and the late Tim Cohane made disparate but important contributions.

Most of all, I thank my wife, Ann. She urged me to write this book, and then helped mightily by lending to the effort her insights and considerable editorial wisdom, while at the same time working in a demanding job of her own. I'm also grateful to our children, Sara and Sofia, who amid a hectic year were a source of great joy.

I began my research in April 1989, less than one month after the first public disclosure of baseball's investigation of Pete Rose. Over the next fifteen months, I interviewed 112 people, a great many of whom had been close to Pete Rose at one time in their lives, were saddened by his problems, and found talking about him painful. To them, and to everyone who consented to be interviewed, including the handful of people who asked that their names not be used, my heartfelt thanks.

I am especially indebted to LaVerne Noeth, Jacqueline Schwier, and Dave Rose for sharing anecdotes from Pete Rose's childhood and for providing the kinds of insights that can only come from family members.

I thank Henry Fitzgibbon, baseball's former director of security, for providing details of his contacts with Rose during the 1970s, and John Dowd, for furthering my understanding of baseball's 1989 probe of Rose.

Earl "Scoops" Lawson was an invaluable resource, as were numerous other members of the sportswriting tribe. In particular, my gratitude to Stan Hochman for loaning me Pete Rose newspaper clippings assiduously collected over the course of two decades, and to Jerome Holtzman, for writing *No Cheering in the Press Box*. Three cityside reporters, Al Salvato of *The Cincinnati Post*, Bill Sloat of the Cleveland *Plain Dealer*, and Rick Tulsky of *The Philadelphia Inquirer*, kept me on top of the breaking Rose story and tried to make sure I knew what was likely to happen next.

The ever-cheerful Jon Braude in the Reds publicity office searched the Reds archives for the answers to dozens of my statistical and biographical questions and found answers to even the most obscure queries.

Three professors at the University of Cincinnati, Zane Miller, Alfred Tuchfarber, and William Baughin, helped me gain a better understanding of the city of Cincinnati. Some of the historical information in the chapter "Mr. Clean's City" is taken from Miller's book, *Boss Cox's Cincinnati*, and Baughin's 1972 Ph.D. thesis, "Murray Seasongood: Twentieth Century Urban Reformer." (Any opinions expressed about Cincinnati are mine alone.)

I would also like to thank the following people whom I interviewed: Sparky Anderson, Buddy Bell, Sheldon "Chief" Bender, Bill Bergesch, Hal Bodley, Bob Bonifay, Marty Brennaman, Asa Brooks, Jim Brosnan, Louis Brunner, Bernie Carbo, Murray Chass, Larry Christenson, Bill Conlin, Murray Cook, and Carol (Schroder) Cornett.

Bill Dantschisch, Willie DeLuca, Sheba Dittus, Robert Dominique, Dallas Doran, Dorothy Ebersole, Nick Esasky, Howard Eskin, Al Esselman, Ray Fosse, Gene Freese, Andy Furman, Dr. Gary Glass, Smoky Glover, Ralph Griesser, Billy Gumz, Danny Gumz, Pat Harmon, Patty Haskin, Thomas Heitz, Tommy Helms, Joe Henderson, Bill Hongash, Tom House, Bob Howsam, and Patricia Hutchinson.

Steve Jacobson, Paul Janszen, Norm Jollow, Roger Kahn, Joe Kaiser, Bill Koch, Andy Kramer, William "Shorty" Leon, Gerry Lynch, Danita Marcum, Jim McCoy, Roy McMillan, Rob Murphy, Joe Nuxhall, Jim O'Toole, Dave Parker, Gabe Paul, Chuck Perkins, Barbara Pinzka, Bill Plummer, Joel Ralph, and Bob Rathgeber.

Merv Rettenmund, Jeff Ruby, Glenn Sample, Jerry Scarlato, Dick Schaap, Al Schavel, Dennis Schrader, Jim Selman, Art Shamsky, Ed Smaldone, Charles Sotto, Jerry Springer, Robert Stachler, Larry Starr, Tim Sullivan, Johnny Temple, Hy Ulner, Rick Van Sant, David Voss, Arnold Wexler, George Yatron, and Hank Zureick.

Contents

Introduction

Not much good has happened in baseball since Pete Rose left.

Eight days after Charlie Hustle's banishment on August 23, 1989, Commissioner A. Bartlett Giamatti died of a sudden heart attack. The following month, an earthquake struck at the World Series.

The taking of a gifted commissioner in the first year of his reign and the interruption of the sport's showcase event—these at least were acts of God. But in the two years post-Rose, the greatest damage to baseball has been man-made. The players at times have seemed to turn on their sport.

One year after the earthquake, the end of the 1990 season was marred by an eruption of a different sort—Roger Clemens's foul tantrum in the final game of the American League playoffs. The flamethrowing Clemens followed up on his on-field embarrassment with an off-field mess, an arrest at the Houston nightclub Bayou Mama's for allegedly trying to choke a police officer. With criminal charges and a five-game American League suspension still pending, the Boston Red Sox rewarded their ace pitcher with a new contract, making him the game's first $5-million-a-year man.

Clemens personifies the baseball story line of the last decade of the century: mind-bending salaries, loutish behavior. I call him the new triple-threat ballplayer: big talent, big money, big jerk.

But there are others, too many others, whose actions and words serve to erode the fans' enjoyment of their performances. Rickey Henderson, for example.

A sure Hall of Famer and possibly baseball's best player, Henderson suggested late in the 1990 season, as he was poised to break Lou Brock's career stolen-base record, that a suitable show of appreciation from his ballclub would be a shiny new Ferrari.

Did anyone who caught wind of Mr. Henderson's humble request get as big a thrill out of watching him steal that historic base? I doubt it.

Here is another notable trend in the game since Rose made his exit: players pelting fans with baseballs. This has been perpetrated by lesser stars than Clemens and Henderson, but is arguably a greater offense. What is more at odds with the concept of family entertainment at the ballpark than the performers assaulting the paying public?

Cleveland Indians rookie outfielder Albert Belle heaved one into the seats in May 1991, targeting a fan who had heckled him about his bout with alcoholism. He nailed the heckler square in the chest and caused a welt. Belle's explanation: "I lost my spirituality for an instance."

That same month, Cincinnati Reds reliever Rob Dibble, frustrated over a poor performance, chucked a baseball into the stands after the game's final out, striking a first-grade teacher in the elbow and causing her to miss two days of school. Said Dibble: "Things happen, especially to me." Later, he was reported to have said of his ill-advised toss, "The scary thing is I could have hurt my arm."

What does all of this have to do with Pete Rose?

I am certainly not alleging any cause and effect, no Wrath of Rose. He wasn't responsible for the earthquake, and although no one can say this for sure, I don't think he caused Giamatti's death. The commissioner's life style—Giamatti was a heavy smoker, overweight, and sedentary—probably had more to do with stopping his heart than any stress Rose put him through.

And Rose can hardly be blamed for making ballplayers act badly. However, the tacky behavior of the current players does go a long way toward explaining the warm feelings that much of the public holds for Rose.

While he was still playing, Pete Rose was called a "throwback." Fans liked him because his style of play, and even the way he carried himself on the field, reminded them of the game's past, when they imagined baseball was better.

Because baseball in 1991 is no longer magical or enchanting, fans are looking backward to a time when it seemed so. How else do you explain the best-seller status of such books as Robert Creamer's *Baseball in '41*, David Halberstam's *Summer of '49*, and Mickey Mantle's *My Favorite Year*?

The moment Charlie Hustle was suspended, he became a part of Baseball Past, a more cherished place than Baseball Present.

I began researching this book in March 1989, just as Rose's runaway gambling and baseball's probe of him were becoming public. The book, which first appeared in September 1990, is hard on Rose. It says he bet on baseball and the Reds, lied about it, and continues to lie whenever he denies wagering on the game. It says that Rose knew his day-to-day cronies were drug dealers and that he laundered their drug money with full knowledge of what he was doing.

I stand by it all. I think Pete Rose did what he was accused of and deserved his penalties.

Having said that, I understand people who miss having Pete Rose in baseball. I share their sentiment. The Pete Rose who breathed the game and played it with such vigor and joy, the one who wasn't obsessed and distracted by his gambling, who didn't bring thugs into his office and onto the field, was certainly more of a credit to his profession than Belle, Clemens, Henderson, Dibble, and their boorish brethren.

I wish the better Pete Rose were still in the game.

No major institution in America is untouched or unmoved by public opinion, not even the Supreme Court. What the public thinks certainly matters greatly to major-league baseball, which converts good feelings for the game into ticket sales.

On the day Pete Rose was placed on the major league's "permanently ineligible" list, I felt he had virtually no chance of ever being reinstated. Fourteen men had preceded him on the list; none had ever come off it. Why would Rose be the exception? And why should he be?

I'm not as sure now that he won't be back. In the public relations arena, Charlie Hustle has been clobbering baseball.

In the two years since his suspension, Rose has at least given the impression of leading the "reconfigured life" that Giamatti said could lead to his reinstatement. After his felony conviction in the summer of 1990 on federal tax charges, Rose was sentenced to five months in prison and three months in a halfway house. As Pete himself has put it, he did his time like a man. He worked as a prison welder. He didn't complain. And his court-ordered work with children in Cincinnati's inner city won him letters of praise from his supervisors.

On the downside, as soon as he was granted his freedom, Rose began selling his signature for money again, a tawdry practice that seems unpopular with the American public, unless you take into account all the people who line up for the autographs. He also talked of investing in a thoroughbred breeding business, perhaps not the wisest endeavor for a recovering compulsive gambler—if that's even what he truly is.

In his first major interview since leaving prison, with Jane Pauley of NBC television, Rose continued to fictionalize aspects of his downfall. He again put forth the preposterous thesis that he fell into friendships at Cincinnati's Gold's Gym with people he assumed were upstanding citizens, only to learn too late that they were steroid pushers and cocaine dealers. "No one told me they were no good," he told Pauley. "Most of the players liked these guys, because all they did was talk about physical fitness. Players today are physical fitness crazy. And these guys would get the players vitamins, legal vitamins. Stuff that was good for their body. Regardless of what you may think, bodybuilders know about taking care of their bodies."

In that same interview, however, Rose sounded genuinely humbled and contrite. He said his confinement had been humiliating, the longest months of his life, but not entirely wasted. "This whole situation saved me," Rose said.

In every dealing with Rose since his banishment, major-league baseball has come off as petty and vindictive. He has already been dealt the game's equivalent of a death sentence, but Commissioner Francis T. ("Fay") Vincent, Jr., has senselessly been trying to improve on that by tailing Rose and citing him for a variety of moving violations.

Rose signed on to play the part of Ty Cobb in a TV movie. The commissioner's office would not grant him permission to wear a uniform displaying the Tigers logo.

Rose attended a ceremony at a minor-league ballpark in Reading, Pennsylvania, honoring former teammate Mike Schmidt. The commissioner's office issued a statement saying that this may have violated Rose's suspension, since the minor-league clubs are part of organized baseball. (Vincent later backed off on this, but too late; the impression had been left that baseball was picking on Rose again.)

By far the most serious of all the actions taken against Rose since August 23, 1989 was the vote by a special committee of the Hall of Fame making anyone on the permanently ineligible list also ineligible to appear on the ballot for election into the Hall of Fame. This could apply only to Rose—he's the only person on the list eligible for election by the writers—but in keeping with the underhanded way this was undertaken, the committee claimed it was simply refining eligibility procedures and not specifically sanctioning Rose.

The commissioner's claim that major-league baseball had nothing to do with the vote—the Hall is a separate corporate entity—would be easier to believe if baseball were not also taking silly shots at Rose like preventing him from wearing the Tigers uniform.

Pete Rose does not belong back in the game; he should not be eligible to work again as a manager. He lost that privilege by flagrantly violating the sport's most sacred rules—by gambling on baseball, consorting with known gamblers, allowing undesirables to linger around the game.

He does belong in the Hall of Fame. (I make the case for this more fully in the epilogue of the book.)

A serious tactical error was made by linking Rose's status in baseball to his eligibility for the Hall of Fame. There is now a reason to let him back into baseball where before there was none: It's the only way for him to get into the Hall of Fame.

One key now unlocks both doors, and the key is held by Fay Vincent, the commissioner of baseball. Someday, the pressure will build and Vincent or one of his successors will turn that key.

—Philadelphia, PA.
August, 1991

Prologue

THE ballplayers sitting at the dingy bar in Tampa's old Union Station on April 3, 1963, had nothing particularly new to say to each other. They had heard it, said it, hashed it over many times before. It was more or less the same gripe session they had been having for two months, and it was fueled, as usual, by beer, whiskey, and the intense dislike they had taken to their new teammate, Pete Rose.

He didn't belong, for all sorts of reasons. The veteran members of the Cincinnati Reds agreed on that. They referred to him as "the rook," which is what first-year men were always called. But in Rose's case, they spit the term out, like a stream of tobacco juice. *The rook.*

The more charitable among them conceded that Rose was certainly a "heads-up" base runner, a hustler who would embarrass any outfielder who wasn't on his toes. Some thought he would be a good hitter, some didn't. Almost certainly, he would be overmatched in the beginning, perhaps have to be sent down for more seasoning. As a fielder, he was an utter disaster, lacking the key ingredients for playing second base, soft hands and graceful footwork. He'd be no comfort to Reds pitchers.

What the players found most troubling about Rose, however, was his style away from the field. A major leaguer, as opposed to a bush leaguer, was *discreet;* he didn't carry on in such a way that stories got around town, or, even worse, back home to the wives. And already, Rose had become an underground legend on the baseball circuit for an incident earlier that spring at a Mexico City strip joint. Not content to just sit in the audience, he had jumped up on stage and become part of the show. That wasn't all. When

11

some of the older ballplayers tried to counsel him that this was not the way a big leaguer should act, Rose showed them no respect.

In a few minutes the Reds would board the train to carry them north toward opening day. To the handful of veterans sitting around the bar, it was nothing less than an affront to their status as big leaguers that this brash kid with the burr haircut and toothy grin would be riding with them.

The veterans wondered why manager Fred Hutchinson seemed so damned determined to bench Don Blasingame, a steady veteran, and impose Rose at second base. Hutch was a reasonable fellow, and a good baseball man. What the hell could he be thinking?

As was the custom in those days, the Reds were scheduled to play a series of exhibition games on the way north, taking four leisurely days to reach Cincinnati. With luck, maybe Rose would slump so badly in those final preseason contests that when he stepped off the train in Cincinnati he'd be handed a one-way ticket to San Diego. Triple A ball.

Or maybe that should not even be left to luck. Maybe, the veterans considered, something could be done to help the process along.

For Pete Rose in that spring of 1963, all was right in the world. He was twenty-one years old. He owned a car, a white Chevy convertible with a nifty decal on the front driver's-side panel of Casper the Friendly Ghost. The previous season he had produced dazzling statistics for the Reds' minor-league team in Macon, Georgia, where he also had dated the prettiest girl in town. And now he was at his first major-league spring training, with a chance to make the extraordinary leap from Class A ball to the opening day lineup of his hometown Reds.

That his teammates openly disliked him hardly mattered. For Pete Rose, the doubts of others, their taunts, the obstacles they threw in his path only nourished his ambition, fed his enormous will to succeed. So what if the great Mickey Mantle, who that spring had pinned the nickname "Charlie Hustle" on him, thought he was a jerk for running to first base on a walk? Screw Mickey Mantle. If that's what he thought, then Pete Rose would keep on running. Maybe faster. That'd show the Mick.

Not that Rose's self-assurance was born of great athletic achievement. Being the glory boy, the hot prospect at the Reds camp that spring, was a new experience. Right up from boyhood Pete Rose had always been a plugger, rarely a star.

Growing up on the West Side of Cincinnati, his friends called him "Pee-Wee," because he was so small, or sometimes "Gimp," because even then he had that chugging, hippity-hop gait that would be the prelude to so many celebrated headfirst slides. He had been no better than the fourth- or fifth-best propsect on his high school baseball team, and his uncle, a part-time scout, practically had to beg the Reds to sign him. After his first minor-league season he was left unprotected and any other organization could have claimed him. If any of this caused Rose to doubt himself, no one ever knew it.

A woman from Rose's part of town remembers in the late 1940s driving every Sunday past Schultes Fish House, down the road from the Rose home, on her way to visit family in Indiana. Each time she would see little Pete Rose, maybe six or seven years old, pounding a ball against the wall of the restaurant. On her way back five or six hours later she would see him in the same spot, still tossing the ball.

At first the woman thought the young boy must be hopelessly bored. Then she feared that perhaps he was daffy. Finally she decided that he was simply determined.

The Chicago White Sox were the opponents in all four of the exhibition games on the Reds' swing north in 1963. These were casual, low-pressure affairs, the idea being to showcase big-league baseball in minor-league-sized towns. Management's sincerest hope for these games was that no one get hurt.

Before the first game, which was in Macon, Georgia, Reds third baseman Gene Freese, formerly a White Sox player, approached his buddy Nellie Fox with a scouting report on Rose. "This little fellow we have playing second base—see if you can get your guys to throw him nothing but high fastballs," Freese told him. "He ain't been gettin' around on them too good, and I want to see if he can hit them."

Fox didn't need to be told what was going on, nor did the White Sox pitchers. The Reds veterans hoped to protect Blasingame's job by getting the opposing hurlers to exploit a perceived weakness in Rose. "I was trying to help Blazer [Blasingame] make the team," Freese recalls.

For four days Rose saw nothing but high fastballs. He responded as he would to all challenges over the next two decades—with a barrage of line drives.

"Hell, he hit nothing but rockets all over the place," Freese says. "To all fields, batting left-handed and right-handed. It didn't matter who we wanted as our second baseman. It was gonna be Rose because the kid could hit."

Even then, Pete Rose had a distinct vision of himself. He was *different*, an exception to just about anything you could think of.

Physically, he was unlike the other players. They were naturals, he wasn't. To achieve as much, he had to work harder. This was a large part of Rose's motivation. It was both a badge of honor (that he was doing more with less) and a license—to invent his own way of playing, of living, to exceed the limits and break the rules.

In Rose's mind, he was squat and slow and logically should never have played major-league baseball. But he did, for more games than anyone in history. Others played just one position or maybe two over the course of a career; Rose played five and was an all-star at each. Others began to fade at thirty and were washed up at thirty-five; Rose batted .325 at the age of forty.

Nearly everyone else slid into bases feetfirst. Charlie Hustle dove headfirst and belly flopped into the bag like a torpedo connecting with its battleship target. It was exhilarating to watch. It looked fun to do. And no one else, in the whole century-long history of baseball, had ever slid quite like that.

The headfirst slide was Pete Rose's trademark, along with running out walks and snapping his head back to follow the pitched ball into the catcher's mitt. He often said his way of sliding got him to the base faster. And then he would wink, and add that it was also a sure way to get his picture in the newspaper.

Rose loved playing baseball, for the joy of the competition, for the money, and, not least, for the acclaim.

He courted his fame, and kept a scorecard. "I'd love to meet Fidel Castro," Rose once said. "Heck, he's been on the cover of *Time* as much as I've been on *Sports Illustrated*."

As he became the best-known player on the best team in baseball, the game's first $100,000 singles hitter, a Wheaties box cover boy, the stalker and finally the conqueror of Ty Cobb—"a modern-day legend," as his lawyers correctly described him in his 1989 lawsuit against major-league baseball—Pete Rose also became, as famous men do, the author of his own myth.

He told the same stories, over and over again, to sportswriters, at awards banquets, in his numerous authorized biographies, to Phil Donahue and Barbara Walters, until they became etched into the myth, until they became part of the Pete Rose Mystique.

The tale of his trying rookie campaign was one of his favorites, and he was still telling it a quarter-century later. The Reds veterans shunned him all that season, except for the black players, who felt sorry for him and took him under wing. Rose survived the rude treatment and flourished, winning Rookie of the Year honors and rapping out his first 170 hits.

He recounted 1963 in a sort of shorthand. It was the Blasingame Story. The taking of a popular veteran's job. The triumph over the entrenched order. The shunning.

Rose's version was essentially true, but as he's told it all these years it leaves an untrue implication—that in later years he won the acceptance and friendship that was denied him as a rookie. He never did, and that is the one aspect of Rose's life that is least understood by the public.

To millions of fans, Pete Rose was baseball, representing everything that was good and pure about the game. But despite all the hits he collected, despite the thousands of high-fives and fanny-pats he exchanged with teammates, despite the records that fell to him and the presidents who called, Rose remained very much an outsider within the game itself.

For Rose, the price of warm relations with his teammates and peers was too high: He would have had to fit in.

When gambling allegations against Rose first surfaced early in 1989, what was perhaps even more shocking to the public was the people with whom he had surrounded himself—the errand boys, small-time hoods, steroid pushers, and cocaine dealers who washed his cars, made his bets, visited his home, kicked up their feet on his desk at Riverfront Stadium. Most people believed that these fringe characters had leeched onto Rose, that they had elbowed out his real friends, his baseball friends, and led him astray.

The truth was, Pete Rose had no friends in baseball. The cocaine dealers, gamblers, and fast-buck memorabilia hucksters *were* his real friends, to the extent that he had friends at all.

One brutally hot day in 1987, with the temperature well over one hundred degrees on the plastic turf at Veterans Stadium in Philadelphia, Rose, who was then the manager of the Reds, decided to take batting practice early in the afternoon, before the press or many players were at the ballpark.

By that time, of course, the little boy who had spent hour after hour pounding the ball against the wall at Schultes Fish House had traveled a long way.

This Pete Rose had Rolex watches, Corvettes, Porsches, and yards of gold chains and bracelets. He had a pretty young wife, and other women, too. He had 4,256 hits, 65 more than Ty Cobb and hundreds more than anyone in his lifetime was ever likely to achieve.

But he had not changed much. He still wanted to play ball. He was greedy for more hits, more magazine covers, more of the pleasure that playing gave him. And he still believed he could do anything he set his mind to.

On this day, Rose was forty-six years old, overweight, plagued by a painful hiatal hernia, and he had not played in a year. But he didn't like the way his team's pinch hitters were performing and he was thinking about putting himself back on the roster. Surely Pete Rose, even fat and rusty, could do better than the fidgety rookies and burnt-out veterans who were failing in the job.

There were people on Rose's coaching staff who might have told him the truth, had he asked them.

Tony Perez was one. He and Rose had first played together way back in 1960, in Geneva, New York, and Rose had once called Perez his best friend in baseball. Tommy Helms was another. He and Rose met up in 1962 in Macon, where the general manager of their minor-league club nicknamed the two pals "Peck's Bad Boys" because of their good-natured high jinks. But Rose no longer had much to do with either man, beyond the businesslike relationship he maintained with them as members of his staff.

As he took his swings against the soft tosses of sixty-two-year-old coach Billy DeMars on that sweltering day in Philadelphia, some of his buddies stood watch. Mike Bertolini, a 350-pound baseball memorabilia dealer from Brooklyn whom Rose called "Fat Mike," shagged balls in left field. Out at first base with a mitt was sportscaster Howard Eskin, who several years earlier had picked an incredible string of winners as the sports handicapper "Vegas Vic" for the *Philadelphia Daily News*.

After each ball that Rose ripped into the outfield, he would call out to another friend, bodybuilder Paul Janszen, who was standing by the batting cage.

"See that knock?" Rose would say. "Did you see that knock, Paulie?"

The hulking Janszen wouldn't have known what a knock was a year before, but he responded in kind after each line drive. "That's a knock, Pete. That's a knock," he would say, using the shortened form for *base knock*, which was itself slang for *base hit*.

That night back in his hotel suite, as the greatest collector of hits in baseball history pondered whether to resume his storied playing career, he did not turn for approval to Perez or Helms, or to anyone else who might have offered an educated opinion. The man he turned to was someone who had not played a single game of organized baseball, not even Little League.

"Should I go back on the roster, Paulie?" Rose asked Janszen, whose testimony two years later would help get Rose banished from baseball.

Janszen answered that the batting display he had witnessed earlier in the day looked better than anything the Reds pinch hitters had been producing. Go ahead, Janszen told him.

"You were gettin' a lot of knocks out there, Pete."

Even if he had drifted from people like Tony Perez and Tommy Helms, even if he was unloved by his peers, Pete Rose was, nonetheless, loved in the way that public people are loved. He was adored. Embraced. By fans. By writers. By owners of ballclubs. Even by bookies, who paid him the tribute of forgiving his debts.

There was so much to admire in Pete Rose, so much to genuinely *like*.

To millions of Americans, he embodied all that was good in the National Pastime, and by extension, so much that was good about America. He was the American ideal of egalitarianism come to life on the field of play; his perpetually dirty uniform, soiled by nothing less than all-out effort, stood as vivid proof that a man who worked hard could triumph over one who was born to greater advantages.

And so the father with the ordinary, lumpy-looking body would sit in the grandstand with his son, who was cursed with the same physique, and he would point down to the Rose and intone: Play like that man. *Be* like that man, for he must have something good inside of him to have achieved so much with such modest gifts.

The sportswriter, like the father, kept his own vigil for heroes and object lessons, and it could be a lonely vigil indeed. Through the years of Rose's playing career, the 1960s, '70s, and '80s, the clubhouse increasingly came to be viewed by writers as a wasteland of inflated egos and salaries, of halfhearted performers and talent abusers.

Rose was the exception, and it was as if there was a beacon above his locker stall that signaled to writers: Here is where the competitive fire still burns, here is where the game is played not just for money but also for fun. The hero search settled on Rose, and he became the beneficiary of the greatest mythmaking machine in America—the daily sports page.

Rose was a fruitful story line—wasn't it *his* father, the legendary local athlete in Cincinnati, who had infused him with his hell-bent style of play?—and also a colorful quote. Without much prompting, he could fill a writer's notebook with twenty minutes of lucid, blunt, sometimes crude, and often outrageously funny material.

Even without regard to their stories, the writers liked being around him because he was simply good company. He treated them with respect, a rarity, and he entertained them. Longtime journalist Dick Schaap, now a sports reporter for ABC News, says he has known only one athlete with a wit quicker than Rose's: Muhammad Ali.

As evidence against Rose mounted in the spring of 1989, as the layers of myth were peeled away and the reality exposed, the nation's sports columnists, virtually en masse, determined that the culprit in the Pete Rose gambling affair was arrogance.

The hero had been too well liked. Too fawned over. The nearly three-decade-long diet of adulation, flattery, and praise had bloated him full of his own importance, causing him to feel that he was above the rules that governed the less exalted.

On the day after baseball commissioner A. Bartlett Giamatti banished Rose, Mitch Albom's column in the *Detroit Free Press* began:

"He leaves the stage still kidding himself, still believing he is somehow above the game, which, let's face it, is what got him thrown out in the first place."

Albom and the others who expressed similar sentiments were correct. Rose *did* think the rules—society's or baseball's—did not apply to him. And far too often, for far too long, events proved him right.

Rose's downfall was preceded by no sudden metamorphosis in his personality. He did not wake up one day a changed person. His gambling was not, as he has insisted, connected to the winding down of his playing career.

He had been drifting for many years, starting from the beginning of his career. His gambling, his shady associations, his debts to bookies were apparent to teammates, managers, owners and others at the highest levels of major-league baseball.

"People say that Pete thought he was invincible," says Rose's former teammate Buddy Bell. "I don't think that. I think he thought he was *invisible*."

In the end Rose came up against someone with a vision that stretched beyond the stadium turnstile, who could express the game's place in the universe by quoting Dante. The late baseball commissioner A. Bartlett Giamatti was many things—long-winded and occasionally pompous among them—but the one thing he was not was someone who was likely to place Pete Rose, or anyone else, above the common interest.

Rose, of course, is no scholar. But he is an avid baseball historian, so as he waited outside the commissioner's office on February 20, 1989, his eyes were naturally attracted to the gallery of pictures on the walls. In their short-brimmed caps and baggy flannel uniforms, some of the game's greats stared down at him.

Walter "Big Train" Johnson was up there, along with the legendary owner and manager Connie Mack. Among the grainy old black-and-white photos were shots of presidents Wilson, Taft, and Harding throwing out the first balls at World Series games. Cobb was up there, too, and Rose would not have failed to notice him.

He had plenty of time to study the photos, for after being summoned to New York from spring training in Florida, he had now been asked to cool his heels.

Beyond the closed door that led into the commissioner's office, two of Rose's lawyers were meeting with the men who at that time were called in baseball circles "the commissioners"— Giamatti and the man he would soon succeed, Peter V. Ueberroth. There were several other baseball executives in the room, including Francis T. ("Fay") Vincent, Jr., who later that summer would succeed Giamatti.

Just the call to baseball's Park Avenue headquarters had sounded an alarm in the Rose camp, and his lawyers suspected that the meeting would be about gambling. But now, for the first time, they were hearing details. The commissioner's office had information that Rose owed large sums of money, that he bet through bookies, and most seriously, that he bet baseball.

Rose's main attorney, the courtly Reuven Katz, told the baseball men that there was no reason for his client to owe large sums to anyone, because of his "substantial net worth." Katz said he didn't know if Rose bet with bookies but he was sure he would never bet on baseball.

The two sides probed each other, each seeking to learn what the other knew without giving away too much itself. Whatever information they exchanged was secondary to the message being passed from the baseball brass to Rose's lawyers: This time, Pete Rose's problems were not magically going to disappear. The living legend would not be granted his accustomed wide berth.

Finally, after nearly ninety minutes, Rose was asked to come in. He entered the commissioner's office with feigned annoyance and his customary smirk. He'd been looking at the pictures outside, he said. Nice collection, but wasn't there one baseball immortal missing?

He turned to Ueberroth. "Why ain't I up there?" he asked.

Everyone in the room laughed.

1

OPENING DAY

I'm the next generation of my father, with an opportunity to show what he could have done.

—Pete Rose

THE cause of the giggles bursting forth from the maternity-floor nurses at Cincinnati's Deaconess Hospital on April 14, 1941, was Harry Francis Rose, who stood, nose pressed against the nursery window, cooing, making funny faces, and gesturing wildly at the typically oblivious newborn on the other side of the glass.

In the bassinet lay the firstborn son. He had been preceded by two girls.

The first was named Caryl, and she was welcomed and well loved, because the Roses were a loving, caring family. The second was named Jacqueline, and she was well loved also, but in an unusual way. Her parents called her "Jackie," and dressed her and cut her hair like a boy. When someone would peer into the baby carriage and comment to LaVerne Rose on her good-looking "son," she would smile proudly and say, "Thank you."

Peter Edward Rose was an uncommonly plump baby at ten pounds, four ounces, spread over just nineteen inches. He entered the world just after dawn, instantly an icon. Although later there would be another boy, the first son completed the Rose family, made it whole.

In time, the fiction would grow up around the family that Peter, as he was called at home, was in all ways an updated version of his father—the fulfillment of Harry Rose's dashed dreams of athletic grandeur, the same man born to a different generation.

21

"He is just like his dad, a carbon copy," Pete Rose's mother told *Sport* magazine in 1979, nine years after Harry Rose, still seemingly vital, had suffered a sudden heart attack and died on the stairs leading up to his bedroom.

"I'm the next generation of my father, with an opportunity to show what he could have done," said the ballplayer himself in 1985.

The truth was that the baby in the bassinet that morning grew to become very much the product of both his parents. In looks as well as temperament he favored his mother, inheriting her severe features—most prominently, the jutting chin—as well as her brown eyes and her fiery, hyperactive nature. If such a thing could ever be ascertained, he also may have inherited from her his baseball talent.

From his father, Pete Rose *learned* how to succeed as an athlete. But ultimately, Harry Francis Rose was as much his son's creation as his son was his.

Pete Rose's father was born in 1912 in the town of Ripley, Ohio, a settlement along the Ohio River about forty miles east of Cincinnati. He didn't stay there long. Before he was two years old, his father, Otto Rose, and his mother, Eva, split up, and Eva moved with Harry and an older son west along the river to Anderson Ferry, a small working-class enclave within the Cincinnati city limits. Harry saw his real father only a handful of times after that.

Harry Rose never liked his given name, and it was not long after the move that he became known as "Pete," which was the name of a horse he had taken a liking to.

The horse was no thoroughbred; it was an agreeable nag that pulled a vegetable cart through the neighborhood. As a youngster Harry would climb up on the horse and refuse to get off, and when his friends began calling him by the horse's name, he took it as his own. And that is the name that he passed to his famous son, and the name his famous son passed on to *his* first son. Years later, after his son became a player for the Reds, many people around Cincinnati began to refer to Harry as "Pete senior," although he had no more formal claim on that name than did the horse.

The small hamlet of Anderson Ferry, and the other tiny settlements along River Road, with their one tavern and one filling

station at each stoplight, today have the look of forgotten places
bypassed long ago by highways and new businesses that touched
more prosperous communities. The clapboard homes slope up
from the Ohio River along streets laid out in zigzag patterns, and
it seems that in the front yard of every third home there is a
collection of junked cars and a pile of bald tires. Even within
Cincinnati's boundaries, this is a rural, backwater place, more
related to Kentucky across the river than the city.

Times were no less grim during the childhood of Harry Rose.
From the very beginning of the River Road settlements late in the
nineteenth century, life along the Ohio was a cycle of floods,
economic blight, and occasional prosperity.

Many of the men in the community worked along the river—
for the area's largest employer, the New York Central Railroad,
whose tracks ran along the highway, or for Ashland Oil, Indiana
Grain, or Morton Salt, whose huge storage facilities blocked the
river views. Still others worked in jobs connected to the running
of the ferryboat from which Anderson Ferry drew its name. The
ferry had operated from the same spot on the Cincinnati side of
the river to Constance, Kentucky, since 1817.

A brewery and a large distillery also operated along the Ohio,
which made the coming of Prohibition, eight years after Harry
Rose's birth, a direct and devastating blow to the place where
he was raised and where he would later raise his own family.
(Schultes Fish House on River Road did continue to operate its
basement beer garden through Prohibition, and it remained the
social center of the community—hosting the weddings, men's
organizations, and card clubs—as much for its illicit brew as for
the fresh fish it brought in daily from Lake Erie.)

Not long after Harry Rose's mother moved to Cincinnati, she
took a new husband. His name was Harry Sams, and he did not
hold one of the jobs on the river. For a time, Harry Sams tended
bar at Hauck's Cafe, in the neighboring hamlet of Sedamsville,
but a number of his former neighbors recall that the main source
of income for Harry Rose's stepfather was the "home-brew joint"
he ran out of the family home.

"Making home brew was the only thing I ever knew him doing," recalls Jim McCoy, a friend and neighbor of Harry Rose's
from boyhood. "This was during Prohibition. There were many,
many brew joints in Anderson Ferry, Riverside, Sedamsville, and
up on Price Hill.

"The beer was actually made in the brew joint. It was German-style beer, very heavy. Harry Sams would sell it to anybody who would come along. There was no bar in the house. You would get a quart and take it home, or you could pour a couple of quarts in a bucket and sit on the porch and drink it, whatever you wanted to do.

"Harry Sams's brew joint was on the first floor. The beer, I guess, was brewed in the basement. But it wasn't separate. The brew joint was part of the house, and the family lived all around it. Harry Sams was a good man. He was a good father to Pete [Harry Rose], even though he wasn't his real father. A lot of people liked to come to his brew joint, and it could get pretty crowded there."

Making beer allowed Harry Sams and his family to survive, but it certainly didn't make them rich. Everyone in the neighborhood knew that to make real money you had to be involved with making or smuggling whiskey. You had to be a bootlegger, not a mere proprietor of a brew joint.

"Pete and me would look in people's garbage cans to see who was rich and who wasn't," McCoy remembers. "Whoever had the most malt cans was the rich ones. When we came home from school we walked by their houses and looked in the garbage cans. We knew who had the money and who didn't. The bootleggers had the money."

Like nearly all the boys along the river, Harry Rose was obsessed with sports. And like many of them, he played well beyond his youth.

Cincinnati's West Side was full of grown men who pulled on shoulder pads and helmets on autumn weekends and bloodied themselves on the gridiron—or who left the house on weekend mornings during the summer to compete on the baseball diamond, a keg of beer going to the winning team. Athletic careers generally ended only when the man's wife screamed *enough!*, which didn't happen to Harry Rose until he was forty-two years old. There had been many hints and gentle threats before then.

"Everybody in Riverside was good ballplayers," says McCoy, who played on numerous football, softball, and baseball teams with Harry Rose. "It was just a good ballplaying area. There were three ball fields down there between the riverbank and the railroad. There wasn't nothing else to do but play ball.

"Big Pete looked exactly like young Pete did when he came up to the Reds. He had that crew haircut that he wore all his life. I played with him on the Riverside A.C. [football] team, and our sponsor was Goodwill Stoves. We also played together on the Tressler Oil team, which was called the Tressler Comets.

"I was a pro, I got three dollars and thirty cents for playing eleven games. Total. For the whole business. That would have been 1933 or '34. Pete got more than me, but not much. I wouldn't think he got more than four dollars for the whole season.

"We played on Sunday afternoons and several hundred people would come out to watch. For a big game we might have a thousand. They would pass the hat to pay for the officials and whatever else. Pete was not the star, but he was around for a long while. And he used to get a lot of headlines, because he was small, five-eight, five-nine, about a hundred seventy pounds, and he would go on these unbelievable runs, sixty, seventy yards, weaving all around, and nobody could catch him."

Harry Rose also fought as an amateur boxer, in the flyweight division, under the name Pee-Wee Sams, and he played baseball and softball. By all accounts, his best sport was football, and his worst baseball.

"We played softball at Bold Face Park, on River Road up in Sedamsville [the ballfield there would be renamed Pete Rose Park in 1970, for Harry's son]," recalls Shorty Leon, another neighbor and lifelong friend of Harry Rose's. "You could play softball there, but not hardball. It had a short right field, and if you hit a hardball good, it would go into some guy's yard who wouldn't give the ball back. It was the guy who owned the movie house. He could afford to give it back, but he wouldn't.

"Pete was an OK softball player. Not great. He also played a little hardball, but he could not hit a hardball at all. Couldn't hit it a lick, which is kind of funny when you think about it."

Harry Rose's approach to athletics could only be described as hell-bent. Every game was a crusade, every play his last one. One time he broke his hip covering a kickoff, but crawled to his feet to make the tackle. When he ran the football, it took nearly an entire defensive team to bring him down—if they could catch him.

He performed mostly for an audience of local West Siders, getting an occasional mention in one of the Cincinnati daily newspapers. But one time television viewers did get a chance to see him in action, and anyone watching that day would not have forgotten it.

Guesting on a weekly sports show, Harry was asked to talk about some of the finer points of the game. This was the early 1950s and TV production was still a primitive art. In the bare studio, Harry and the show's host, *Cincinnati Post* sports editor Pat Harmon, sat on chairs and chatted about how to punt, how to burst through a hole, how to pass—all without the benefit of film clips of Harry or anyone else in action.

This dry, theoretical conversation hardly gave a taste of what it must be like to play so violent a game as football, so to spice things up, a chair was set up in the studio for Harry to demonstrate tackling.

The host thought Harry would lower his shoulder into the piece of furniture and gently roll it, slow-motion, to the floor. Not a chance. Harry saw red. At just about the time the chair was set down, he took off on a flying leap and tackled it, shattering the wood into several pieces.

"Now that," he explained to the astonished host, "is how you bring a man down in the open field."

All through his life, Harry Rose was a ferociously fast walker, always giving the impression that he was on his way *somewhere*. He was not a cold or aloof man; on the contrary, most people found him quite friendly. But he was rarely frivolous, and there was nothing of the clown in him.

Pete Rose's father was a quiet man who spoke volumes by remaining mostly silent. He was classically handsome, with a square jaw and blue-gray eyes. He was a clean liver who did not drink, and although he sometimes kept an unlit cigar in his mouth, he was rarely seen to smoke it.

Even as early as his teen years, Harry Rose carried himself with a sense of purpose, of import.

"Everybody looked up to him," remembers Shorty Leon. "I don't know why exactly. In my case, him and me was about the same age. As I recall, he was just about exactly a year older. But there's just certain people who you respect, because of how they are. Harry was a great, great athlete, and everybody respected that. But I think he would have got a lot of respect even if he wasn't a ballplayer."

Harry Rose took business courses in high school (typing, accounting, filing), which prepared him for clerk-level work in government or private industry. A year before his graduation he landed a job as a messenger at the Fifth-Third Bank in downtown Cincinnati, where he worked for the next forty-two years, until his death.

His studies, sports, and work could not have left time for much else, but he did allow himself one outlet: On weekend evenings, Harry Rose sometimes sneaked down to the public pool in Sedamsville to play craps with the itinerant Mexican laborers who worked on nearby farms. It was the beginning of a lifelong fondness for gambling, which was the only interest, besides ball-playing, that Harry passed down to his firstborn son.

At about the same time he started at the bank, Harry was introduced after a softball game to LaVerne Bloebaum, the daughter of a streetcar motorman from the neighborhood. Her four older brothers were all fine ballplayers, and one of them, Buddy Bloebaum, was the one who introduced them. The introduction came at Harry's request.

"He said to my brother, 'That cute girl, who is she? Can you introduce her to me?' " Pete Rose's mother recalls. "Buddy says sure, and he brings him over and says, 'I'd like you to meet my sister.' "

LaVerne was outgoing, flashy, and considered quite pretty. Less than two years later, LaVerne, eighteen, and Harry, nineteen, were married. It's fair to say their union was a case of opposites attracting.

LaVerne liked to dance. She took an occasional drink. She liked to dress up, although the skimping she and Harry would later do on behalf of their children limited her to one new fancy outfit a year, and sometimes not even that.

And unlike Harry, LaVerne was anything but quiet. If Harry was controlled and dignified, she was mercurial, explosive. Say something to anger LaVerne and you got an earful back—or more. She was not averse to scrapping physically with other women. (That's just one of the similarities she shared with Karolyn Rose, her son's first wife.)

One thing LaVerne did have in common with Harry Rose was

that she, too, was a fine athlete. On the same fields where Harry
Rose played, and where her children would later play, LaVerne
Bloebaum had made quite a reputation as a softball player.

"She could really wallop the ball," says Shorty Leon. "But she
was also a sort of a cocky person. I think that's where little Pete's
personality comes from, because his father was as far from being
cocky as you could be."

Pete Rose's mother is still called "Rosie" by her friends, although,
formally, she is now LaVerne Noeth, having remarried after Harry
Rose's death to Robert Noeth, a neighbor and widower, who also
has since died. She is seventy-five years old, utterly without pre-
tension, and has a gift for blunt, colorful language.

Like mother, like son.

"I didn't take nothing from nobody," Pete Rose's mother boasts,
recalling a couple of her more notable brawls. "I wouldn't stand
back from a fight. A couple of times I pulled a girl out of a bar and
whooped the hell out of her. One time, I was already married. I
was in my mid-twenties and I already had a couple of kids. She
was telling somebody I was running around with her husband. I
went right in the Trolley Tavern and I dragged her out and I
knocked the living hell out of her. We were real, real good friends.
I don't know why she ever started something like that, but I just
went in and grabbed her.

"Another time, I was still in school, about eighth grade. And
this girl, Mildred Bailey, she was saying things that were bugging
me. It's like I can still see that girl now. I followed her home, and
I grabbed her before she got in the house. She got in a couple of
good licks, but I whooped the hell out of her, too."

The marriage of opposites worked.

"He was a real easygoing person, and I wasn't," Mrs. Noeth
explains. "We never argued, and maybe that's why. The four children could swear, each of them, that they never heard us argue."

The family made their home at 4404 Braddock Street, in the
two-story, seven-room house where LaVerne had been raised.
There was plenty of room and plenty of food. Money was a
struggle, but the parents tried mightily for the children never to
know it.

If Harry never bought the Christmas tree until Christmas morning, because by then the prices had dropped, that was not how it was represented to the children. It was, instead, a Rose family tradition, which made Christmas Eve all the richer with anticipation: before dawn, everyone knew, Dad would steal out of the house and return with the tree before they awoke.

Banker's hours, if such a thing even existed, were unknown to Harry Rose. He left for work before 8:00 A.M. and returned in the evening around 6:00, at which time he washed his hands and promptly sat down with his family for dinner.

"We all talked at dinnertime," says Jackie (Rose) Schwier, the daughter who was dressed like a boy until the coming of Peter Edward. "It wasn't the kind of house like you have today where people are getting up and down or just leaving the table when they're done. Our parents were very interested in everything we did, and dinnertime was when they would ask us about our day."

After dinner, it was Harry's job to bathe the children before bed. When they were young, he took his turn diapering them. Once a week, when LaVerne had her card club, he took charge of the house.

Harry Rose, who had barely known his own biological father, was, LaVerne says, "A great daddy. When God made him, he threw away the mold."

Discipline was left to LaVerne. "My husband never touched my kids," she says. "I used to paddle them with my hand when they needed it. If they sassed me, then I would crack their little butts for them."

The only change in the household routine was when Harry came home from work with a headache, which was as frequently as once a week. "When he came in, if he walked right upstairs, then we knew he had one of his bad headaches," Jackie Schwier recalls. "He probably had migraines, but I don't know if that's what they were called then. He would go to bed and not get up until ten or eleven P.M. Then he would take a bath and go right back to bed. I've always assumed that the headaches came from him looking at those columns of numbers at the bank all day long."

The Rose family was not particularly religious, but all the children, including Pete, attended Sunday school at a nearby Methodist church. Both LaVerne and Harry grew up Protestant, in families that were mixes of German, Scotch, and Irish stock.

Their family was affectionate, says Jackie Schwier, but not overly so. "We weren't real kissy-kissy, but we were affectionate."

At the bank, Harry Rose advanced, but slowly. There was some thought in the family and the neighborhood that Harry's progress was impeded because the cut of his clothes was not quite conservative enough for downtown, although no one knew that for sure. The Fifth-Third Bank sent him to several training sessions over the years, to learn how to use the latest IBM calculating machines, and by the end of his life he had risen to supervisor of the calculating department.

His work at the bank, as well as his reputation as an athlete, made Harry a figure of great respect in Anderson Ferry and its environs, where most men still worked with their hands and some of the work was seasonal. But even though he walked to and from the bus in a suit and tie, the most he ever earned was just a little more than $200 a week. He never bought a new car; his automobiles were a succession of recently repossessed Chevrolets that he purchased at cut-rate prices from the bank.

Only once does anyone remember him chafing at his low salary. "When he was helping my husband and me with our taxes one year, he discovered that my husband made more than him, and he didn't think that was right because my husband didn't graduate high school," Jackie Schwier recalls. "Daddy had, and he was very proud of it. I think that hurt him."

Harry's modest salary was enough, however, to support the Roses' life-style. They did not take vacations, entertain, or go out much. Their life was Harry's work, his sports, and their children.

After the first son of Harry and LaVerne Rose became a major-league ballplayer and began to make public appearances, a line that got a laugh every time was when he said that his family had been so poor that his sister came out of the womb stamped "Made in Japan."

Throughout his career, when teammates or others could find no other explanation for Pete Rose's behavior, they pointed to his upbringing. What could you expect from him, considering where he'd come from? It was as if he had grown up without shoes or indoor plumbing.

Rose encouraged this view of his childhood. It was another

license to operate outside the norms, but it was also misleading.
Sure, he came from humble beginnings, but no more so than a
great many other big leaguers. He was the son of a bank clerk, but
how many big-league ballplayers were the sons of bank presidents?

"I say to Mom I get really irritated when somebody says we
were underprivileged, because we weren't," says Jackie. "When
we sisters were fifteen and thirteen, Mom and Dad got us diamond rings. And that was just one thing. At Christmastime, you
couldn't get in our living room. We always had a big Christmas.
We dressed as well or better than a lot of kids who went to school
with us. It irritates me because it seems like people are saying my
father didn't do a good job taking care of us, and he did. I know
now that maybe my mom would wear the same dress to a dance
or a function more than one time, but we didn't do without anything."

Life at 4404 Braddock Street, as described by its former occu-
pants, was a sort of children's paradise. Fun did not come in a
package from a store or over the television screen. It was invented, improvised.

In the summertime, Harry Rose took his children camping
down on the banks of the Ohio. They would sleep on top of
newspaper, no tents, and sometimes in the morning everyone
would find that they had slid down during the night and their feet
were almost in the river. (Or perhaps it was just that the river tide
had come up, but that was not nearly so delicious a thought as the
notion of inching down the hill while sleeping.) Breakfast was
peanut-butter-and-jelly sandwiches.

In the winter, they would go sledding down Intersection Street,
the steepest incline in Anderson Ferry. The man who owned
Schultes would bring out his big sleigh, and everyone would jump
on. Harry Rose would build a bonfire. Afterward, LaVerne would
make hot chocolate for her four children and what seemed like a
hundred others. The home at 4404 Braddock was the social center
for the neighborhood's children, and Harry and LaVerne used to
joke that they didn't even know they had a lawn until their children left home.

On Saturday mornings the entire Rose clan frequently went to
River Downs, the local thoroughbred track. Harry Rose, the teen
who had played craps with the Mexican laborers, was a racetrack
bettor all his life. "Two dollars, maybe four at the most. I think

Dad mostly liked the competitive aspect of it," says Dave Rose, the younger brother of Pete by eight years. "Dad would go out for doughnuts on Saturday morning and bring them back, then we'd all pile in the car and go to the track. Mom would go, our sisters would go, but it was strictly for fun. Dad was never there any three, four nights a week."

When the children were left to their own devices, they made the river and its bank their playground. Pete Rose, his brother, Dave, and their friends built foxholes on the bank, connecting them with an intricate system of tunnels that took most of the summer to construct. The tunnels were washed away by the fall's higher tides, and the following spring elaborate searches were conducted to find traces of them. And then new tunnels were built.

Everyone could swim across the river to the Kentucky side, although Pete was not as strong a swimmer as his brother or sisters. He could make it, but with much effort and a lot of thrashing.

Down the river about a mile was the small farm that belonged to the family who owned the ferry. The Rose children, on the sly from their parents, would sometimes pinch watermelons and sugar melons or raid the farm's bean patch and tomato vines. In the same general vicinity, there was also a crude nine-hole golf course with fairways that criss-crossed each other, and it was said that the only safe way to play it was in a helmet and catcher's gear.

The Rose boys, of course, played plenty of baseball, and much of it was informal, without uniform, lineups, or coaches. If they didn't have nine to a side, they played "Indian ball," which meant right field was closed off and made foul territory, there was no first baseman, and the batter was out if a throw to the pitcher beat him to first.

Harry Rose reveled in his family, but he would have been a sad man had it included only daughters. On the joyous day that he had pressed his nose to the nursery window, he was nearly thirty. He had begun to despair. *A son! A son!* No man could have wanted one more. It was as if he had a family business to pass along, and no suitable heir. He was desperate.

"I think every father wants a son," LaVerne Noeth says. "He especially wanted one because he loved sports so much. When we got pregnant, he said, 'If this isn't a boy, we're quitting.' But I don't think we would have, because he wanted one that badly. I don't even want to think about how many girls I would have had to have before we stopped."

Jackie Schwier says her father was "just as good with the girls as he was with his boys," but everyone understood that Peter was his father's special project. As soon as he could sit up, Harry rolled balls at him. At the age of two, he bought him his first baseball glove. Two years later, Pete Rose, at age four, took a mighty swing with a baseball bat as tall as he was and somehow connected, sending the ball on a beautiful arc through a first-floor window of the Braddock Street home.

The shattered glass was not cause for a home-repair crisis but rather for a celebration. Harry, even then, had a sense of destiny about his young son. He ordained that the window was a piece of history, never to be repaired. It would be left, instead, as a monument to Pete's hitting prowess. Years later, after the Cobb record, the windowpane was offered to the Smithsonian, which politely refused.

LaVerne Noeth says her late husband never contemplated that his son might not be interested in sports. He just assumed he would be. "If he hadn't been," she says, "he would have just had a fit."

The adults in the community began to call Pete by the nickname "Re-Pete," because everywhere big Pete went, little Pete tagged along. From 1945 on, he's in all of Harry's team pictures, although he's sometimes hard to spot. He's the batboy, the water boy, a crew-cut speck of a child kneeling in front of two rows of large men wearing uniforms emblazoned "Trolley Tavern" or "Schultes" or with the name of whatever other local establishment put up the sponsorship money.

Soon enough, Pete was playing on his own.

When he joined his first organized team at the age of nine, his father told him, "You're an athlete, now I can watch you," and Harry set about grafting part of himself onto little Pete. From that point on, the heart of Harry Rose, the heart of the athlete, would beat inside his first son.

The son would not have to be a *better* athlete, because that would be too tall an order. In his own understated way, Harry held his athletic abilities in as high esteem as did others; he was good and he knew it. But if Pete could not be better, he could be more recognized; he could redeem his father's life of anonymity.

The world had changed. There were more pro teams, more opportunities. Young Pete would not have to take a job at the age of sixteen. He would not even have any chores or responsibility around the house. All that was asked of him was that he prepare for stardom.

The Rose dinner table became a classroom, a never-ending sports seminar.

Runners on first and third, you're playing catcher, the runner takes off from first. What do you do?

You're on second base, one out, the batter hits a roller to the shortstop. Do you try for third? How about with none out? Do you chance it then?

Most of Harry Rose's lessons were less complicated. He had a simple formula for success—work harder than anyone else. That's all. The man who crunched numbers for the bank would tell his son, "If you and your opponent are equals in talent, and he gives 100 percent and you give 110 percent, then you'll win every time. Simple mathematics."

Pete Rose never asked how a person could give "110 percent" of himself. He just did it. And throughout his life he parroted his father's advice. It was as useful as it was illogical.

His father also told him that whatever success he did achieve, never to be satisfied. Strive for more.

"His daddy never let up on Peter," LaVerne Noeth says. "If Peter got four hits and he came home with a smile on his face, his daddy would want to know about the time at bat he *didn't* get a hit. And if, God forbid, his daddy ever saw that he wasn't hustling, he would really let him have it.

"Did Peter ever mind? Maybe sometimes he would feel disappointed that his daddy didn't praise him without always including a lesson. But he didn't show it. I don't think he got upset, because he wanted the exact same thing his daddy wanted for him. He wanted to be a pro player."

Family memories of little Pete involving anything except sports are nonexistent. Playing ball was all that was expected of him. "Pete didn't do anything else," Jackie Schwier says. "From the time he was little, that was his life. That's it."

In grade school, Pete Rose was a good student who earned a smattering of *A*'s and nothing else but passing grades, even though, his mother says, "He liked to cut up and be silly." But he lost interest in schoolwork. He failed tenth grade and had to re-

peat it, although he could have been promoted to the next grade
had he made up the courses during the summer. But his father
wouldn't allow the summer sessions because it would have interfered with American Legion baseball. "His daddy said, 'You're
not going to summer school, you're taking the grade over, because
if you go to summer school you'll miss playing ball.'"

At Western Hills High School, Pete Rose typically walked the
corridors in a T-shirt, Levi's and pointy black shoes. For some
reason, nearly everyone remembers the shoes. "They came to a
pretty sharp point," says high school buddy Jerry Scarlato.

If someone brushed up against him he shot that person a nasty
look. He was the kid from the other side of the tracks, and he
fancied himself a tough guy.

"They should have named an alley after me the way I acted in
high school," Rose said after the street in front of Riverfront
Stadium was renamed Pete Rose Way by the city.

Pete Rose was, in fact, a bad student. But he wasn't a bad kid,
although later he liked to romanticize his high school years, to
remake himself into the thug he never was.

"Our basic attitude was, if you screw with us, we'll beat you
up," recalls Scarlato, who played on the Western Hills football
squad with Rose. "We were into a very macho thing. We got in
fights. We cheated on some tests. But we never robbed anyone or
anything like that. We weren't criminals. We didn't do anything
we could go to jail for.

"Pete was a so-called river rat, and those types were looked
down on by the rest of the school. That was his whole persona. He
saw himself as a punk, or a greaser as it was called then. But we
were harmless."

Says Ralph Griesser, the team's quarterback and another Rose
pal: "Pete had his scrapes, but he was not a kid who got in that
much trouble. Maybe he appeared to others as a dead-end kid,
because that was his look. But I don't think anyone considered
him a problem, other than academically. He had a few borderline
friends from the neighborhood, but he also had friends who were
solid people. Christ, one of his close friends became a high school
principal and another became a priest. How bad were those guys?"
Griesser himself went on to the University of Michigan and then
Columbia University for a master's degree before returning to
Western Hills as its football coach.

Western Hills High School has produced a remarkable fourteen major-league baseball players, as well as four managers—in addition to Rose, Don Zimmer, Jim Frey, and Russ Nixon. In Rose's era, it was such a gold mine of baseball talent that he very nearly got lost in the shuffle. For a time it seemed that Pete Rose's best sport, like his father's, would be football.

"Pete was very small, but quick," says Griesser. "He would do things like you would see on the cartoons—disappear into the pile and come out on the other side. Even on film, you couldn't tell how he did it. He was very competitive, very tough, and had great hands. I would throw him little dump passes and away he would go, without blocking. He put on a show one game. We beat a team sixty to six and he gained some phenomenal amount of yards and scored a bunch of touchdowns."

Rose may also have been the first athlete with an incentive clause in his allowance: His mother paid him a quarter a touchdown. Before one game he told her that the opposing team was very good on defense and there probably wouldn't be much scoring. In the unlikely event he crossed the goal line, could she raise the touchdown bonus to fifty cents?

No problem, said Mom, which was her response to nearly anything Pete asked. "I was so damn happy to have a boy, and he was such a good kid anyway, that I spoiled him rotten," she says. "Whatever he asked for, he got."

Against the impenetrable defense, he scored four touchdowns. Two dollars' worth. Could that have been the 60–6 game?

"Knowing Peter," says his mother, "probably."

At 5' 9" and no more than 140 pounds, Rose, were he more academically inclined, might have been attractive to a small-college football team in search of a scatback. But he held little allure for baseball scouts. At his size, it was hard to imagine him holding up over the course of a professional baseball season.

Roy McMillan, the former Reds shortstop, remembers the high schooler Rose working out before games at Crosley Field. "You had to admire his effort," McMillan says. "He was Pete Rose then as he is now. Determination. Desire. Hustle. He was always seeking advice, help, direction. I gave him some. Johnny Temple [a Reds second baseman] helped him some, too. But he was so small. Even after you watched him play, that's what you were left with, how small he was. I don't think anybody could have projected what he was to become."

Most scouts attending Western Hills games weren't focused on

Rose anyway. First and foremost in their minds was Eddie Brink-man, who had pitched his American Legion club, which allowed players as old as eighteen, to a national title as a ninth grader. Brinkman pitched and played shortstop for Western Hills, and he became one of baseball's first bonus babies, signing with the Washington Senators for $75,000. Although he was just four months older than Rose, he broke into the big leagues a full two years sooner.

Years later, a picture of the old Sedamsville Civic Club team, on which Brinkman also played, was included in *The Official Pete Rose Scrapbook* (1978). Rose, who supplied the caption information to writer Hal McCoy, is quoted as saying: "Eddie was one heckuva fielder, and he's in the record book, too. I hope he doesn't mind me pointing it out—fewest hits in a season, 82, made with Washington in 1965."

Besides Brinkman, the squad included a polished infielder named Jerry Painter, who accepted a baseball scholarship to Bowling Green, and Ron Flender, a fleet outfielder with a powerful throwing arm and classic swing. Flender was signed by the Reds and played on two of Rose's minor-league squads, but he didn't make it and ended up as a Cincinnati cop.

Rose couldn't even play high school ball his senior year, because failing his sophomore year had made him ineligible. He played instead that season in a semipro league in Dayton—6:00 P.M. games on ruddy diamonds, with men who worked during the day and changed into their baseball uniforms in the car. Without the intervention of his mother's brother, Buddy Bloebaum, that might have been the pinnacle of his baseball career.

Pete Rose's uncle might have had his own major-league career if he had not declined when baseball first came calling. Buddy Bloe-baum was a big man at about 6' 3", an outfielder and—a rarity for the times—a switch-hitter. When he was coming out of high school, numerous big-league organizations were eager to sign him, but he turned them all away. The Great Depression was on and Bloebaum could not afford to embark on a new career. He was doing just fine in the one he was already in—pool hustling.

Bloebaum is reputed to have once beaten Willie Mosconi in a big Midwest tournament, but mostly he played for grocery money in the pool parlors of downtown Cincinnati and across the river in

Newport, Covington, and Louisville. "He played a lot in Ben Bleski's pool hall in Sedamsville," recalls Shorty Leon. "But that was for practice, because nobody there was stupid enough to play him for money. So he went downtown, in the market area where there were a lot of pool halls, and he traveled around a lot, too."

Bloebaum did later play a couple of years in the minors, "but I think it was too late, then," LaVerne Noeth says. "He should have gone when they first called."

By the time the Rose children came to know their uncle, he was married with a family, living in Dayton, and working for National Cash Register. Dave Rose remembers that his uncle, in the colder weather, always wore a full-length overcoat and a big-brimmed hat. "If you look at old film clips of football games from the twenties or thirties, you know, like a Bears game at Soldier Field, he looked like all those guys you see in the stands. Big coat. Big hat pulled down low. He had a very old-fashioned style."

Although he lived a couple of hours away, Pete Rose was nearly as much his uncle's project as he was his father's. On weekend visits Bloebaum coached him in the game's finer points, and he was the one who convinced Harry Rose to make his son a switch-hitter. When the nine-year-old Pete joined his first youth team, his father gave the coach an ultimatum: Let my son switch-hit, or he'll play on some other team. It was really Bloebaum's message he was delivering.

"I think we got our intensity and our drive from my father," says Dave Rose, who also had a brief minor-league career. "But we got our ability through my mom's side of the family. They were the athletes."

In 1960 Bloebaum was a "bird dog" scout for the Reds, a part-time position of some minimal status and no authority. Basically, a bird dog combs his territory for prospects, then turns their names over to higher-level scouts who watch them play and grade them. A bird dog might continue to attend a prospect's games and file reports, but normally he will not have much say in whom the organization signs. That is left to the full-time scouts and their supervisors.

But with Pete Rose's professional career seemingly stillborn, his uncle went directly to the Reds front office to plead for him. Included in what he promised was the unknowable: that his nephew would grow. The men in both the Rose and the Bloebaum families develop late, Bloebaum told Gabe Paul, the Reds general manager, and Phil Seghi, the farm director. By the time he's big-league ready, he argued, he'll be big-league sized.

Bloebaum's appeal touched a sensitive nerve. The Reds had recently made a couple of mistakes by passing on prospects they thought were too small. There was even some lingering regret in the organization from a decade before when Don Zimmer, another little man from Rose's neighborhood, had been allowed to leave the city and sign with the Dodgers. Zimmer in 1960 was an established big leaguer, and might even have been a star if not for two serious beanings.

"Phil Seghi was very high on Pete, because he liked his aggressiveness," remembers Paul, the former Reds GM. "I myself had not seen him play. But I did know Bloebaum. He worked hard, and he was a good judge of talent. We decided to take the chance."

On the Saturday morning after he graduated high school, Pete Rose, with his father and uncle looking on at the Red's Crosley Field executive offices, signed his first contract. It called for a $7,000 bonus, an additional $5,000 if he ever stuck for thirty days on a big-league roster, and $400 a month to play for the Geneva Redlegs in the Finger Lakes region of New York.

The money hardly mattered. Pete Rose was a professional.

Harry Rose's dream lived on.

Pete Rose's sister sits in the living room of her modest two-story home in suburban Cincinnati. Jackie Schwier, a gray-haired grandmother, wears a sweatshirt with her brother's picture on it, and under the picture is the number 4,192. As everyone in Cincinnati knows, that is the historic number of hits it took to pass Cobb.

With her husband, Al, Jackie Schwier once owned a tiny corner grocery in the old neighborhood. They sold it, and now Al works a day job and a night job to support them.

The other members of Pete Rose's family live much as they always did. They struggle.

The oldest sibling, Caryl, is divorced and living in Indiana in the home Pete bought her several years ago. He paid the medical costs of a child of hers who needed surgery for a cleft chin, showing up at the hospital on the day after the birth with the assurance, "Don't worry, Sis, I'll take care of it."

Dave Rose, the youngest, played a couple of years of minor-league baseball, served in Vietnam, then came home and got in a motorcycle accident that busted up his knee as well as whatever was left of his baseball career. Dave might have been the better natural athlete of the brothers, but he wasn't committed enough. He had other interests, like tinkering with cars, which no one in the family could quite understand. He was the first Rose boy in anyone's memory to want to do anything but play ball.

Dave lived in Tampa for several years, where he worked as a paramedic. One year down there at a spring training game, he punched out three guys in the stands who had been heckling his brother. He returned to Cincinnati in the early eighties, where he's held a variety of jobs, including the overnight shift at a chili parlor. Married now for the second time (he has three children from his first marriage), he thought he and Pete were about to become partners in a restaurant, but that didn't work out.

Dave Rose is a gregarious, likable man who has never found a niche, and people who know both brothers say they see a lot of Pete in Dave. The popular thing to say is that if Pete hadn't found success in baseball, he'd be like Dave: a good guy, kind of lost.

Pete Rose's mother, LaVerne, also is back in Cincinnati after spending the better part of a decade in Thonotosassa, Florida, which is inland from Tampa. She lived in a trailer park, and on her living room wall she kept a framed poster of Pete from a 1984 Fan Appreciation Day at Riverfront Stadium. It was inscribed, *To mom, a great fan who I love very much, Pete Rose.*

Pete Rose's mother and siblings have a distinct vision of themselves as a family. They are the Roses of Cincinnati. A clan. Together through thick and thin, whether they see each other once a week or once a year.

What gives the clan its identity is the family member who is largely not there. Pete sees Dave frequently, the others hardly at all. Family gatherings go on without him, even when he's in town. What the others know of Pete's current life is largely through Dave, and also from watching him being interviewed on TV.

But they think about him all the time. And, inevitably, they compare him to Harry Francis Rose. In their hearts, they know he doesn't measure up. Jackie Schwier sighs. "Well," she says, "we always did say he would never be half the man Daddy was."

Everything that was great about Harry Rose, the athlete, was incorporated by his son. Young Pete could zigzag around tacklers just the way Harry could. He could play from morning till dark and never stop hustling.

But the parts of Harry Rose that had nothing to do with sports—his decency, dignity, and integrity—were lost on Pete. And so was the part that had to do with being a father. Harry Rose was good at that, but he didn't pass it on to Pete. He didn't value it enough even to try.

Maybe Pete Rose could have picked it up by observation, by osmosis, but he didn't. He could have learned, for instance, to be "just as good with the girls as he was with the boys," as his sister insists Harry Rose was. Instead, he shunned his first daughter, Fawn, and told people she embarrassed him because she was fat.

"I used to feel sorry for Fawn," says Earl Lawson, a baseball writer who covered Rose his whole career in Cincinnati. "He wanted nothing to do with her. When I went to the all-star games, I would bring her back souvenirs, because I knew Pete wouldn't."

What Pete Rose took from Harry Rose was that a father's role is to coach his son.

"What'd I learn from my dad?" writer Pat Jordan quotes Pete Rose, Jr., the second child of Pete and Karolyn Rose, in the April 1989 *Gentleman's Quarterly*. "My dad told me to hit the ball where it's pitched."

In that same story, Fawn is quoted as saying, "My father is the world's worst father."

Pete Rose couldn't believe his daughter would say that. "What are you talking about?" he said when reporters confronted him with the quote. "I'm a great father. I just bought my daughter a Mercedes-Benz."

He wasn't kidding. To Pete Rose, love was simple enough: You bought it.

Harry Francis Rose and his son were not carbon copies and Pete Rose wasn't the next generation of his father. Saying so only made a nice newspaper story. Fathers and sons. Baseball.

Harry Francis Rose was an everyday hero, his son a hero for the ages.

The father got some mentions in the newspaper during his lifetime and a couple of nice obits: Harry F. Rose, Father of Pete.

The son's accomplishments took an incredible forty-six lines to chronicle in *The Baseball Encyclopedia*.

By making Harry Francis Rose the most prominent supporting character in his life story, Pete Rose meant to compliment his father, to make *him* famous, too, and he largely succeeded in that. But he also demeaned him.

The father was *more* than the son.

Harry Rose died on December 9, 1970, at the age of fifty-eight. At the funeral, Pete Rose cried for the first time in his adult life. Harry had lived just long enough to see Pete's transformation from local hero to national superstar.

Although he had won back-to-back National League batting titles in 1968 and 1969, what really catapulted Pete Rose into national prominence was the 1970 all-star game at Riverfront Stadium, which had just opened that season. A national television audience watched as he scored the winning run by crashing through and injuring catcher Ray Fosse. It was one of the most violent, and most famous, baseball collisions of all time.

Pete Rose gave credit for that play to his father. Or blame, depending on what you thought of the play. He had to crash through Fosse, he said, because it was how Harry Rose had taught him to play. All out. Every game, every play. Fosse might just as well have been the chair set up in the TV studio.

Fifteen years later, on the night of his greatest baseball moment, September 11, 1985, he had a vision of his dead father. He had just smacked the historic hit to put him past Cobb, a typical Pete Rose single, a crisp, slicing line drive to left field.

Standing at first base, he felt naked. First they took the ball away. And then they carted off first base. And all the while, a seven-minute standing ovation washed down on him.

Pete Rose's son Petey came out on the field, and as he hugged him he cried again for the first time since the funeral, and he knew that his father was there. They were three generations of Pete Roses. The two embracing at first base. And one watching from above.

After the hit, Pete Rose said afterward, he had gazed into the night sky, and beyond the glare of the stadium lights he had seen two men. One was Ty Cobb.

The other was Harry Francis Rose.

He was watching. Approving. He had seen the hit.

2

I'M YOUR NEW SECOND
BASEMAN, MISTER

Pete Rose Jr., the native Cincinnati Redleg second-
sacker, has more bounce to the ounce than a hot golf
ball on concrete.

—*Cincinnati Post*, April 1963

By the time he was nineteen, the farthest Pete Rose had been
from 4404 Braddock Street was a day's drive into Kentucky or
Indiana. He'd been to visit no distant relatives, been recruited by
no faraway colleges. Much of his out-of-state travel still consisted
of those swims across the Ohio River.

On June 21, 1960, he took his first airplane flight, Cincinnati to
Rochester, New York. From there he boarded a bus for Geneva,
New York, and upon arriving at the downtown Greyhound station, he hailed a cab and told the driver to head directly to the
ballpark.

Just inside the front gate of ancient Shuron Park, Rose approached Asa Brooks, general manager of the Geneva Redlegs,
public address announcer, town police chief, and sporting goods
store owner. Brooks had just picked up the evening's starting
lineups from the rival managers and was headed back upstairs
when the kid accosted him.

He remembered something about a new infielder due in from
Cincinnati, but this skinny youngster couldn't be him, he hoped.

Rose wore a Cincinnati Reds cap pulled down so low on his

head that his ears seemed to grow up the sides of it. He carried an
old beat-up suitcase with a couple of baseball bats tightly strapped
to it. He didn't look like a ballplayer; he looked like a runaway.

"Hey, mister," he called out to Brooks, "I'm Pete Rose. Where
do I get my uniform?"

Brooks, salty and straightforward, asked him, "Who the hell do
you think you are?"

"I'm your new second baseman, mister," Pete Rose shot back.

"All right then," Brooks replied, "go out and tell the manager
who you are. If he wants to use you, he will."

"Who are *you?*"

"I'm the general manager."

"OK, I'm gonna make your ballclub," Rose said. "I'm gonna be
the second baseman."

If he had not been so deadly earnest, someone meeting Rose for
the first time in 1960 might have thought he was acting, that he
had cast himself in a role. He was the dead-end kid, the river rat.
Impatient. Blustery. Hungry. Bats strapped to the suitcase, ready
to play.

*Just point me to second base, mister, and I'll worry about
gettin' a room after the game.*

Rose's great charm was that all this was real.

Having established that Brooks was someone of influence, Rose
lobbied him to get in the lineup. Hadn't he just two days earlier
signed a player's contract? Did it say anything about watching?

"He wanted to get into the game. He didn't want to sit on his
butt and watch," Brooks recalls. "I said, 'Son, it's twenty after
seven, and the game starts at seven thirty. You can't play tonight.' "

Asa Brooks wishes that he had taken a photograph that evening.
It would have been a beauty, something to cling to now: Pete
Rose, with the endearing braggadocio of youth, the brash crew
cut, clutching those bats, taking his first step into professional
baseball. "When I think about how Pete went on to become one
of the all-timers, I wish I took a snapshot of him," he says. "But
how can you know at the time? Back then all I was thinking was,
Who the hell's sneakin' into my ballpark?"

*   *   *

Art Shamsky, one of the few Jews in professional baseball, was Rose's best friend in Geneva, and they boarded together in a private home. Ever tactful, Rose referred to him, affectionately, as "Jewman."

"We were so consumed by baseball," Shamsky says. "I don't even remember much about us eating. We were hungry for baseball. We weren't hungry for food. Our lives were different then. We didn't have to eat three meals a day. If we were hungry, well, maybe it would pass, and we would go out and play catch somewhere instead."

As a last-place club in a league for first-year pros, Geneva was on the very bottom rung of organized baseball. The club's home games were attended by 350 to 400 people a night, which was not enough to pay expenses. When the team hit the road, Brooks staged wrestling shows in the ballpark to bolster revenues. One night a card headlined by the heavyweight Argentine Rocko filled the place, which kept the Redlegs in bats and balls for another few weeks.

From Geneva, it was a long, long way up.

What Shamsky remembers about Rose from 1960 is not so much how he performed in games, but how he practiced. Even then, Rose had something that many major leaguers, even good ones, never achieve: a realistic view of his strengths and limitations. If he hit a home run in the previous night's game, he did not imagine himself a power hitter. The next day in batting practice, Rose would watch and cheer his teammates on as they swung from the heels, trying to reach the fences. Ballplayers, even on the major-league level, never grow tired of playing home-run derby. Then Rose would step in the cage and calmly, repetitively, stroke ball after ball up the middle. When he was through with that he would work on his opposite-field stroke.

"There were very, very few young players taking that kind of approach," Shamsky says. "It wasn't that Pete put in more time, but he practiced right. It was all work for him. The rest of us were *hoping* we'd make it. Pete was preparing."

Rose had a good but not great debut season. He batted .277, but just 14 of his 89 hits went for extra bases. He also committed the ghastly total of 36 errors, nearly an error every two games.

"When he undressed he was black and blue all over," says Brooks. "I used to say to him, 'If you would use that goddamn leather glove instead of your body, you wouldn't be so black and blue.' And he'd say, 'But Mr. Brooks, I throw 'em out, don't I?' "

The Cincinnati Reds organization wasn't impressed. "Rose hustles a lot, but he can't field, throw, or hit" was the succinct organizational scouting report filed on Rose after that 1960 season.

Every player remembers his first major-league at bat or pitching appearance, but there is another milestone, not so easily pinpointed in time, that is equally significant. It is the moment in his minor-league career when he establishes that he'll be given a shot at playing in the big leagues. It hasn't happened yet, and may not for a year or two or even more. But it's going to happen, the only question being when. For Rose, the progression from prospect to big-leaguer-in-waiting occurred sometime during his 1962 season with the Macon Peaches.

The season before that, at Tampa, he had begun to make a name for himself in the organization, hitting .331 and crashing out a league-record 30 triples. But that only earned him the promotion to Class A Macon, where the competition was faster and he was placed, for the first time, with some of the Reds' glitzier prospects.

"By the end of his season with us, anyone could tell he was a very special player," recalls Bob Bonifay, who was the Macon Peaches' general manager. "I'm not going to say that the organization considered him the top prospect on that team, because he wasn't. Tommy Helms, for one, was further along to my way of thinking, and the Reds felt that way also. Tommy was a very polished infielder, which Pete was not. But as good as Tommy was, he didn't have the charisma Pete had. Pete put out electricity when he played. If you watched him play, you knew that this boy was not going to be denied from reaching his goal."

The Peaches were a phenomenal hitting team, the most dominant offensive club Rose would play with until his days with the Big Red Machine. They routinely scored in the teens, and in one game they beat a Dodgers farm club 32–5. In that game one of Rose's 6 hits was a prodigious home run to dead center field, well over a wall 405 feet away.

Rose was capable of hitting a ball that far because he had fulfilled his uncle Buddy Bloebaum's prophecy: He had grown bigger and stronger. Nothing that occurred during Rose's minor-league years was more important than the development of his physique.

No one looked at him anymore and called him Pee-Wee or wondered if he could survive the rigors of the long season. In the two years since his signing, he had grown two inches and gained nearly forty pounds, and by the time of his major-league debut the following year, Rose would be a rock-hard 195 pounds and just a shade under six feet.

The baseball establishment in those days discouraged weight training, but Rose had bulked up the traditional way: He had eaten big meals, and turned the calories into muscle by loading boxcars on Cincinnati's waterfront during the off-seasons.

Harley Bowers, the sports columnist for the *Macon Telegraph*, was struck, as was Shamsky, by how savvy the young Rose was about his skills. "Pete adjusted his game. I was convinced after watching him that season that he could have been a home-run hitter. He was always a lot stronger than people think. I think he knew that he could hit twenty-five, thirty home runs, but not for a very high average. So he opted to go in the other direction. I don't know if he's a smart guy or not. Certainly, he's not an intellectual. But he had a plan and he followed it."

Rose also had a plan that related to his play at second base. If he could not become a better fielder, he could, at the very least, make himself *appear* to be a better fielder. So every day, when he arrived at the ballpark in Macon, the first person he looked for was Smoky Glover, who was not a fielding coach but the grounds-keeper at Luther Williams Field.

Even early on, Rose knew some veterans' tricks. He knew there was more to grooming a ball field than cutting the grass and lining the baselines. The field could be altered, and often was, in ways that gave competitive advantage to a team or a particular player.

While his teammates were still home napping or in town watching a matinee, Rose was already at the ballpark, giving himself an edge. "He would come out in his shorts and sneakers, one, two o'clock in the afternoon, and he would take the shovel and the rake and take charge of the second-base area," the lanky, slow-talking Glover recalls. "He had a way he liked the dirt. He liked it a little thick, a little muddy. The rest of the field would not be that way, but that's how Pete wanted his area. I never asked him why, but I'm sure it made it harder for the ball to go by him."

Rose played a passable second base at Macon, but he shone as an offensive player, hitting a hard .330, with 9 home runs, 17 triples and 71 runs batted in.

Impressive as those statistics were, a page of numbers hardly did justice to the young Pete Rose. The fans loved him, and, without fail, so did the older men who made the important baseball decisions. "He was so taken with himself, but in a wonderful way," says Bonifay. "He was so brimming with confidence, so effervescent, that people wanted to be around him. You just had to love him."

Macon was a couple of notches below the big leagues, and in most cases, players there were at least two years away from the majors. Shamsky and Tony Perez, Rose's teammates on the '62 Peaches, did not become full-time big leaguers until 1965. Helms had to wait until 1966.

Although he didn't know it at the time, Macon would be Rose's jumping-off point to the Reds. He was going home to Cincinnati, well ahead of schedule.

Like a great many ballclubs with a championship in their recent past, the 1963 Reds were a smug bunch.

"Most of the key players had been there in 1961, and we were all living off having had career years then," remembers Jim Brosnan, a Reds pitcher of that era. "It was a good ballclub, but as a team, and as individuals, we probably thought more highly of ourselves than was warranted."

If the '63 Reds were not a club you would have expected to be welcoming to rookies, few teams back then were. All across baseball, first-year men routinely faced a certain amount of hazing and rude treatment. The reason had everything to do with money—and the lack of it. A promising rookie was a dire economic threat.

In 1963, there was just a fledgling players' union, free agency was a decade away, and salaries more closely approximated those of the general work force. Young players were paid not much more than school teachers. An established player who was not a star made enough to be comfortable but not wealthy, and if he had a large family he struggled. A star was paid about what a successful attorney might make.

Only the tiniest percentage of big leaguers were what could be called "set for life" at the end of their playing careers, and some of those only because they'd been clever investors. Much more frequently, a man cut loose to make room for a rookie was forced to go out in the world and scrap for a living, and almost always at something less pleasant than playing baseball. It wasn't unheard of for a released player to end up pumping gas.

On the 1963 Reds, outfielder Frank Robinson's $35,000 contract, won after bitter bargaining, made him the team's highest-paid player. Pitcher Jim O'Toole was the only other to make better than $30,000.

Many of the Reds took off-season jobs. O'Toole, whose family then numbered three children and would eventually grow to eleven, sold insurance during the winter. First baseman Gordy Coleman pushed season tickets and did promotion for the club. Pitcher Jim Maloney sold used cars in California, and got a big laugh every spring training when he joked that once again he had succeeded in selling stick shifts to one-legged veterans.

Most Reds players carried themselves like the workingmen they were. Despite all the time they spent on the road during the season, few were adventurous travelers. They didn't seek out new restaurants or visit cultural and historical sights. Like birds, and like most other big leaguers, they tended to return to the same spots year after year: the good steak joint, a convenient movie theater, the closest respectable bar to the team hotel.

"A big group of us—the pitchers, plus Wally Post and Eddie Kasko and Blasingame—we would migrate to a bar after the games and play coins for a round of drinks," O'Toole explains. "You would have three coins in your hand, and it was a guessing game to determine where the coins were. We would go to whatever bar was the closest to the hotel, because in those days players still couldn't drink in the hotel bar. That was reserved for the manager and the coaches."

The '63 Reds came together in common purpose only at game time. Otherwise, the club was composed of whites and blacks, pitchers and nonpitchers, drinkers and nondrinkers, golfers and nongolfers, early risers and late risers, cardplayers and noncard-players. As on most teams, players associated, or not, by position, race, habits, interests.

There were also a couple of lone wolves. Brosnan was one. He not only read books, which made him an oddity in a big-league clubhouse, but he also had written two, *The Long Season*, a diary

of his 1959 campaign that was a sort of PG-rated forerunner of
Ball Four, and *Pennant Race*, about the 1961 season. The other
players called Brosnan "Professor."

Another loner was relief pitcher Al Worthington, who was once
part of the drinking crowd before he became religious. Worthington was one of the first of the born-again ballplayers and later an
activist with the Fellowship of Christian Athletes. Shagging balls
in the outfield during batting practice, he would sometimes try to
witness to the other pitchers. "Don't try to save *me*," they would
gibe him. "Save my *game*."

The manager of this crew was Fred Hutchinson. The players
called him "Stoneface" because, as they said of him, "He smiles
but his face never knows it."

Hutchinson, who would die the following year of cancer, was
6' 2" and about 200 pounds, with big bushy eyebrows and dark,
almost black, curly hair. He was an extraordinarily strong man,
the type who could drink all night, sleep for an hour or two, and
then get up and play eighteen holes of golf.

In eleven seasons as a right-handed pitcher for the Detroit Tigers, wrapped around four years' service in World War II, he won
95 games. And he was an accomplished hitter, batting better than
.300 in four different seasons. Hutchinson, at forty-four, was still
a more commanding physical presence than most of his younger
players.

"Hutch wasn't matinee-idol handsome, but he was ruggedly
handsome," says Earl Lawson, who worked the Reds beat for the
Cincinnati Times-Star and later the *Post* for a remarkable thirty-
four years. "He was a man, that's the only way to say it. A man's
man. Women liked him. Men liked him. Most of the players liked
Hutch, but they were also scared to death of him."

Hutchinson was given to occasional explosions. One night in
Milwaukee after a tough loss, he stormed down the tunnel leading from the dugout to the clubhouse, ripping the wire cages off
each light bulb along the way and shattering the bulbs with his
bare hands. After a game at Crosley Field, he threw a bag of balls
through his glass-enclosed office and sprayed shards of glass onto
the team trainer, who happened to be walking by. Hutchinson
was also in the habit of ripping his uniform top straight off, and
the clubhouse man spent a lot of time sewing the buttons back
on. The players gave Hutch lots of space.

"Once after the second game of a doubleheader," Lawson says, "he just sat in the dugout by himself for five or ten minutes. We had lost both games and hadn't looked too good doing it. Then he called in from the dugout phone and told the clubhouse man: 'I'll be there in twenty minutes. See that that place is cleared out.' He didn't want to see anybody's face, and when he came in, he didn't. Everyone was gone."

More than anything, though, Hutchinson was a dedicated base-ball man, obsessed with winning and, as all good managers are, obsessed with the game down to its most minute detail. Getting beat because of a botched double play, a missed sign, or a badly executed bunt literally kept him up at night. On the road, coaches and writers covering the team knew that if they got a knock on the door after midnight, it was probably Hutch. He couldn't sleep and wanted to talk baseball.

Hutchinson had certainly heard of Pete Rose before he saw him play. He would have seen his name on the minor-league reports and taken note that the kid hit for a high average and banged out lots of doubles and triples. But the Reds had about a hundred and fifty other minor leaguers, and quite a few of them were consid-ered a lot closer to the big leagues than Rose.

Normally, Hutchinson concerned himself with players who could help him right away, not Class A boys who might surface with the big club two or three years down the road, if ever.

But after the 1962 season, Hutchinson swung by Tampa for a few days to observe the Reds' Instructional League team, and that's where he saw Rose play for the first time. He was smitten, instantly. The young man was his kind of player. He was, in fact, any manager's kind of player.

Rose was aggressive and fearless at the plate. If he was unpol-ished, he was also smart, giving the impression that what he didn't yet know he would learn. He never threw to the wrong base. He knew what he was going to do with the ball before he got it. He backed up plays. On the bases, if he tried to stretch a single to a double or a double to a triple, he didn't get thrown out. Someone had taught Rose the right way to play baseball.

"It was almost unheard of to promote a guy from that low in the minor leagues," says Lawson. "But as soon as Hutch saw Pete play, he fell in love with him. At the winter meetings that year, he told me, 'If I had any guts, I'd stick Rose at second base and just leave him there.' "

The young player's mannerisms on the field were another matter. Hutch was a traditionalist, and ordinarily he might have been rubbed the wrong way by a man who ran to first base on a walk or belly flopped into bags instead of sliding feetfirst. But the manager knew his holdover players wouldn't exactly cotton to Rose, and he didn't mind that at all.

Sometimes a veteran team, especially one that tends toward complacency, *needs* to be bothered a little bit. Hutch's incumbent second baseman, Don Blasingame, was perfectly serviceable, but nothing more. Subtracting him would not change the balance of power in the National League, but it might, on the other hand, send a nice little message to the rest of the ballclub.

Hutchinson thought that maybe Pete Rose could be his second baseman and—a bonus—a kick in the pants, a wake-up call, a warning shot to the rest of the squad. The more he thought about it, the more Hutch liked the idea of accomplishing two things at once.

Pete Rose's new teammates were at first put off by him, then mystified. Didn't he want to be liked? Didn't he care about being one of the boys? Their shunning him didn't make him change his ways at all. It seemed to make him even more stubborn. He didn't defer to them, or conform in the ways they thought he should. He just turned his back and walked the other way.

Often when he walked off it was with a woman on his arm, and that was another thing that mystified them. The kid hadn't even been around the circuit once. How could he already have a date waiting for him in every city? Had he called ahead from the minor leagues?

"He was just so cocky, so wild," says O'Toole, the best pitcher on that '63 club. "He never rode the bus with us. All the veterans, the older guys, rode the bus [from the airport]. He would walk by with a young stripper or something twice his age and say, 'See you guys,' and he would wave. In Philadelphia, Pittsburgh, sometimes he'd have one on each arm. That really was Pete. He didn't care about anything, he just knew he could play ball. That's what he wanted to do, and at night he did other things.

"Pete had his own world. He never liked to sit around and drink beer. I knew he liked to talk baseball, but back then he didn't. At night, he was like the sailors, you know, one at every port. He wasn't the only one, but still we had time for our teammates.

From day one, some of the unusual things Pete did set him apart. Pete was never one to be secretive. He didn't care who saw him; he was always arrogant or whatever. He didn't care."

Probably the most unusual incident involving Rose in 1963 was the one that took place before the start of the regular season in Mexico City, where half the Reds squad had traveled to play in a series of exhibition games. Rose and a group of his teammates went to a local strip joint, and after ascending the stage, he engaged in what amounted to a live show with one of the performers. Rose ended his portion of the program with his head between her legs.

Not many of his teammates would have found this morally wrong. A major leaguer certainly didn't need high morals. What bothered them was Rose's utter lack of discretion. Having fun was one thing; being a loose cannon was another. Rose was a loose cannon. Dangerous.

Later, after he married Karolyn Englehardt at the end of his rookie year, he routinely ignored an important baseball custom by taking his wife into nightspots where married ballplayers spent time with their girlfriends. On one of these occasions Karolyn assured O'Toole that he and the other players shouldn't worry about her presence. According to O'Toole, Karolyn told him: " 'I know Pete gets fucked on the road all the time: I say as long as he doesn't do it at home, I don't care.' And then she says, 'Have a good time.' I said to myself, 'Boy, what a nice wife.' "

The Mexico City incident even pained Rose's sponsor. "It broke Hutch's heart," says Lawson.

If others were put off by Rose, he either didn't get the point or didn't care. What might have embarrassed someone else had no effect on Rose. At an exhibition game in Florida late in the spring of 1963, Joe Pepitone of the Yankees needled Rose around the batting cage about the strip-joint performance.

"I hear you're the best pussy eater in the National League," Pepitone called out to Rose.

As Lawson recalls, "Pete just grinned, like someone had just told him he was going to be the batting champion."

On the field, things were going more smoothly. Through the whole of his career, the ballfield was Rose's refuge, just as it was in that summer of 1963. He drew a four-pitch walk in his first at bat on opening day, sprinted to first base, and came around to score the first of his 101 runs that season, making 1963 the first of a record ten seasons in which he would score better than 100 runs. He did go hitless over the next three games, beginning his career in an uncharacteristic slump.

On April 13, Rose lashed his first-ever major-league hit, a line-drive triple to right-center field at old Forbes Field in Pittsburgh off the Pirates' Bob Friend. But he wasn't quite over the hump yet. After getting just 3 hits in his first 25 at bats, he was benched by Hutchinson for three games, Blasingame taking his place, but the move was only to relax Rose; the manager was not one to reverse a decision too quickly. Reinserted in the lineup, Rose began to hit, and by the end of the month he was entrenched as the Reds' second baseman. There would be no return trip to the minor leagues.

The first Red to earn a ticket down to the bushes that season turned out to be Gene Freese, the veteran who had conspired against Rose with the White Sox pitchers. In May, Freese was shipped to San Diego; he returned later in the summer but was traded at season's end. More significantly, on July 1, Blasingame was sold to the Washington Senators.

The end of the competition between the rookie and Blasingame might have finally been the impetus for the veterans to relent, to warm to Rose, but it was not. By that time, there was another problem: They didn't like the company Rose was keeping. He had found companionship among the team's black players, and that was yet another reason to dislike Pete Rose.

The Reds in 1963 played in Crosley Field, which is remembered today for the one feature that set it apart: In left field instead of a warning track, the ground sloped up, and when an outfielder felt himself starting to climb the terrace he knew he was approaching the wall.

Except for that quirk, Crosley held the precise charms of most of the other ballparks of its era. It was an intimate place where a fan sat close enough to see a bead of sweat on a player's brow, or to see a muscle bulge under one of the sleeveless uniforms then worn by the hometown club. When a fielder settled under a pop fly and shouted, "I got it!", a good part of the crowd could hear him.

The grass, of course, was real, and the fan walking into Crosley Field from the working-class neighborhood that surrounded it felt the momentary thrill, the quickened heartbeat, of passing from the concrete urban environment to the rich green of the diamond and outfield.

Rose, being a local boy, was an immediate Crosley Field favorite. Each night he had dozens of family members and friends in the stands, and he received a warm ovation every time he stepped to the plate. But the cramped players' clubhouse where he proudly pulled on his Reds uniform was another story. No more than three miles from his boyhood bedroom, it was a foreign, hostile outpost.

"Charlie Hustle, my ass," some of Rose's teammates used to crack. "How about 'Charlie Diaper'?"

The one patch of friendly territory for Rose was across the room from his assigned locker stall, where Frank Robinson and Vada Pinson dressed. It was not long into the season before Rose was spending most of his time in the clubhouse sitting on the floor between the two black outfielders.

Soon he was also splashing on the same cologne they wore— "very strong-smelling," Brosnan recalls—and wearing his baseball pants the same way they did.

"Robinson wore his pants long to hide his skinny legs," says Brosnan. "Pinson wore his pants long to imitate Robby. And here we found Pete doing the same thing. It was like wearing a very tight pair of jeans. Hutch would say to Pete, 'You silly son of a bitch, you're gonna split your pants one day reaching for a ground ball.' "

It's not so surprising that white ballplayers in the early sixties would have believed that a man should find his friends among his own kind. Elsewhere, the rest of the nation was beginning to awaken, ever so slowly, to the civil rights movement. The summer of Rose's first major-league season was also the summer of Medgar Evers's slaying in Jackson, Mississippi, the summer of a huge march on the nation's capital for equal rights and Martin Luther King's famous "I Have a Dream" speech. But then as now, baseball lagged behind the rest of the nation in its race relations.

From the time Jackie Robinson broke baseball's color line to Rose's rookie year, just sixteen years had passed, and in 1963 there remained plenty of players, coaches, and managers who had begun their professional careers believing that they would never have to compete with or against a black man.

What is somewhat surprising is that some of the Reds from that era speak so freely about the episode now, and without regret. Over the course of nearly thirty years, neither their feelings toward Rose nor their attitudes on race have changed much.

O'Toole was one of the veterans who tried to "counsel" Rose. The pitcher's wife, Betty Jane, was the unofficial den mother of the ballclub, hosting the baby showers, recommending schools and neighborhoods, finding doctors for sick children. O'Toole saw himself in a similar role with the men, and midway through the year he tried to smooth Rose's strained relations with the white veterans.

In O'Toole's mind, Rose had established his playing credentials. He was on his way to an excellent rookie season—more than 600 at bats, 170 hits, a .273 average, 25 doubles, 9 triples, 13 steals. A man with statistics like that could fit in easily; that was the kind of ballplaying that could make everyone a little money at the end of the year. The only other thing Rose needed to do to be accepted in the clubhouse, O'Toole believed, was to pull away from the black players.

"He would sit there and talk [with Robinson and Pinson], 'jab, jab,' more or less nigger talk," says O'Toole, who has remained in Cincinnati and works selling waste disposal contracts. "And I said to him, 'I don't know who taught you the facts of life, but there are certain things you do and certain things you don't do.' He more or less hung around with the colored guys on the team. They liked him. They got along fine. If he was going out and didn't have a date, that's who he would be with.

"I might have just said little innuendos along the way. Like, 'Say, Pete, some of the things you do, you just shouldn't do. You know, like talkin' that nigger talk. Not if you want to have people accept you.' "

The Reds' white veterans were racist enough in their outlook, and the team sufficiently divided, that it did not boost Rose's stature one bit that one of the black men he had become buddies with was the team's best player and maybe the best in the National League.

Frank Robinson himself was resented by some of the team's surlier white veterans because he had recently become too vocal, in their view, in a series of players-only meetings. The man who would become baseball's first black manager was a notoriously tough player who stood right on top of the plate, daring pitchers to hit him, and he thought the Reds stood a better chance of recapturing the pennant if some of the other players took his rugged approach.

"In that time, it was not usual for a black player to point out the mistakes of white players without engendering resentment," says Brosnan. "He wanted everyone to play the way he played. In the temper of the times it was rare for any black player to do that."

Robinson and Pinson made up their own clique, along with another black player, Tommy Harper, who had come up from the minors to play a handful of games the previous season. But in the beginning, even the two black veterans shared the team's sentiment for Blasingame.

"We were upset, too," Pinson says. "We couldn't understand why Blasingame was being edged out. But Frank and I had been through plenty of discrimination ourselves—having to board with black families in spring training because we couldn't stay in the team hotel, being barred from certain restaurants. The way Pete was being treated was not something we were going to go for.

"It upset me. He was a rookie, untried. But he had a uniform on, he was a teammate, and we were trying to win. The way I was raised was to treat people as human beings, fellow human beings. I think that's all we did with Pete."

Robinson, in his 1988 autobiography, *Extra Innings*, wrote about his friendship with Rose:

> When I saw that Pete was being ostracized by most of my teammates—guys hardly talking to him, never inviting him out with them—I asked Pete one night if he would join Vada and me for dinner.
>
> "Damn right, Frank," he said, "I'll be honored."
>
> No other players warmed to Rose all season, so Vada and I became his friends and showed him the ropes around the league. We'd warm up together throwing a ball around before games. After games if Vada and I were going out for a bite to eat, we always tried to bring Pete along. He loved to talk baseball as much as I did. Being black and having gone through some hard times with aloneness myself, I felt for Pete and he said he appreciated my thinking of him.
>
> . . . A couple of years later Karolyn Rose told Barbara [Robinson] that Pete's father had told him not to hang around with the

black guys. Pete came to me and said the same thing. He loved
and respected his father, but he totally ignored that advice about
who he shouldn't hang with.

Pete Rose had no black neighbors when he was growing up. As
late as 1979, a cross was burned in Sedamsville at the home of a
newly arrived black family. Of all the hundreds or even thousands
of teammates of Harry Rose's over the years, not one was a black
man. LaVerne Noeth doubts that her late husband ever played
against a black man.

Pete Rose was proud that his racial views and his friendships
transcended his upbringing, and he tried to transfer some of the
credit to his parents. "My father and mother taught me to treat
everybody equally," Rose was quoted as saying in a 1975 UPI
story. But the truth was, Rose's father was among those putting
pressure on him to break with his black friends.

"He was getting phone calls at the bank—calling him a nigger-
lover and every other name you can think of," Mrs. Noeth recalls.
"He didn't like that one bit. Then Phil Seghi [a Reds executive]
called big Pete at the bank and asked him if he could do something. He said, 'I'll talk to him, that's all I can do.'

"When he talked to Peter, he said, 'Aren't there any white guys
you can hang with?' He would have rather that, sure, that Pete be
with the whites. He told him, 'Let the coloreds go. Leave them
alone.' But the problem was, his wife hung with the colored, too.
The white wives didn't want to have anything to do with her. The
black players were his good friends. They treated him good. And
that's what Peter told his daddy. Him and Pete talked it out, and
that was the end of it. But I know big Pete wasn't happy about it."

Pete Rose often has said that he was called in by a member of
the front office in 1963 and asked to disassociate himself from
Robinson and Pinson. In his 1989 autobiography, *Pete Rose: My
Story*, written with Roger Kahn, he refuses to name the club
official, although fifteen years earlier, in *The Pete Rose Story*, he
said the front-office man was club president William DeWitt.

Whatever DeWitt did or didn't tell him, Rose would certainly
have known that the member of Reds management who was most
disturbed over his friendships was none other than Hutchinson.
The Reds manager carried on bravely and through great pain as he
managed his club in 1964 while his body literally wasted away,
and he is remembered by baseball people with great fondness and

a respect bordering on awe. Rose has said that one of his greatest regrets is that Hutchinson, who believed in him so strongly, never lived to see him hit .300 or win a batting crown.

But for all his attributes, Hutchinson was a racist.

"He was not very progressive on the race issue, I must say," Hutchinson's widow, Patricia, recalls. "He wasn't very diplomatic with the blacks, he was short with them. Frank Robinson was not one of his favorites, although toward the end they established a better relationship. Frank was very vocal. He had a lot to say at the time, and Fred did not appreciate that. He was going to do his own thing, regardless of what anyone thought. And Vada Pinson was a boy from California who had gone to college, and he couldn't understand the segregation in spring training.

"Pete was a raucous kid, and he very much preferred the company of the blacks. That rubbed Fred the wrong way. He didn't like that. He couldn't understand why Pete had chosen that companionship. He felt Pete could take care of himself on the field, but he worried about him off the field. And he had promised Pete's father that he would look after him."

Very early on, Hutchinson saw Rose with great clarity, in all his dimensions. He had seen the remarkable drive, the impeccable baseball instincts. And he had also judged that Rose needed to be reined in. By "bumming" with blacks, the youngster was drifting outside the sphere of baseball's powerful, albeit unwritten, social codes and mores. It made Hutchinson, and many others, uncomfortable, and the manager determined that he would do something about it.

After Rose's rookie season, Hutchinson complained to his friend Lawson: "Earl," he said, "Pete's turning into a nigger. I need to do something to get him away from the blacks."

To dislodge Rose from Robinson and Pinson, Hutchinson came up with a plan. His idea was to bring in cast-off veteran Johnny Temple, cut loose after the 1963 season by the lowly Houston Colt .45s. Temple wasn't much of a player anymore, but, as Hutchinson pointed out to Lawson, the veteran second baseman was a "Toots Shor" man, which in baseball's lexicon meant he had a semblance of refinement, dressed nicely, and knew how to order a meal in a good restaurant.

Temple, who had been with the Reds from 1952 to 1959, would return as a player-coach. He could room with Rose, take him to dinner, "polish him up."

Hutchinson's plan was misguided, as attempts at social work in baseball often are. And the thinking behind it was ugly. But the manager's effort to influence Rose, and Rose's response to it, were nonetheless instructive, revealing much about the racial and social climate of baseball at the time Rose broke in—and also a great deal about Rose himself.

At least on one count, Hutchinson chose the right man for the job. Someone else might have balked at his agenda, but Temple, a native of Lexington, North Carolina, warmed to it.

"Hutch called me in and told me, 'Pete Rose is your project,'" Temple recalls. "He said, 'The first thing I want you to do is to teach him to use a knife and fork.' The second thing Hutch told me is, 'I want you to keep him away from the goddamn niggers.' And I said, 'How am I gonna do that, Hutch?' He said, 'That's what you're here for, you figure it out.'

"Pete was always with the blacks. He related with them, and had trouble with the white people. Maybe it was an inferiority complex. I think it was. But we kind of resented it. His wife even sat with the black wives. As far as the knife and fork goes, I think Pete did know how to use a knife and fork. That was just a term Hutch used. But he didn't have good manners in anything he did. He was reared in a real tough neighborhood, and I think what Hutch was trying to tell me was that Pete needed some polish."

For all of Temple's supposed sophistication, he and Rose had some distinct similarities. Temple was described by a Cincinnati sportswriter in his 1952 rookie season as "a throwback to the hell-bent-for-leather, tobacco-chewing players of the old times." Like Rose, the intensely competitive Temple was not particularly popular with other players. His wife complained at the end of his career that he had never been "understood" by teammates who mistook his intensity for arrogance.

Temple played a little *too* hard. Such players may be respected, but they're rarely liked.

Rose and Temple also had a past acquaintance from Rose's high school days when his great-uncle, an assistant clubhouse man named Curley Smart, used to get him onto the field before games. Temple, along with Roy McMillan, had given tips on second-base play to the teenaged Rose.

In his last minor-league season, Rose was asked by columnist Gordon Stem of the *Macon Telegraph* who his hero was. He didn't name strongman slugger Ted Kluszewski, one of the Reds stars he had watched at Crosley as a teen, or the slick-fielding McMillan, or even Frank Robinson, who began his Reds career when Rose was fourteen years old. According to Stem's column, Rose's baseball hero was the gritty Temple.

Temple began with Rose in 1964 by resuming the second-base tutorial. He tried to get him to relax his body, to loosen up. No need to tag those big outfielders between the eyes, the veteran told Rose. Give 'em a nice sweep tag and step out of the way.

Temple also tried to get him to bunt and to fake bunt more often, so he could pull the third baseman in and slap the ball by him. He thought Rose would get more hits that way. "Looking back, we talked more about baseball," Temple says. "I was hoping that by example, from being around me, some things would rub off on him.

"I did try to counsel him in a fatherly way. Every time we ate, we would talk about things, and I let him know that he didn't have the respect of any of the white players. But Pete was a cornpone, tough kid, and very headstrong. His answer was, 'I'll do what I want to do. These people are my friends.' "

Temple was failing in his mission. Eventually, Rose got away from him altogether. "I didn't see Pete that much late at night," Temple admits. "I couldn't go to the places Pete went. They were too lowbrow. I couldn't stay with him. I'm not even sure where he went. I had tried to take him to the better places, but he wouldn't go."

Temple did not last the season. He was released in June following a clubhouse brawl with Cuban-born coach Reggie Otero. As he cleaned out his locker, Pete Rose's onetime hero gave Lawson this rather melodramatic quote, which appeared in the next day's *Cincinnati Post*: "I came to Cincinnati as a nobody, became a star admired and respected by the fans," Temple said."Now I'm leaving as a bum, battered and bruised."

Facing down Temple, O'Toole, Hutchinson, his father, and all the others who wanted him to end his friendships with the black players was a rare moment in the life of Pete Rose. He had stood for something outside of himself—a cause unrelated to the accumulation of base hits, records, or money. "Listen, these colored guys are the ones who treat me like I'm a human being," Rose told DeWitt, the Reds president, in 1963, according to his own account in *The Pete Rose Story.*

The episode showed a remarkable strength of character on the part of the young ballplayer: Right at the beginning of his career, not yet established as a big leaguer, he resisted the will of the highest-ranking members of management and the overwhelming majority of his teammates. He rejected the prevailing racial bigotry in baseball, and he was loyal to friends. It might have been easier to cave in, but Rose didn't.

Wrapped up in all those positive traits, however, was another quality that in the coming years would not serve Rose nearly so well: his stubbornness. He was, as they called it on the streets where he grew up, a "hardhead," impervious to advice or guidance related to how he lived or should live his life. As Rose got older, richer, and more important, this trait became exaggerated. Well-intentioned advice, good advice, guidance from friends and teammates, was repelled.

As a ballplayer, Rose was highly analytical. After each game, he checked his bats for marks to see where the ball had come into contact with the wood. Then he rubbed them down with alcohol, so they would be clean and he could make the same check after the next game. But if the same sort of examination were possible with human beings, to determine if what they were told had left an impression, Rose would have been unscuffed. People who tried to offer advice were sure they had not left a mark, and they rarely tried again.

"In the sixteen, seventeen years I've known Pete, any time you talk about something he doesn't want to talk about, he assumes the irritating posture of letting you know he's not listening to you," says longtime Reds broadcaster Marty Brennaman. "He stares you straight in the eye, but in such a way that you know he's not listening. Like he's looking right through you."

When he felt like it, Rose could also reject advice in such a way that it didn't make the advice-giver angry. Instead, he could provoke a laugh. William Giles, the president of the Philadelphia Phillies, was one of the many who tried to tell Rose that his extramarital affairs during his first marriage were unnecessarily public.

"I said to Pete, 'You got a nice wife. If you chase women, why do you flaunt it so much?' " Giles recalls.

Rose countered; "Let's look at the four sins of the world, Bill. There's drinking, there's gambling, there's smoking, and there's woman-chasing, right? Now let's look at you. You drink, I don't drink. You smoke, I don't smoke. And you gamble, and I gamble. We're both gamblers. I don't think you chase women. So I got two vices and you got three."

The conversation left Giles speechless, smiling, and convinced that there wasn't much point in trying to reason with him.

Pete Rose already had all the answers he needed.

3

THE UNNATURAL

Pete doesn't have a lot of great physical abilities. He
made himself into a ballplayer.

—5′ 7″ Joe Morgan, on longtime teammate Pete Rose

AMONG the answers Pete Rose had was the one to the great riddle
of his life: How had he become such a great ballplayer? How had
he placed himself in the most exclusive gallery of baseball greats,
apart from the run-of-the-mill Hall of Famers and alongside such
magic names as Ruth, Cobb, DiMaggio, Clemente, Musial, and
Mays?

To Rose and so many others, it was such an unlikely outcome.
The Reds executives who had signed him in 1960 would not have
been shocked if after a year or two he had returned home to take
his father's old spot playing for the Trolley Tavern.

Instead, he played in more major-league games (3,562), accumulated more at bats (14,053), and stroked more hits (4,256) than
any player in the century-long history of baseball. In ten different
seasons he got 200 or more hits, another record. He made sixteen
National League all-star teams, won three batting championships
and a Most Valuable Player award.

How had he done it? Not with inherited physical abilities, he
was sure of that.

One day not long after the close of the 1982 baseball season,
Rose dressed up in a suit and tie, swore on a Bible, and explained
his grand and improbable success. His audience was not the usual
one of sportswriters or banquet attendees, but was instead a jury
of his taxpayer peers.

At stake was whether he could properly claim as a business deduction the $50,019 he had spent to purchase Jeeps for Reds coaches and clubhouse personnel after the 1978 season. The IRS had disallowed it, ruling that the automobiles were simply gifts. Perhaps they were given in gratitude for a job well done, but they were not *necessary* business expenditures; in the government's view, Rose could still hit .300 and make the same salary without giving away Jeeps.

When it came time for him to take the stand, Rose respectfully pointed out that the nation's tax collectors didn't understand baseball, and in particular they did not grasp the essence of Pete Rose. He argued that he was not like the other big leaguers. Most of them were bigger, faster, stronger. The game came easier to them.

To keep up with these superathletes, to outperform them and win the batting titles and other honors that had come his way, Rose testified that he had to practice more than his teammates. And he couldn't very well practice alone. He needed coaches to pitch to him, to hit him ground balls, to help push him and drive him toward excellence.

"I needed [the coaches] more," Rose testified. "The whole secret of my success was to work day after day. Other guys didn't need as much as I did. I needed more work because I am not blessed with special talent."

Rose, one of the most celebrated athletes in American history, held a curious view of his own body: He considered himself the equivalent of handicapped. He usually made this case on the sports pages, rather than in court.

"I've got to be unique," he mused to *Philadelphia Daily News* sports columnist Stan Hochman in 1978. "Two of my strongest assets are my arms and my legs. But I don't have a good throwing arm and I'm not a fast runner."

That same year, Thomas Boswell of *The Washington Post* wrote, "Of the primary baseball skills, Rose is deficient in the majority. He can't run, throw, field or hit for power any better than hundreds of players who have passed unnoticed through the majors during his 16 seasons."

In naming Rose the Player of the Decade for the 1970s, *The Sporting News* observed, "So what if he wasn't blessed with the greatest natural ability? He combined guts, determination and stunning single-mindedness to make himself one of the game's biggest stars. He went from a player no one wanted to the man who replaced Ty Cobb in the record books."

Rose, in that same *Sporting News* story, said, "I don't think anyone of equal ability can beat me."

During the Cobb chase, the ballplayer frequently made reference to his physical deficiencies. "I think I'm probably the most bear-down guy in baseball," he told *USA Today*. "I bear down more than anybody. Maybe it's because I had to."

Rose had no trouble sorting out who among his peers was gifted with natural talent, who was not, and who, based purely on physical ability, was more or less likely to succeed. In his mind, it was all fairly simple.

Others, however, have found that identifying the components of athletic success is a complicated endeavor. Scientists in various disciplines have attempted it for the better part of a century, with only moderate success.

In some sports, the task is relatively easier than in others. To give one example, physiologists believe that a sprinter must have a predominance of "fast-twitch" muscle fiber in order to compete on a world-class level. A person without this genetic head start is only going to run so fast, no matter how hard he tries. And since running fast is the only thing that matters in sprinting, he's obviously not going to succeed.

In basketball and football, there is another sort of equation at work, one that is more easily ascertained by a nonscientist. To play either sport, it helps to be oversized.

The smaller the player is in relation to the size required by his position, the quicker he has to be. To survive in the NBA, a 6' guard has to be quicker than a 6' 6" guard. A 260-pound NFL tackle has to be quicker than a 295-pound one. There are exceptions, but this is generally the way it works.

These parameters do not determine who is going to be a professional football or basketball player, or who among them will become an all-star performer. What they do is *eliminate* the great majority of people with average physiques and average speed and quickness from competing on a high level—just as the wrong sort of muscle fiber prevents someone from becoming an Olympic sprinter. Once the field is narrowed, then other factors less easily measured (such as opportunity, quality of coaching, motivation, and luck) determine who will make it and who will fall by the wayside.

Professional baseball, by its nature, is less exclusive. People of normal size can play, and a ballplayer's body type is not a reliable predictor of how good or what type of player he'll be.

Men like Bo Jackson or Jose Canseco, who overwhelm on first sight with their physical gifts, are the exceptions among professional baseball players. Less impressive-looking athletes possessing a more subtle mix of gifts and skills take up most of the spots on the all-star rosters and win most of the postseason awards. Perennial all-stars such as Don Mattingly, Tony Gwynn, Wade Boggs, Steve Sax, Ozzie Smith, and Robin Yount are average in size. None has blinding running speed, although by baseball standards Gwynn, Sax, Smith, and Yount are considered fast.

The raw materials required to excel in baseball are not as readily apparent as they might seem. Consider a few of these premises:

• *A pitcher needs to have a lively throwing arm.* Yet Tommy John, with his surgically reconstructed left elbow, threw no harder than an average high-school hurler and survived in the big leagues until age forty-six. (One of the game's brightest new pitching stars, Jim Abbott, does indeed have a powerful left arm, a gift from God, capable of delivering the ball to the plate at speeds better than ninety miles per hour. But he has no right hand, the result of a birth defect, and he fields his position by adroitly switching his glove to his left hand after delivering to the plate.)

• *A hitter should have superior eyesight.* Ted Williams did— 20–10 in each eye. Yet Dick Allen slugged 351 major-league home runs, won an American League MVP award, and hit for an excellent .292 career batting average even though he stepped up to the plate wearing Coke-bottle-thick glasses. Plenty of other good hitters have worn glasses or contacts to correct flawed vision.

Hitters even give varying testimony about what they see. Some have said they can see the seams rotating on a pitched ball, indicating to them that it's going to break. Other major leaguers say they've never seen the ball rotate, yet they hit breaking balls anyway. Some have talked of hitting the "top half" of the ball; others say they could not possibly discern the top from the bottom.

• *The shortstop, the most important defensive player on the field, must possess a throwing arm powerful enough to make the long throw to first base in time to beat the runner.* Yet Ozzie Smith, who will enter the Hall of Fame based on his defense alone, plays the position with a weak, often-injured throwing arm, and has compensated by inventing a new way to play the position, charging every ball and throwing quickly and on the run.

There *are* physical prerequisites to playing big-league baseball. It's not open to the entire population. A hitter needs reflexes that are well above average, because once the pitcher lets go of the ball he has less than half a second to decide whether to swing. (With a Tommy John, he'd have slightly more time.) And to make actual contact and drive the ball with authority, he must have superior hand-eye coordination.

The game is tilted in favor of the more physically gifted. The stronger-armed pitcher begins with an advantage over the one whose pitching elbow is pieced together with tendons and ligaments taken from other parts of his body, and the quicker-reflexed hitter is more likely to succeed than the one who is a millisecond slower at starting the bat in motion.

But it is not tilted in such a way that it excludes the weaker-armed, the slower-footed, the smaller, or even the less sighted from stardom. They may just have to work harder. Or, possibly, they may be endowed with other, less obvious genetic advantages.

By the time Pete Rose reached the halfway mark in his long career, he started having younger teammates who liked to pose in front of clubhouse mirrors to admire their unnaturally sculpted bodies. These players were the types who after a bad game were as likely to find solace in the weight room as in the batting cage.

Rose, to some of these young men, did appear to have one physical vanity, which was expressed in the very tight slacks he favored. He never carried a wallet and he seemed overly concerned about smoothing any creases in the back of his pants, which usually were caused by the thick wads of currency he carried. This mannerism would cause some of the younger men to remark that, "Pete sure does love his ass."

Whether or not this was true, Rose's real affection was for his baseball uniform and his baseball equipment. In the idle hours before game time, as he held conversations with teammates or writers, his left hand would already be stuffed into his baseball mitt, like an overeager Little Leaguer. Or he might be "boning" one of his bats, rubbing it with a hambone, a practice many players believe hardens the wood. For several off-seasons, Rose also soaked a couple dozen bats in a tub of motor oil in his basement and then hung them up to dry, in the belief that *that* would harden them.

If he wasn't fussing with his equipment he was polishing his shoes. The clubhouse boys didn't do a good enough job, so Rose worked them over again himself, polishing them to such a high gloss that they twinkled under the stadium lights. In later years, as the shoes progressed beyond basic black, he would sit in front of his locker, dipping a cotton swab in alcohol and wiping clean the white stripes and trim.

He insisted on a new pair of sanitary socks (the long white hose that go under the baseball stirrups) for every game, even in spring training. If anyone objected, he had the same retort every time: A big leaguer never wears a pair of sanitaries twice. Never. Case closed.

When he was traded to the Phillies in 1979, Rose for the first time was required to wear a uniform with pinstripes, which was not something that would have engaged the minds of most ballplayers. But it was a concern of his, and before taking the field he would painstakingly tuck in his shirt in such a way that the pinstripes would match up with the pinstripes on the pants. If they weren't right or if the shirt was too bunched up inside the pants, he would take it out and start all over again.

Standing for the National Anthem, everything on Pete Rose was polished, lined up, perfect. No player ever wore a major-league uniform with more pride. None ever looked cleaner. And no player, over the course of nine innings, ever got dirtier.

He would get so dirty that the hair on his arms and wrists retained the dirt, and he needed to use a brush in the shower to get clean.

Rose kept a sort of unspoken bargain with his body. His part of the deal was to give it plenty of sleep, regular meals, no alcohol, and no nicotine. And to put it through no rigorous conditioning. If he felt at a disadvantage physically, he solved the problem by making himself a better baseball player, by practicing harder and playing with greater savvy.

It was an old-fashioned approach. No weight training. No endurance or speed training. No fancy exercises to strengthen his inferior throwing arm.

In the winter, Rose played tennis several times a week, usually doubles, against opponents ranging from his lawyer to his business partners to the baseball writers who covered him. Now and then, to shake the winter cobwebs off his baseball swing, he took a couple hundred whacks against a pitching machine. Early in his career, he played in adult basketball leagues during the off-season.

Mostly, when he wasn't playing baseball, he passed the off-hours at home, watching TV and supplementing his three squares by eating fistfuls of junk food. His first wife, Karolyn, once described the staples of his diet as "Fritos, circus peanuts, cold hot dogs, cold hard-boiled eggs, cheesecake, pound cake, and Rice Krispies."

What Rose got in return from his body was unswerving loyalty. Injuries were something other players got—particularly those other players who spent all that time grunting and sweating in the gym.

In his first two decades of major-league baseball, Rose missed an average of about three games per year due to injury. In eight of those seasons, he played every game on the schedule. At one point, he played in 745 consecutive games, and he is the only player in major-league history to have two consecutive-games streaks of 500 or more. If he was hurt, he usually ignored it and kept on playing. On those rare occasions he needed treatment, he sought it furtively.

One Saturday afternoon in the early 1970s, Rose suffered a slightly pulled muscle while running down a ball in the outfield. No one would have known it because he never allowed himself to limp. After the inning he took a seat in the dugout next to Reds trainer Larry Starr.

"All of a sudden I feel somebody grab my hand, and it was Pete," remembers Starr. "I can remember this because it was a national-TV game. He says, 'Don't look at me, just keep looking straight ahead.' And he puts my hand on his left thigh and says 'Rub that, my thigh's killing me.' And that's what I did. I stared straight ahead and I rubbed it. And I'm thinking, If these guys see me doing this, or if the camera does, it's gonna look awfully strange."

With another player, Starr would have wanted to ice the leg, and he might even have asked manager Sparky Anderson, as a precaution, to lift the player from the game. He knew better with Rose.

"One of the things he hated was for me to come out on the field," says Starr, who became the Reds' trainer in 1971. "I think I went out after him twice in all the years he was with us. One time was on a pop-up down the left-field line. [Shortstop Davey] Concepcion pulled up short and Pete went *pop*, right into the wall. He stayed in, but later his right elbow was all swollen and black and blue and it had some fracture symptoms. I said after the game, 'Let's get an X ray,' and he said, 'No, I don't think so.' And so we didn't. He just wouldn't do it.

"Pete had this absolute confidence in his body. He didn't talk about it or think about it that I know of. He wasn't a big off-season conditioner. He just figured it was going to work and do the things he wanted it to do. And it did."

Rose at one time was considered a fast runner. "He can get down to first base faster than anyone in our league," Augusta manager Ernie White said in 1962, when Rose was tearing up the Sally League as a member of the Macon Peaches. "He is a major-league prospect, a fiery competitor who instills the desire to win in his teammates. He's an Eddie Stanky who can hit and field better than Stanky."

The following season, in Cincinnati, a stopwatch clocked Rose running to first base from his left-handed stance in 3.8 seconds, which made him an above-average runner, although he was never able to convert that to base-stealing ability.

In the spring of 1969, Rose met Ted Williams for the first time and the Splendid Splinter paid him an extraordinary compliment. "Do you know what he told me?" Rose gushed after talking with Williams. "He told me I could be the next .400 hitter, that it was possible because I switch-hit, make good contact, and can run."

Rose's fielding problem at his original major-league position, second base, was mostly an inability to move laterally to his right and throw, which was as much a baseball-skills deficiency as it was an athletic one. Rose at one time could dunk a basketball, which is not something the average man of 5' 11" can do.

Because he fashioned his game like a little man—choking up on the bat, hitting ground balls and spraying line drives to all fields—it was sometimes overlooked how big and strong he really was.

When one of Ty Cobb's sons was asked in 1985 how his father would have felt about Rose eclipsing his record, he replied, "He would admire Pete's determination. He would recognize Pete as a little fellow who always gave his best, a guy who hustles and overcame shortness in size." Rose, in his playing years, was just two inches shorter and about twenty pounds heavier than the 6' 1", 175-pound Cobb.

Unlike most singles hitters, Rose was one by choice.

He hit 160 lifetime home runs, an average of about 6.6 a season. In the last week of the 1978 season, he hit three home runs in a game at Shea Stadium. If he had wanted to alter his approach and hit more balls in the air at the expense of his batting average and total hits, few people in baseball doubt that he could have far exceeded his home-run total.

"My God, Peter was strong," says Sparky Anderson, who was his manager from 1970 to 1978, during which time Rose hit better than .300 in all but one season. "People do not understand this, they can't believe how strong this man was in his hands."

Larry Starr, a jockey-sized graduate of Ohio University, knows his athletes the way a good mechanic knows the cars he services— their good features, their bad features, when they're likely to run well, and when they're likely to break down. He's spent a lot of time thinking about Rose.

"When you look to his raw ability, he did not have the greatest speed. He did not have a gifted throwing arm. He did not have good endurance. He could not run five miles. Ever. He would have been dead. But that's not important in baseball.

"But what he did have was great leg strength and great upper-body strength. That came naturally. His throwing and running skills were enhanced by his great baseball intelligence. His vision was twenty-twenty all the way through his career. And the one other thing he had, which is probably unteachable, is terrific hand-eye coordination. To hit a baseball, that's the number-one most important attribute. You have to be able to quickly translate what you see into a physical response, and Pete could do that as well as anyone."

Says Billy DeMars, who was Rose's hitting coach for the last decade of his career: "What made Pete a great hitter, besides all the work he put in, was he had great eyes. And he was so quick. His hand actions and reflexes were quicker than any player I've ever seen."

Sparky Anderson says Rose's gift of great vision went beyond following the flight of the pitched ball. "He had that tremendous vision. I mean vision of the whole field. All these people who are truly great, Magic Johnson, Joe Montana, Gretzky, they cannot do it without that vision. They make the play, the pass, whatever, because they see everything and they know what's going to happen. You can't teach that. It's vision, instinct. They see it happen before it happens. That was Rose.''

People who spent time around Rose noticed something else about his vision: He seemed literally able to see more than most people, or at least to sense more. At times he seemed to have an almost feral instinct.

One day in 1987 while he was managing the Reds, Rose stood against the first-base side of the batting cage before a game at San Francisco's Candlestick Park. He was talking to a handful of writers while watching his team take batting practice, and his eyes seemed directed toward the batter. Suddenly, he interrupted what he was saying and interjected, "Fucking Mariotti just walked in,'' referring to columnist Jay Mariotti, with whom he had been feuding.

Rose's listeners looked around and spotted the columnist about three hundred feet down the right-field line, in a spot where it seemed impossible for Rose to have sighted him. But he had.

"I used to think Pete had three sets of eyes,'' says former major-league pitcher Larry Christenson, who played with Rose in Philadelphia. "We had this thing, we used to sit together on the front step of the dugout during the game. That was our meeting place. We were both single. Well, I was single, and he was sort of single. He acted single, anyway. And we used to like to watch the women. But at the same time, he was keeping track of every game on the scoreboard.

"He kept track of everything going on in the ballpark—on the field, in the stands, on the scoreboard. They have those numbers of the pitchers up there on the scoreboard, not the numbers on their backs but the numbers from the programs. Pete knew every one of those goddamn numbers—both leagues.

"At the same time he'd be saying—'Did you see that girl over there? Who's that guy sitting in the box over there? Who's the other guy sitting in the box with that other guy?'

"He knew some of the corporate execs. 'Who were some of the corporate execs around?' Or, 'Did you see Carly Simon over there behind the Mets dugout?' He would know where the pass seats were in each stadium. He would know whose wife was there, whose girlfriend was there. 'Who's the visiting team have here?'

"And all of a sudden in the middle of this, he'd say, 'Oh, look, must be a long inning in Chicago. It's been a few minutes since the inning changed.' And then he'd be right back at it. 'Oh, look, so-and-so's here with the owner. Look at those boobs on that babe walking up the aisle. Looks like the pitcher's losin' it. So-and-so's girlfriend's leaving.' It was unbelievable."

Rose did not define himself as a physically gifted athlete, and the sports commentators and writers who sort out the "self-mades" from the "God-givens" followed his lead. Athletes had to be one or the other, born or made. Rose, even with his strength, his speed when he was younger, his perfect vision, and his extraordinary hand-eye coordination, was one of the mades.

But the question was rarely asked: What is a great "natural" athlete? Why couldn't Pete Rose be considered one?

Eric Davis, a Reds outfielder who played under Rose, is generally accepted as one of baseball's finest athletes. He has a sleek build, supple muscles, and a combination of speed and power that gives him the potential to hit 40 or more home runs a year and steal up to 100 bases. But he's never reached those figures because he's brittle and struggles to play much more than two-thirds of the schedule.

Davis is gifted—and impaired, too. What makes him necessarily a better athlete than the blocky but durable Rose, who plodded on day after day, year after year, until one day he had accumulated so many records that, as he has said, "You know, I should have the record for most records"?

Only one thing does: Athleticism has come to be defined almost exclusively by speed, and, particularly in baseball, by the much-desired mix of speed and power.

Rose's durability, the basis for all of his most important records, was rarely defined as a "gift," although that's what it was. His father played semipro football into his early forties, competing against men twenty years younger, and while Rose inherited his mother's facial features, he took his father's body type. "You're looking at my father's body," he once said. "Same body."

Rose, a fancier of flashy, powerful sports cars—Ferraris, Porsches, BMWs—was himself a Volvo, well-made, dependable, and long lasting. It might not have been what he would have chosen for himself, but it served him well.

"You can't play as long as Pete did, and as many games a year as he did, unless you have the will to do it," says Starr. "But there are other guys with his desire, and they still break down.

"Part of it's luck, and Pete was very lucky in avoiding major injuries. But a big part of it is physical makeup. Pete was like his dad. He had a body that wore very well."

What if other players approached the game as Rose did—making headlong dives on concrete-hard Astroturf, chasing every foul ball, even the ones that seem unreachable for sure, playing both ends of doubleheaders in the thickest August heat?

"Most guys couldn't," says Starr. "They wouldn't make it to the all-star break. Pete's physical and mental makeup was unique." Naturally.

After the 1983 season, Rose, for the first time since his days loading boxcars during his minor-league off-seasons, embarked on a physical conditioning program. He was coming off a .245 season, with a paltry 17 extra-base hits in nearly 500 at bats, and he had lost his first-base job with the Phillies to minor-league journeyman Len Matuszek. This was two years before he broke Cobb's record. To surpass Cobb, he would have to persuade some team he could still play.

Starr, who felt close to Rose (he was one of the recipients of the Jeeps), agreed to become his personal trainer for that off-season, but not without first getting him a comprehensive physical examination. At that point he considered Rose less a competitive athlete than a middle-aged man, with all the inherent health risks. He also had in mind that Rose's father had died young, and the last thing he wanted was for the famous ballplayer to collapse under a Nautilus machine.

The physical confirmed Starr's suspicions. Rose had become too old for his off-season regimen of TV, tennis, and junk food. He was in decent condition for a forty-two-year-old man, but not for a professional baseball player.

"What we found was that he still had great leg strength, some limited upper-body strength, poor endurance, poor flexibility, and was a little bit overweight," Starr says. "He had about seventeen percent body fat. That's good for an average American, but was below average for an athlete of his caliber."

Besides their friendship, what kept Starr coming to the gym three days a week during that off-season to push Rose, what kept him believing in Rose, was his knowledge that the ballplayer retained extraordinary abilities. Not speed or power, but the other attributes that had fueled his success all along.

Off the field, as far as the trainer knew, Rose did nothing to abuse his body. "The first thing I tell people about Pete Rose, when I'm asked about his durability, is that his habits were so good," says Starr.

"He wasn't a big conditioner. He did not do the routine off-season work of running or lifting weights. But at the same time, he never smoked and he never drank. And he always got his sleep. On the road you never saw Pete Rose. He went to his room, he got room service. He was not one of the partiers. He didn't sit in the lobby.

"Pete would talk about this and I think some people would snicker. But what they don't realize is, you can be the greatest conditioner in the world, you can spend hours in the gym, but if you drink a lot or smoke a lot or if you run your body down at night, you negate everything. And there are guys who do that."

That off-season, Rose canceled all his public appearances. From the end of the World Series until the beginning of spring training, he did not miss one of his Monday-Wednesday-Friday sessions with Starr, which were two hours long and consisted of "circuit training"—a series of aerobic and flexibility exercises at different stations. The workouts took place in a Nautilus showroom made available by Rose's high school friend, Ralph Griesser, who sold training equipment. Rose's second wife, Carol, to whom he was engaged at that point, often went through the workouts with him. There was fifties music playing over the showroom's stereo system.

"You had to make things interesting for Pete," says Starr. "He still hated to run. You couldn't tell Pete go out and run two or three miles; he would get bored with it. Pete was someone who liked games; he didn't get any kick out of conditioning. But we made it a challenge for him. We gave him certain goals to shoot for.

"He worked his butt off, and it definitely had an effect in allowing him to play for two or three more years. I doubt he would have put himself through it if he had had a better season, but he knew he better do something."

*   *   *

In the second half of his career, Pete Rose increasingly came to be viewed as an athlete who had been cheated at birth. It was an impression that was furthered by the passing of time.

For one thing, the game itself changed. The coming of artificial turf, which made the baseball skitter through infield holes and outfield alleys, created a premium for speedy players who could cut the ball off before it did damage. There were more fast runners in professional baseball when Rose left the game than when he entered it. Even had he not lost any of his original speed, he would have *seemed* slower in the seventies and eighties than he did in the sixties.

There was also a racial element to the perception of Rose as physically inferior. The game's top base stealers tended to be black. So did the great majority of the players who could both steal a base and hit with power—Mays, Aaron, Bobby Bonds, and later Rickey Henderson, Eric Davis, Darryl Strawberry, and Bo Jackson.

In baseball as well as in other sports, the writers and broadcasters, by narrowly defining athleticism in terms of speed and power, also left the impression, intentionally or not, that to be a great athlete you had to be black.

Rose was the stereotypical white athlete—slow, plodding, determined, heady. By the end of his career that was an accurate description; he played so long he really did get markedly slow, less mobile and less powerful, although he denied it. "I haven't slowed down any because I never was what you would call a fast runner," he said during his 44-game hit streak in 1978, when he was thirty-seven years old, conveniently forgetting Ted Williams's words from just nine years earlier.

At the other juncture of his playing career when he was the object of intense national attention, the final leg of his Cobb chase in 1985, Rose was forty-four. At neither time, with the eyes of the nation upon him, did he look like anyone's idea of a superior athlete.

And that, of course, was a great part of his appeal. Pete Rose—achieving so much with so little, outworking, outsmarting, outlasting the *übermenschen*. There was a time when he could also outrun and outmuscle quite a few of them, but nobody remembered it, and he had considerable reason not to remind them. By the time he reached his greatest fame, few people could imagine a Pete Rose who could dunk a basketball.

The notion that he wasn't gifted worked for Rose. He believed it himself, which was the most important thing. It drove him to hit in the batting cage until his hands bled, to practice longer and play harder. Whatever he would have accomplished, his work ethic allowed him to accomplish much more. The guys with the talent could coast; he never could.

This view of Rose tended to win him more credit: He was less likely to succeed, more admirable for having done so. That was, essentially, what he argued that day in his testimony in the Jeep giveaway case. He must have made quite an impression. Even the judge seemed quite taken.

With the jury out of the courtroom, U.S. District judge Carl Rubin, who years later would play a key role in delaying Rose's banishment from baseball, spoke glowingly of the hometown hero. "Who do you compare him to?" the judge mused. "There are lots of baseball players. They come and go, but this man doesn't. I guess the only man you could compare him to now is Ty Cobb."

The jury in the case must have liked Rose, too. They had heard him speak of the immense obstacles he faced as a professional athlete, his struggles and triumphs against superior, more naturally gifted ballplayers. It was easy to understand why he had wanted to reward those who had helped him.

Perhaps Rose was not blessed as an athlete, but on that day he was blessed with a tax write-off. After deliberating less than an hour, the six Cincinnati-area citizens returned with their verdict. The $50,019 deduction for the Jeeps was restored.

There was one exception to Pete Rose's laissez-faire approach to his body through most of his major-league career, and that was his long-term use of amphetamines. They were an edge, or so he believed. Like muddying the infield in Macon to slow down the ground balls.

When Rose broke into major-league baseball, the use of amphetamines, or "greenies" as the players called them, was an aboveboard practice. There were more players who took them than there were who lifted weights. The greenies were frequently dispensed by team trainers. Some clubhouses had a big jar for anyone to simply reach into and take what he wanted. Amphetamine use was so ingrained that when a player was having a particularly good game, he might hear someone shout from the opposing dugout, "Hey, whatever you're on, I gotta get some!" Everyone knew what that meant.

Some players took a greenie before every game. Others popped them just before the second game of a doubleheader, to get a needed lift, or on selected days during the long season when they weren't feeling peppy.

The drug worked on the central nervous system and elevated the player's heartbeat, giving him, at the very least, the illusion of more energy. Most medical professionals now believe that amphetamines have no proper application, and equate any use of them with abuse. But at the time, greenies were what doctors were prescribing to millions of American housewives; college students studying for exams took them so they could stay up all night, and so did long-haul truck drivers. They were called diet pills, pick-me-ups, speed, or greenies, depending on who was using them.

A ballclub's heavy drinkers tended also to be its heavy greenie users. A hard-drinking, swashbuckling group of Phillies players in the mid-1950s who called themselves "the Dalton Gang" were said to wake up around noon every day, have a cup of coffee, take two greenies, and proclaim, "OK, let's go get 'em, guys." Rose's roommate in his first Reds spring training in 1963 had been one of the members of the notorious Dalton Gang.

The amphetamines taken by ballplayers sometimes also came in a liquid form, which around baseball was known as "red juice." In Rose's early years, that's what was available in the Reds clubhouse.

"You wonder where he got all the energy," says Jim O'Toole, Rose's teammate on the Reds until 1966. "Well, it wasn't pure energy all the time. It was greenies, which is about the only thing guys took back then."

No one really thought Rose needed to take greenies, energy being one thing that all agreed he came by naturally. Earl Lawson remembers Dave Bristol, the Reds manager from 1966 to 1969, trying to persuade Rose to stop taking them. "He used to say, 'Pete, you don't need that shit. Don't drink it.' " But Rose did anyway.

"I got metabolism or something," Rose said in 1966. "That's what the guys call me, 'Mr. Metabolism.' "

A new wave of trainers, better educated than their predecessors, drove the use of amphetamines underground by the 1970s. The pills were potentially addictive, and while they might temporarily mask fatigue, the new trainers, Starr among them, did not consider them helpful to performance and did not dispense them. They also stopped giving vitamin B_{12} shots, another supposed pick-me-up.

The use of greenies was still prevalent, even winked at by club officials, but they were not openly dispensed in the clubhouse. Players needed to find a source other than the trainer. Often the source would be one of the Latin American players, because amphetamines were less carefully controlled in their home countries and were sometimes even available over the counter at pharmacies.

There is evidence Rose continued his amphetamine use right through the end of his playing career.

An associate of Rose's, Donald Stenger, told baseball investigators who were looking into Rose's gambling in 1989 that his girlfriend, Linda Kettle, picked up amphetamines from a Cincinnati doctor and delivered them to Rose at the ballpark in 1985.

In 1979, Rose admitted to using amphetamines in a *Playboy* interview. "Have you taken greenies?" he was asked by writer Samantha Stevenson. "Well," he's quoted as replying, "I might have taken a greenie last week. I mean, if you want to call it a greenie. I mean, if a doctor gives me a prescription of 30 diet pills, because I want to curb my appetite, so I can lose five pounds before I go to spring training, I mean, is that bad?"

Rose continued to be coy in his replies. A greenie, he said, *might*, at the very least, give you a greater sense of well-being or confidence. And you *might* want to take one in the dog days of August or before the second game of a doubleheader. Finally, he was asked: "You keep saying you *might* take a greenie. Would you? Have you?"

"Yeah, I'd do it," he's quoted as saying. "I've done it."

Two years later, Rose testified in the case of a Reading, Pennsylvania, physician who was accused of improperly prescribing amphetamines to Rose and other Phillies. His name, along with the names of five other Phillies, had been found by law-enforcement authorities on prescription records. What the doctor needed to prove was that he at least knew the players, so he could mount a defense that he had the sort of physician-patient relationship necessary for him to be permitted to prescribe the medication legally. All but one of the players denied knowing Dr. Patrick Mazza. Rose actually may not have known the doctor, who was the unofficial club physician for the Class AA Reading Phillies, but several of the other Phillies, who had played in Reading, certainly did.

Under questioning by the doctor's lawyer, Rose was asked: "Are you denying it now that you have ever taken any greenies or Dexamyl?"

He replied: "What is a greenie?" A few questions later, as the lawyer continued to press him, Rose asked again, "What's a greenie? Is that a—what's a greenie?" He denied in court that day ever having taken any form of amphetamine.

The Pennsylvania assistant attorney general who took Rose's deposition recalls that it was not a pleasant encounter. "I met him at Veterans Stadium," says Andy Kramer, who prosecuted the doctor. "He was arrogant. That's not unfair to say. The first thing he said was, 'I want to know who's saying these things about me.' That was even before we could tell him what we wanted or how we were going to proceed. I'm not even sure we said hello. He was yelling—'Who's accusing me? I want to know!' He was not the focus of any investigation. The question was the abuse of the doctor."

When it came time for Dr. Mazza to testify, he explained that he had prescribed the pills for Rose because he was getting on in years, and playing a 162-game schedule had become increasingly difficult. "He was thirty-eight years old," says Mazza, who was acquitted largely because the players' testimony was not believable. "Basically, it was a whole lot of strain on a thirty-eight-year-old body." Mazza's defense lawyer during the case referred to Rose and his teammates on the 1980 World Champion Phillies as "world-class liars."

Given the accounts of his amphetamine use and his admission of it in Playboy, Rose's testimony in the Reading case was utterly incredible. His denial that he even knew what a greenie was, two years after telling Playboy that he had taken them, was audacious even by the standards he would later set.

Beyond the lack of candor there was something else at work. Pete Rose, as America's greatest example of a "self-made" athlete, had an image to protect. He hustled all the time, gave his all, because of his well-known and well-advertised love for the game. His father signed the letters he wrote to him, "Keep Hustling." If

Harry Rose ever saw him fail to hustle, he left his seat at the ballpark in disgust, or confronted him about it after the game. This was after Rose was an established major leaguer.

All this was part of the Rose mystique. It was written about, included in his autobiographies, raised again and again during the pursuit of Cobb. Needing an artificial stimulant to pump him up was most definitely not part of the Rose mystique. Charlie Hustle got high on life, on baseball. He would not want his legions of admirers to believe his enthusiasm was partly fueled by chemicals.

Rose claimed to have been misquoted by *Playboy* in 1979. The writer, he said, "made a mountain out of a molehill." When the Phillies amphetamine scandal first hit the news a year later, Rose again denied ever having taken greenies.

"Why would I need them?" Pete Rose said. "I'm a natural."

4

CHARLIE HUSTLE

I play to win. Period.

> —Pete Rose, on why he ran over catcher
> Ray Fosse in the 1970 All-Star game

THE collision was left shoulder to left shoulder. Sudden and violent. Pete Rose, a runaway truck with no brakes. Young Ray Fosse, a stalled vehicle blocking his lane.

Baseball's most famous traffic accident, witnessed by 51,838 at steamy Riverfront Stadium in Cincinnati and a national television audience of 60 million, was the seminal moment in the public perception of Pete Rose.

From that point on, Rose was baseball's ultimate competitor, the man who put winning above all else, even in an all-star game, an exhibition, in which the winning and losing was of no great consequence—except to Charlie Hustle, who knew only one way to play.

Sure, there might have been another route home, a detour around the catcher. A dainty two-step to the left or right. Base runners do it all the time, so often that the radio play-by-play men have an expression for it: "Tiptoeing around the catcher." Sometimes it works: just as often the runner gets tagged out.

He tried to tiptoe around him, Joe, but Fosse leaped, came down with the ball, and tagged Rose before he reached the plate.

Hard to imagine Pete Rose tiptoeing.

*　*　*

The bottom of the twelfth began with Joe Torre grounding to third base. Brooks Robinson gobbled it up and fired across the diamond to Carl Yastrzemski. (Riverfront Stadium, opened just two weeks earlier, was graced by some pretty fair players on July 14, 1970.)

Next up was Roberto Clemente, who hit a hopper to second baseman Sandy Alomar. Two outs. With lefty Clyde Wright of the California Angels breezing through his second scoreless frame, it looked as if the all-star game, tied 4–4 since the ninth, would roll into a thirteenth inning.

But Rose, batting right-handed, kept the inning alive with a solid single to center field. He moved up a base on another single by Billy Grabarkewitz. That brought the Cubs' Jim Hickman to the plate.

Rose took a generous lead. He checked the outfielders to see where they were positioned, although in this case it really didn't matter. He'd try to score on any base hit through the infield. No need even to pick up the third-base coach.

When Hickman cracked a single to center field Rose was off with the swing.

Amos Otis charged the ball aggressively, fielded it on the run, and unfurled a strong but errant throw; as it sailed over the pitcher's mound, it bent to the right, up the third-base line. To meet the ball, Fosse, the Cleveland Indians' twenty-three-year-old catcher, moved three steps to his left, toward the onrushing Rose.

About two-thirds of the way down the baseline, Rose began to lower himself for his headfirst dive. He planned to launch himself into the air, then skid in on his belly with the winning run. He usually came feetfirst into home plate, but this was high drama, an all-star game on his home turf, a riveting extra-inning contest. He chose performance over prudence.

At the last moment, he saw his path blocked. Going in headfirst would have taken him right into Fosse's shin guards. Rose was hard-nosed, not suicidal. He aborted on takeoff, staggered for an instant, then straightened up and drove through Fosse with a frightening, teeth-jarring force.

It was a tough play. An instinctive play. A clean play.

"He hit him hard and he hit him clean. This is exactly the way the game is supposed to be played, and that's the way Peter played it," says Sparky Anderson, who is the only person besides Rose's mother who calls him by his full first name.

"Rose was one of the cleanest players I've ever seen. You knew exactly what to expect from him. He came in headfirst or he drove you with his shoulder. But he never came in spikes high.

"The Fosse play was a credit to him. He gave his all, every play, because he believed that's what the fans deserved. That's the highest tribute there is."

The catcher in the base path is fair game. Rose drew no distinctions between all-star, regular-season, or any other type of game. He played them all the same. (He even played tennis that way, skinning his knees and elbows diving for forehands.)

Nor did he consider that he might be risking injury himself by running into Fosse. He was convinced of just the opposite: To compete at anything less than full throttle, he believed, was the surest way to get hurt. He'd seen too many players twist knees or pull muscles when they slowed up or tried to dance away from a collision. Rose programmed himself to seek contact and deliver the more punishing blow.

"More than any athlete I've been associated with, he just *knew* he wasn't going to get hurt," says trainer Larry Starr. "That was because he was always the guy running into people, running into the wall. He was the aggressor."

Rose's blow knocked Fosse onto his back and into a backward somersault. Rose went down, too, and tagged the plate with his right hand as he rolled by it.

Then he got up, somewhat dazed, stood over Fosse, and asked him if he was all right.

Baseball was Pete Rose's sacred calling. His daughter Fawn once called it his religion. He sought payment for nearly everything he did, but he spread The Word free of charge.

He gave clinics, gratis, at baseball camps. He stopped by University of Cincinnati baseball practices to lend his expertise. He was known to pull over by the side of the road and give impromptu hitting lessons at batting cages.

The saddest thing that Pete Rose could think of was not being able to play baseball. He was truly sorry when someone's career ended, because he couldn't imagine what came next. He mourned for older players and for younger ones whose playing days were cut short.

While he was managing the Reds, one of his pitchers, a fine

Dominican hurler named Mario Soto, tried to return from shoulder surgery but failed in his comeback after pitching a handful of games. A newspaper story in Cincinnati questioned whether Soto's convalescence had been too brief, whether perhaps he should have recuperated longer. Rose read the story to say that he had been the one to push Soto, and he was stung by the suggestion that he was responsible for ending a career.

It didn't matter that Rose despised Soto personally, or that he knew Soto despised him. It only mattered that Soto was a ballplayer.

To Rose, all major leaguers were fellow holy men, part of the priesthood. He particularly liked to befriend younger players, the newly ordained.

He met Fosse for the first time at a banquet the night before the 1970 all-star game and invited him back to his house later that evening, along with Fosse's teammate Sam McDowell. Along with Karolyn Rose and the wives of Fosse and McDowell (Carol and Carol), they talked baseball until 3:00 A.M.

The collision the next night left Rose so bruised and sore that he sat out the next three games. Fosse didn't miss any games, but he should have. He had suffered a shoulder separation that went undiagnosed until the next spring training, and he never again was the same hitter. Going into the all-star game he had 16 home runs for the season. He hit just 2 the rest of the 1970 campaign, and his best home-run total in any of his eight remaining major-league seasons was 12. "When I went back to Cleveland to start the second half I could not lift my left arm above my head," Fosse says. "It limited my power. I got the strength back in my shoulder but I never regained my home-run power. My swing had changed."

After the play, both ballplayers said it had been just something that happened in the course of a ball game, a confrontation between two tough men who wanted to win and wouldn't back down. A split-second thing.

But over time, a mythology was built up around the play, most of it created by Rose. After his father died in December 1970, he harked back to the Fosse incident in a piece for *Sport* magazine titled "Memories of Dad."

"It's strange, but Dad and I never got to discuss that play because right after the game I left on a road trip with the Reds," Rose said. "But I would have to say he ate it up because I did what

I had to do and what he taught me to do. Fosse was playing to win and so was I. He stood up there and tried to make a tough tag, tried to make a good play, and I suppose I just made a better play, and that's the way it is."

Later, Rose said he wouldn't have been able to face his father if he hadn't steamrollered Fosse. He could sound surprisingly callous when discussing the collision, as if he had grown tired of having to defend it. "Yeah, it screwed him up," he commented on the eve of another all-star contest.

Eventually, Rose came to define the confrontation as a test of his manhood. Easing up would have been girlish, which was something Rose never wanted to be. "Look, I'm the winning run in the all-star game in my hometown," Roger Kahn quoted him as saying in *Pete Rose: My Story*. "I just want to get to that plate as quickly as I can. Besides, nobody told me they changed it to girls' softball between third and home."

Lumping the Fosse play together with another famous confrontation, his rumble in the 1973 playoffs with the Mets' Bud Harrelson, Rose told Kahn: "Both times I made the right play. I wasn't trying to hurt anybody and I wasn't trying to get hurt myself. There was nothing mean, and there was nothing sissy."

Ray Fosse still thinks the play was clean. He and Rose agree on that. Fosse has looked at the replay countless times and seen himself straddling the third-base line as he waits for Otis's throw. Someone else might have gotten around him with a hook slide, a more conventional maneuver, but Rose has told him that his momentum was such from starting into his headfirst slide that he could not swerve around him.

"As far as I'm concerned, you don't come in headfirst at the plate, not with the catcher wearing shin guards," says Fosse, now a broadcaster for the Oakland A's. "But on the replay, it looks like that's what he started to do, which would have made it hard for him to change directions when he saw I was in his way."

Fosse doesn't understand why Rose insists that he made such a great play. The throw was high and wide, and he never had the baseball in his mitt. He never even touched it. If Rose had found a path to the plate, he could have scored without flattening him.

Fosse has always viewed the incident as unfortunate. He used to think Rose thought the same thing, but knows now that's not the case. Rose got a lot of mileage out of the collision, two decade's worth. It helped make his reputation.

"I thought that it was a play that just occurred," Fosse says. "And then I saw the quote where he said he would never have been able to face his father if he hadn't bowled into me. I didn't understand him saying that. It was something that brought me to reality."

Pete Rose played in 1,972 winning major-league games. It's a record, *most winning games played, career,* that wasn't even kept until he pointed out that he held it, and it's not one of the hundreds of official major-league records. Rose invented it, and has said it's the one he cherishes most.

It certifies to him that all his other records were not achieved selfishly. They came in the pursuit of victory. When citing the record, he adds, "I'm the biggest winner in the history of baseball."

No one worked harder at baseball than Rose, for victories or for personal goals.

If he was slumping at the plate, he didn't attribute it to the vagaries of the long season, as many players do, or invoke the baseball cliché that every player goes through slumps. Instead, he crunched baseball after baseball in the batting cage, sweating and grunting and working until the slump was dead. It was nothing for Rose to take two hundred swings.

"I can hit all day and never get tired," he told Thomas Boswell of *The Washington Post.* "I've got these big old arms and thighs that don't wear out. And I'm stubborn, too. I've never seen a slump that I couldn't hack my way out of in the cage."

Rose didn't take days off during the season. When there was no game scheduled, he came to the ballpark and found someone to pitch to him. Sometimes he had to pay a teammate to do it. "The year he broke [Ty Cobb's hit] record [1985], we practiced every day," recalls Billy DeMars, Rose's hitting coach for the last decade of his career. "He didn't take one day off. On off-days, he took a minimum of forty-five minutes of batting practice. We had guys hitting .210, .215, and I couldn't get them to come in on a day off. But Pete was there."

Rose gave himself no credit for God-given physical skills, but he believed his appetite for hard work was a genetic trait. "You see, I think working hard is a talent," he explained before a Reds game in July 1989. "I think it's a talent you're born with. Don't you think some people are born aggressive? Don't you think some people are born with enthusiasm? You can't give someone enthusiasm."

In the course of a game, no one competed harder than Rose. "Everybody gets tired by the end of the season," Tommy Helms says. "Petey didn't, and I think the reason was that the game was so much fun for him. He played the second game of doubleheaders and got that big finish every September because he was mentally fresh. And that was because he was still having fun."

An Associated Press feature story about Rose in 1968 observed: "He is addicted to hustling."

A case in point was when Rose was caught in a rundown. Every major leaguer knows the trick of escaping one: You run straight at the infielder's glove. Stay hung up between the bases long enough and there's a chance you'll get in the way of the ball. The trouble is, the infielders know the trick, too, so it rarely works. They direct their throws around the runner.

Staying in a rundown is tiring. A great many runners surrender, or give a halfhearted effort. Rose never did, and every now and then he'd get plunked in the back or the elbow and wind up safe instead of tagged out.

Says Anderson: "The best way and the only way to explain Rose is he's the one greatest competitor I have ever seen. I have never seen one in baseball like him. He's the only player I have ever seen with total tunnel vision. Every single day he would drive. He was obsessed with it. That's the best way to describe him—an obsession for competing."

Along with his work ethic and competitive spirit, Rose approached the game with an unmatched baseball intelligence and savvy.

He prepared himself mentally for pitchers by tracking the rotations of opposing teams. He knew weeks in advance what pitchers he'd be facing, and he scouted them on television if he could.

Rose studied the mental makeups of opposing players and took advantage of their weaknesses. He knew, for instance, that after a bad plate appearance certain outfielders sulked in the field and didn't hustle after batted balls. When the time was right, he tried to take an extra base on them. He rarely guessed wrong.

Of his 746 career doubles (second on the career list), quite a few came because he had "caught an outfielder napping." Rose never had a lazy day in his whole twenty-four-year major-league career, but he knew when others were likely to let up and he victimized them.

"It helps to know the personalities of rival players in the league," he told Earl Lawson. "And I feel I know most of them. What I'm saying is that if an outfielder offers to give me an extra base by playing one of my hits casually, I'll take it."

Baseball humbles even its very best players because the game gives so much more failure than success.

The basketball player Michael Jordan is the high scorer and the star of nearly every game he plays. The only question is whether he'll play up to his own high standards. A football receiver can go a decade without playing a game in which he doesn't make a catch.

Baseball offers no such guaranteed success. The best pitchers get knocked out of games and must place the baseball in the manager's hand and take the lonely walk back to the dugout. The best hitters fail more than half the time. The most dominant teams lose four out of every ten games.

An axiom in sports is that all athletes enjoy winning, but the real "winners" are the ones who cannot tolerate losing. They so despise it that they don't allow it to happen. A baseball player with that kind of aversion is unlikely to thrive. Defeat is too inevitable.

Over the whole century-long history of baseball, of all the thousands of players who have populated major-league rosters, it's possible that no player was more mentally suited for the game than Pete Rose.

And one reason is that he was such a surprisingly good loser.

Personal failure never put him into a funk. He didn't bash watercoolers, turn over clubhouse food trays, or pick fights with teammates or writers. He didn't take the game home with him and he didn't sulk. Whether he got four hits or went hitless, he was the same person after the game.

"Pete's confidence was at such a high level that if he had a bad week, he figured that was more hits he had coming to him the next week," says Merv Rettenmund, the Oakland A's hitting coach and a former teammate of Rose's on the Reds. "He turned it into a positive. Good hitters learn from their failures, but they don't dwell on them. Pete was the ultimate example of that."

Rose also handled his team's losses with great grace. He much preferred winning, and few players were more dogged, aggressive, or inventive in the pursuit of it. But what really thrilled him was the quest, the competition.

He didn't play to win. He played to play.

And that was the best of Pete Rose: The manchild, caked in dirt, driven by joy.

The 1975 World Series featured a pair of powerful teams, the Cincinnati Reds and the Boston Red Sox, a contrast in ballparks between symmetrical, plastic-turfed Riverfront Stadium and Boston's Fenway Park, with its odd angles and ugly-but-beloved left-field wall, and a galaxy of stars and colorful players—Rose, Bench, Morgan, and the rest of the Big Red machine cast for the Reds, and Carlton Fisk, Fred Lynn, the aging Carl Yastrzemski, junk-balling wizard Luis Tiant, and retro-hippies Bill "Spaceman" Lee and Bernardo Carbo for the Red Sox.

Five of the seven contests were decided by one run. Two went extra innings. Six runners were thrown out at the plate. Six home runs were clubbed in game three but the contest turned on a tenth-inning bunt.

The series captured the imagination of the nation as few have before or since. Of all the baseball fans in America, no one was more enthralled than Pete Rose.

In the final game, he delivered the crucial play, although it cannot be found in the box score. With the Reds trailing 3–0 and looking listless, Rose's ferocious takeout slide spooked the Red Sox's little second baseman, Denny Doyle, kept an inning alive, and set up the home run that brought the Reds back to life. Peter Gammons captured the moment in his book *Beyond the Sixth Game:*

> By the sixth inning of the final game, Rose was stomping around the dugout like a whiffling Che Guevara. He screamed, hollered, and slapped his teammates, then stomped up to the plate and led off the inning with a single, one of the extraordinary eleven times he reached base in his final fifteen plate appearances. An out later, Bench pulled a Lee sinker into the ground for what appeared to be an inning-ending double play to [shortstop Rick] Burleson. "There are some things you just can't allow to happen," said Rose. "At that moment, a double play

was one of them." He sent himself in a kamikaze orbit toward Doyle. "He saw me coming for ten feet in the air," Rose later chortled. "I made sure of it." He wanted his takeout slides to go to Cooperstown with his base-hit records.

Doyle's relay throw ended up in the first-base dugout, even though the sliding Rose had never touched him. Tony Perez followed with a two-run homer, and the Reds won the game, 4–3, with a two-out single in the ninth by Joe Morgan.

As great as that seventh game was, the very best game of the series, perhaps of any World Series, was, as the title of Gammons's book suggests, the sixth game. The Red Sox, having tied the game in the eighth inning on a pinch-hit, three-run homer by Carbo, won it with a postmidnight, twelfth-inning fly ball off the bat of Fisk that had just enough steam to clear Fenway's left-field "Green Monster."

Two innings before the home run, Rose, between pitches of an at bat, had turned to catcher Fisk and observed: "This is some kind of game, isn't it?"

On the way to the chartered bus that would return the Reds to their hotel, Rose was still prattling on about what a wonderful contest it had been.

"But we *lost*, Peter," Sparky Anderson protested.

"I know, Sparky," Rose countered. "But it was a great game, wasn't it?"

Five years later, Rose found himself involved in another thriller, Philadelphia's 8–7 extra-inning victory over the Houston Astros to earn a place in the 1980 World Series. It was probably the greatest League Championship Series game ever.

In the seventh inning, Pete Rose's buddy Larry Christenson came in as a reliever and pitched a disastrous two-thirds of an inning, giving up a walk, a single, a double, and three earned runs. Before the Phillies rallied for five runs in the next frame off Nolan Ryan, it appeared he would be the goat. Each team had two wins in the five-game series: the winner continued on, the loser was done for the season.

"Until the day I die," says Christenson, "I will never forget the look I got from Pete Rose after I gave up those runs. I'm sitting on the bench, and I feel about two inches high. It looks like we're going back to Philadelphia, and I've given it all up. Everything we've hoped for. Everything we've worked for. It happened so fast. It's hitting me, it's sinking in. I've given up the whole shitterooni.

"I'm sitting on the bench, close to the bat rack, behind the batting helmets. I'm in an area where I'm almost hidden. And Pete comes in after the inning, and I see those piercing eyes. He's looking right *into* me. And it's like he's saying, *You mother-fucker. You just screwed up everything. You blew our chances.*

"I was being sworn at, scolded, ripped apart with one look that lasted maybe two seconds. There was disgust in that look. Pure hatred."

Five years earlier Rose had bubbled over with delight at his involvement in losing the sixth game of the 1975 World Series. A loss. Why was he now so enraged? This was a great game, too, win or lose.

"I don't think Pete liked that we were losing," says Christenson. "Not one bit. But what I think really had him pissed off was that if we lost, that was it. The end. No World Series. We weren't going to get to play anymore that year."

The bigger the game, the more press attention, the greater the potential distractions, the keener was Rose's concentration.

In the third game of the 1973 National League playoffs, Rose engaged in his celebrated scrap with Mets shortstop Bud Harrelson. With the Mets leading the Reds 9–2 in the fifth inning of an otherwise drab ball game, Rose came in hard on a takeout slide at second base—too hard for Harrelson's taste—and the two exchanged words.

Rose told Kahn that Harrelson called him a cocksucker. Rose, ever alert to his masculinity being called into question, replied, "You don't know me that well."

Why slide so hard in a lopsided game? "Me sliding hard into Harrelson trying to break up a double play was baseball the way it's supposed to be played," he explained in 1978. "I'm no damn little girl out there. I'm supposed to give the fans their money's worth and play hard and try to bust up double plays—and shortstops."

The two men tussled. Rose wrestled Harrelson to the ground and ended up on top of him while some Mets pummeled him with punches in the back.

The most outstanding feature of the brawl was Reds reliever Pedro Borbon ripping apart a Mets hat with his teeth. Other than that, it was a fairly typical baseball fight, with lots of shoving and shouting but little real boxing. The real violence occurred afterward, and it was directed at Rose from the unruly Shea Stadium crowd.

As he stood at his defensive position in left field in the bottom of the fifth, all manner of debris came whizzing down at him from the stands, including, finally, an empty whiskey bottle that caused Rose to come walking in toward the dugout and Sparky Anderson to pull his team off the field. The game resumed after New York City police officers were posted in the left-field grandstand.

The real measure of Rose's competitiveness, and fearlessness, came after the fight, when he came to bat in the ninth inning with his club down seven runs.

With the drunken mob in Shea targeting him and the game seemingly out of reach, the last thing he needed was to be on base when the game ended. It would have been understandable if he tapped out to the infield and hustled into the clubhouse. Instead, he ripped a single up the middle. When the game ended, he sprinted to the clubhouse, with police sealing off the field from fans.

The next day, with the Reds trailing two games to one in the best-of-five series and needing a win to stay alive, Rose came up to bat in the twelfth inning of a 1–1 game. As he stepped into the box at Shea Stadium, he was easily the most hated man in New York. Harrelson was as tall as Rose, but at least thirty pounds lighter. Mets fans had cast Rose as the bully.

At such critical moments you expected something exciting from Rose. And with the Reds on the brink of elimination, Mets right-hander Harry Parker, winner of eight games that season, made the mistake of grooving a fastball in Rose's hitting zone. Rose put his home-run swing on it—he had one, but usually kept it stashed away—and lifted the ball over Shea's right-field fence, the winning hit in a 2–1 victory.

Take that, New York!

Rose pumped his fist into the air as the ball cleared the fence, galloped jubilantly around the bases, and stomped on home plate as his teammates mobbed him.

In a final touch of poetic justice, Borbon, the hat chomper, pitched the bottom of the inning to pick up the save.

*   *   *

More often than hitting home runs, Rose did the little things that won games. But he had a knack for making those subtle plays at incredibly dramatic moments.

One example was the takeout slide in 1975 that caused Denny Doyle's wild throw. Another was Rose's unusual catch—owing to hustle and alertness—that became the signature moment in the Philadelphia Phillies' 1980 world championship.

The Phillies club that Rose joined in 1979 was a good but underachieving group that had won division titles but failed to advance to the World Series in each of the three previous seasons.

The Phillies' best player was Mike Schmidt, who despite his immense talent was a brooder and self-doubter. The team assumed Schmidt's personality. Talented as they were, they played with none of the swagger of the great Big Red Machine teams in Cincinnati.

The hope was that Rose could give the Phillies a heart transplant, as it were, but it didn't work out that way, at least not immediately. The Phils fell to fourth place in 1979, and the next year, the championship season, they were six games out of first place in mid-August and playing so lethargically that manager Dallas Green blasted them as "gutless" and "crybabies."

Everyone knew Green wasn't referring to Rose. At the age of thirty-nine, he played in all 162 games, batted .282, stole 12 bases, hit a league-leading 42 doubles, and performed with all his usual vigor.

And there was even one player whom Rose had been able to boost up: Schmidt. Just Rose's presence on the team and the press coverage he attracted took some of the attention and pressure off the great third baseman. In addition, Rose spent a lot of time telling Schmidt how good he was, injecting him with megadoses of confidence. "He pumped him up and up and up until Mike finally believed it," says Christenson.

Schmidt hit 48 home runs in 1980, and his blistering final two months led the Phillies past the Montreal Expos to the Eastern Division crown, which they clinched with one game left in the season.

On October 21, 1980, the Phillies, leading the Kansas City Royals three games to two, stood poised on the brink of their first-ever World Championship. Rose was stationed at first base, not far from where a line of police dogs and riot-helmeted police on horseback ringed the field.

In the wake of a couple of ugly postseason scenes in New York—the Harrelson episode, and more recent mayhem at Yankee Stadium—the dogs and horses were there to deter any fans from pouring onto the field.

But there was some business to attend to before anyone could celebrate: The Phillies needed two outs. The Kansas City Royals, trailing three games to two in the series and 4–1 in the game, had loaded the bases in the ninth inning with one out. At that point, Royals batter Frank White lofted a pop-up toward the Phillies dugout, not far from the growling German shepherds, the horses, and the delirious crowd.

Catcher Bob Boone flicked off his mask, moved out from behind the plate, and drifted uneasily under the ball. At the lip of the Phillies dugout, the foul pop floated down and ticked off his glove.

Sixty-five thousand fans gasped as one. The air was sucked out of the stadium. The home team had committed that unpardonable baseball sin, giving the opposition an extra out. And in the ninth inning of a World Series game. Disaster would surely follow.

Right after the gasp came an explosive cheer.

Rose, his hat having flown off during the run into foul ground, his Prince Valiant haircut flapping in the October night, had snagged the ball before it fell to earth. He had been standing under Boone, as if he knew the ball would float down to him.

He pounded the ball hard into his first baseman's mitt, returned it to pitcher Tug McGraw, slapped him on the butt, and trotted back to his position. Then he turned toward the' outfield and punched the air with his right hand, the index and little fingers pointed up.

Two outs!

Watching Pete Rose play, anyone could have guessed he was the first one at the ballpark, that he put his glove on three hours before game time.

Despite episodes like the Fosse collision and the Harrelson scrap, he didn't play with the angry edge of a Cobb, an Eddie Stanky, or a Billy Martin. He played happy. The late columnist Red Smith wrote that he played with a "lascivious enthusiasm."

If someone bought a ticket just to see Pete Rose, it was for a simple reason: It felt good watching him.

But there were elements to Rose's success that were not so attractive. There was, for one, his maniacal single-mindedness. Baseball came first, always.

His first wife, Karolyn, once said that she ranked fifth in her husband's life, behind baseball, their two children, and his maroon Rolls-Royce.

On the day in 1979 when she served him with divorce papers, Rose remarked to teammates and writers, as they rode on the team bus to Shea Stadium, that it looked as if he'd better go out and get a bunch of hits. They were somewhat taken aback. Why did Pete suddenly need some special incentive to get hits? After all, he always wanted hits.

My wife just filed for divorce, he explained. More hits might mean more money, which would be needed to pay off a divorce settlement.

Remarkably, Rose did precisely what he said he would. Not that anybody would have doubted him. In September 1979, the month the papers were served, Rose banged out 51 hits, hit .421, and was named National League Player of the Month.

Nothing interfered with his concentration on the game.

"Pete had this incredible ability to focus," says Larry Starr. "I've been involved with greater players, with great intensity, but eventually you see there's other things on their mind. One day they come to the ballpark and something's bothering them, usually a problem from home. And it affects their play. It has to. With Pete, you never saw that. Nothing ever bothered him to the extent that he took it on the field with him."

There was also an element of greed in Rose's approach to baseball. Not a money greed, although he certainly had that too, but something else. Baseball greed. A boundless baseball greed.

Old-time pitcher Rube Bressler, in Lawrence S. Ritter's *The Glory of Their Times*, said of Ty Cobb: "It was *his* base. It was *his* game. *Everything* was his." The same could be said of Rose.

If it was part of baseball, Rose wanted it. Wanted *more* of it. Games. At bats. Hits. Money. Girlfriends. Doubles. Dirty uniforms. Skinned forearms. Astroturf burns. *Sports Illustrated* covers.

Big leaguers begin playing for keeps in early April. The games go on, just about every day, through the heat of the summer and they don't end until the leaves begin to change. A great many of the games are not packed with drama. Some of them are damn boring, not just to the fans, but also to the participants.

The player whose attention ebbs is penalized. He loses at bats, games, entire weeks. They can't be reclaimed. His string of zeros, his ghastly pitching line, his error for the booted ground ball, is duly recorded at the Elias Sports Bureau, keeper of major-league statistics. His line in *The Baseball Encyclopedia*—career average, career ERA—is debited.

Rose knew everything counted. And he played like it.

Why give up an at bat? It was *his*. It belonged to *him*. If he sat down because his elbow hurt, if he let someone else play because his team was leading 12–2, who was going to get the at bat? Not Pete Rose, that was for sure.

It was just what his father told him all those years around the dinner table in Anderson Ferry: *Never be satisfied*. The lesson still applied. Get a hit, take a big turn around first, and look to stretch it to a double. If you've got 3 hits, go for 4. If you've got 4, go for 5.

It was no accident that he set a National League record by getting 5 hits in a game on 10 different occasions. Each time he had stepped up to the plate with 4 hits, unsatiated. He wanted more.

Merv Rettenmund was Rose's teammate in Cincinnati. In Baltimore he played with Frank Robinson. As the batting coach for the Oakland A's he has tutored, among others, Jose Canseco. Just about all good hitters, he says, have the same type of personality.

"They're all selfish," Rettenmund says. "I don't mean this as a compliment. They're selfish, one-dimensional people. They're not giving-type people. They want what they want and everything else, families, teammates, comes after that. Pete committed himself more than any athlete I've ever seen. To me, Pete got more out of his ability than anyone. He maybe even exceeded his ability.

"One time I saw Pete get hit with a pitch by Bob Gibson, who was one of the most feared pitchers ever. He stood up there and argued with the umpire that he didn't get hit. One thing that showed is that Pete had very little fear of the ball, and believe it or not, major-league hitters *are* afraid. The degree of a hitter's success is limited by the amount of fear he has. Pitchers find out who's afraid, and they use it.

"But even with Gibson out there, Pete didn't want to go to first base because it was robbing him of an at bat. He was missing his chance to get a hit. Other times, I saw him swing at three–one pitches [out of the strike zone] and miss on purpose. His commitment was total.

"There's another type of player who only plays according to the situation of the game. That was Joe Morgan. He could have stolen a hundred bases, but there weren't enough game situations for him to do it. When the game was out of reach, when it was nine to one or ten to one, he was showered and gone. For him to stay in there, he couldn't put the same effort in. He was strictly a winning-type player.

"Pete on the other hand, he'd say, 'OK, it's ten to one, now we're facing the weak pitchers. Let's get some more hits.'"

Yes, Rose was a fierce competitor and a winner. Most of the time, these two attributes were not in conflict. But when they were, particularly toward the end of his career, the greed for hits, for numbers, for glory in the record book even more than on the field, won out all too often.

5

CHASING LEGENDS

Take my advice. Don't ever tell Pete Rose he can't do
something. You'll lose.

—Sparky Anderson

So much of the beauty of baseball is in its flashes of teamwork.

The right fielder digging the ball out of the corner and relaying
it, shoulder-high and on the glove-hand side, to the second baseman, who wheels and fires the strike to the catcher.

The hit-and-run play—the infielder lured from his position, the
batter deftly poking the ball through his unguarded territory.

The third-to-second-to-first double play. Around the horn, an
infield poem.

This is the beauty of the game, but not its essence.

In its gut, baseball is one man versus one man. Pitcher against
batter. An individual sport masquerading as a group effort.

Pete Rose would not play along with the charade. He set personal goals and trumpeted them, too loudly. Two hundred hits
every season. One hundred runs scored.

In just his third big-league campaign, he led the league with 209
hits, after which he was asked, What about a batting crown?

"I'll get that, too," he promised.

He aimed to be the best switch-hitter in baseball, and by 1966
he figured he was. "Why not?" he boasted. "I look around and I
don't see anybody better."

"Ever hear of Mantle, Tresh, Wills?" a teammate gibed him.

Yeah, he'd heard of them.

He set out to become the first $100,000 singles hitter. In 1970, he became it, signing for $105,000, a hefty salary at the time.

In contract negotiations, Dick Wagner, the former Reds general manager, used to tell Rose that he was not a team player, that all he cared about was getting his 200 hits and his 100 runs scored.

In the clubhouse, Rose was known as a "me-me-me" player, which is surely the most peculiar term in baseball's rich vocabulary, and not a flattering one. Rose accepted the label and turned it on its head.

That's right, he would say, and if everyone put up the numbers I do, we'd win the pennant every year. He was right. What manager wouldn't want to field a team of nine men as hungry and goal-driven as Rose? And who would want to play against them?

"Yeah, he was a me-me-me guy," says Anderson. "Some people don't like that, but I believe in me-me-me players. Give me twenty-five players who want to go to the Hall of Fame, and I'll take them. He set goals, but nobody sat down with a typewriter and typed Pete Rose's numbers in there."

In the beginning, Rose's selfishness served him.

By the end of his playing career, his greed, the baseball greed, had consumed him and forever cheapened his records.

Years before, they had toured Vietnam together, traveling from point to point in a low-flying helicopter. Where it was safe to touch down, Joe DiMaggio and Pete Rose did what they could to boost the morale of the American GIs. They shook hands, they told jokes, shared some baseball stories.

Rose had said then he was in awe—of Joe D's accomplishments, his stature, his "class."

Now it was 1978, a midsummer night, and DiMaggio was again on Rose's mind. In his sights. The unbreakable record, the 56-game hit streak, was still well off in the distance. But because it was Pete Rose, the pursuit was being taken seriously.

The streak began on June 14 in Cincinnati with a first-inning single against the Cubs' Dave Roberts. Rose stretched the streak to 7 games, and 15, each time with a single in his last at bat. As he moved through the 20s and into the 30s, mostly with hits in the early innings, the national baseball press began to climb aboard. A man here, a man there, until an unwieldy entourage of writers, sportscasters, and cameramen was moving from city to city with Rose and the Reds.

Something big was happening. Tommy Holmes's National League record of 37 games was in peril, and beyond that, who knows? It had always been a mistake to underestimate Rose.

On July 19, the streak would have ended except for a stroke of good fortune. In the ninth inning, Rose, hitless, walked. Almost miraculously, the Reds batted around, bringing him back to the plate. In the process, they also took a 7–2 lead over the Phillies.

Rose took his stance in the left-hand batter's box. He was crouched, coiled, ready to hit—or so it seemed.

As Phillies relief pitcher Ron Reed delivered, Rose, at the last possible moment, laid the bat out across the plate and dropped a bunt between home plate and third base. Had he walked out onto the plastic turf with the baseball in his hand, he could not have placed it more perfectly.

Third baseman Mike Schmidt had been playing well back, as the game situation dictated. Bunting for a hit with a 7–2 lead in the ninth inning was not usually done, not even by a player in the midst of a hit streak. Schmidt tried to bare-hand the ball on the run but couldn't get a handle on it. He could only watch as Rose, taking no chances, steamed across the first-base bag, pounding it with a long, last stride.

On the mound, Reed, a 6'6" former professional basketball player, showed his displeasure at Rose's breach of baseball etiquette by stomping around for a while, then glaring for a few long seconds at Rose. (Two years later, after Rose and Reed became teammates, they got in a fistfight on a team flight, which around the Phillies became known as "the scuffle in the sky.")

After the game, Rose was happy but sheepish. "You hate to do it when you're up seven–two," he admitted. "That's not me. I don't want to show anybody up. But it took me sixteen years to get thirty-one in a row. If they're going to give me the bunt, I'm going to take it."

Rose, who was thirty-seven years old, then added, by way of further explaining the bunt, "I've given enough to baseball."

Six days after bunting to save the streak, Rose ripped a third-inning single at New York's Shea Stadium to set a new National League mark of 38 consecutive games. On July 28 at Riverfront, he passed what was then the fifth-longest hit streak ever, a 40-

gamer by Cobb in 1911. His method of doing so was familiar—another bunt, again in front of Schmidt, this time in the sixth inning. This one was a much better baseball play: The Reds led 1–0, and Rose's bunt gave them a base runner with one out.

(A decade earlier on the season's final day, Rose had bunted in a nonbaseball situation, with a runner on second base and two outs in the inning, to clinch a tight batting race against Roberto Clemente. "Look," he said after that game, "I bunted my way into a hundred grand. It was my shortest hit and my most important.")

The day after the second bunt at Schmidt, Rose passed George Sisler of the St. Louis Browns (1922), and the following day he overtook the ancient 42-gamer of Bill Dahlen, accomplished in 1894 with the Chicago Colts. Two days later he tied Wee Willie Keeler's 44-game string with a single off knuckleballer Phil Niekro.

On the first day of August, Rose's historic hit streak came to an acrimonious end. His last at bat, and its bitter aftermath, should have been a sign that his competitive spirit, once so admirable, had become warped.

The pitcher was Gene Garber, a bearded thirty-one-year-old who was a slight 5'10" and 175 pounds. Garber threw with a sidewinding, almost underhanded delivery and survived on deception and a mix of off-speed junk that came dipping and diving toward the plate.

His fastball, if it could be called that, was something he threw only if he absolutely needed a strike, and sometimes not even then. Garber hadn't established himself as a full-time big leaguer until he was twenty-seven years old, but by the time of his 1978 duel with Rose, he had become one of the league's better relievers.

Rose came up for the last time with the Reds trailing 16–4. Twice earlier that night he had hit the ball hard but right at a fielder. On Garber's first delivery he tried to bunt, but pushed the ball foul. "They didn't expect a bunt in a sixteen-to-four game," Rose commented later, which was a funny thing to say since he had bunted to keep the streak alive four times.

In the ensuing series of pitches, Garber threw nothing but slow curves and change-ups, all of them off the plate or borderline strikes. They were pitcher's pitches. The best Rose could do was foul a couple of them off.

Finally, with the count at 2–2, Rose struck out swinging on a change-up. Out of character for him, the momentum of the swing caused him to spin completely around. He had overswung. Garber, energized by the duel and the excitement surrounding the streak, leaped off the mound and pumped his fist. So did his catcher, journeyman Joe Nolan.

In the clubhouse later, Rose was in a sour, bitter mood. Why did Garber have to throw him all that junk? And what the hell was he so happy about? Why couldn't he have challenged him with a fastball?

"I guess he thought I *was* Joe DiMaggio. A sixteen-to-four game, and Garber's pitching me like it was the seventh game of the World Series," Rose groused. "In that situation, most guys try to throw hard, or get you with sliders. They won't try to jerk you around. Nah, maybe they do nowadays. Pitchers aren't happy with getting you out, they want to make you look bad."

That night Rose stayed up late to watch a replay of the wretched 16–4 game. It made him even angrier, if that was possible. As Sparky Anderson pointed out, no one had typewritten all those hits into the box scores. But now, Rose sounded as if he thought someone should. The baseball greed had caused him to expect special treatment, even on the field. He wanted things that others, too, had a stake in.

Did Gene Garber need another base hit in his pitching line that season? Not many people knew who he was. Maybe Garber wanted to be famous, too.

The following day Rose told reporters that the next time he faced Garber, "I want to drive one at him right through the box, and I mean hard. That would give me more satisfaction than if I would have hit a rope to keep the streak going."

As for Nolan, the catcher, Rose found him beneath contempt. A goddamn backup catcher, and the guy had ripped him for trying to bunt, mocked him for hinting that he should have been served an easier pitch to hit. "A second-string catcher doesn't like me, it doesn't bother me," said Rose. "He's got his own problems playing the game."

Rose stepped away from the moment, looked back on his streak, and wondered why he hadn't been luckier. He had hit .385 (70 for 182) over the 44 games, with a lot more line drives than bunts.

"I went forty-four games and I didn't get lucky one time," he said, overlooking his team's contribution the night they batted around in the ninth. "I didn't hit anything off anyone's glove. I didn't hit anything the official scorer had to rule on. No checked-swing hits.

"I was swinging the bat good. You get up where I did, the opposing players are rooting for you, the opposing management is rooting for you, the opposing fans are rooting for you. You got everything going for you."

Except a pitcher who wouldn't get caught up in the spirit.

During Rose's great hitting streak, sports columnist Steve Jacobson of the Long Island newspaper *Newsday* asked Joe Morgan to look into the future and predict what the end of Pete Rose's playing career would be like. The vision conjured by Rose's long-time teammate was harrowing, and stunningly accurate.

"At the end, I don't want to be around him when it comes," Jacobson quotes Morgan as saying in the 1978 column. "I know what it will do to him. I don't know what he's going to do.

"I'll miss it as a passing thing in my life. He may disappear, that's true. It is his life. I'm not like that. At the end of the season, he feels bad; a week after the end he wants to take batting practice. That's wrong. Any psychologist will tell you that's wrong. When I'm through, I'll still be Joe Morgan. He won't be Pete Rose, and I worry about that.

"You know the movie where the guy sold his soul. Pete would do it to do it over again. A lot of guys would like to play forever. But I don't know how far they'd go. He'd go as far as he had to."

After observing during the hit streak that he had "given enough to baseball," Rose went on to play eight more seasons. He spent five of them, 1979 to 1983, with the Phillies, and was a productive player for the first three. In strike-shortened 1981, he hit .325, but after that his performance fell sharply and the Phillies cut him loose.

He signed with Montreal for the 1984 season, and he was even worse there. He hit .259 with the Expos, but by then he had completely lost the ability to drive the ball with any authority.

The younger Rose had been no slugger, but neither had he been a Punch-and-Judy hitter. For his career, he averaged an extra-base hit every 13 at bats. He averaged just 1 extra-base hit every 34 at bats for the Expos, which meant that if he had been playing full-time, Rose would have hit something other than a single about once every week and a half.

On the rare occasions someone had the temerity to point out how dramatically his skills had eroded, Rose denied it. "Age don't mean a thing," he would say. Then he would invent his own standards of performance.

One of his favorites was to keep count of how infrequently he "swung through" pitches, missed them completely. This was meaningless to everyone but Rose, who would tell reporters that it had sometimes been a week or more since he failed to connect, however feebly, with a pitch he had offered at. No one could argue because no one else kept track.

After his last year in Philadelphia, he had tried to put a better face on his season by pointing out that he had led the club in sacrifice flies, another obscure fact.

Rose knew better than most the games that can be played with numbers. Sometimes they didn't add up to anything. Rose played so long he held all kinds of wacky, even contradictory records.

One was for fewest sacrifice flies/most at bats in a season, which he set in 1973 when he batted 680 times without a sacrifice fly.

In 1975 he set the record for fewest stolen bases/most at bats in a season—662 at bats, 0 steals. Five years later he stole three bases in one inning, tying the major-league mark.

If it was remarkable that Rose at forty-three could still make contact with major-league pitching, it was also a fact that in his final five seasons he was the very worst offensive first baseman in all of baseball. His friend, the statistics, said so.

Once so prideful, he had become a liability on the baseball field. A dead weight in the lineup. His hits consisted almost entirely of dinked, semi–line drives over the left side of the infield.

If he weren't Pete Rose, no baseball club would have employed him as a player. But with Rose struggling in Montreal, there was a club that needed the one thing he could still provide—hype.

Back in his hometown of Cincinnati, Rose's old team had big problems of its own. The Big Red Machine had been unceremoniously dismantled, piece by piece.

Tony Perez was the first to go, traded to the Expos in 1976. Two years later, Rose was gone, and so was manager Sparky Anderson. Little Joe Morgan, the dynamo of a second baseman, signed with the Astros as a free agent in 1980. Slugger George Foster, unable to come to contract terms, was dealt to the Mets in 1982. Johnny Bench retired after the 1983 season. Among the stars, only Davey Concepcion was left.

With each departed player, the Reds lost more fans. The trading of the hugely popular Perez, the failure to sign Rose, the shocking firing of Anderson were taken by Reds fans as outright betrayals by management.

The city responded by turning viciously on its baseball franchise. In 1976 the Reds drew 2.6 million fans; by 1983, attendance had dwindled to 1.2 million.

There was even talk that the tradition-rich Reds, baseball's oldest franchise, might have to leave town. The Reds had an unusually large crop of good young players who would soon make the Reds contenders again, but the team's fans were in no mood to wait.

If this moment in Reds history had been captured in the style of a newsreel, the camera would have scanned a section of empty seats and the narrator would have intoned, in a booming voice: *Only one man could save the Cincinnati Reds!*

On a Sunday morning in August 1984, several hours before game time, team president Robert J. Howsam summoned into his Riverfront Stadium office his son, Robert junior, who was called "RJ," along with longtime player personnel director Sheldon "Chief" Bender.

"I have something to ask you," Howsam began. "I'm going to throw something at you, and I don't want you to answer right away. After I ask, I'm going to go in and shave, and when I come out, then you can give me your answer."

On his way to the bathroom Howsam finally said what was on his mind: "What do you think of Pete coming back here as manager?"

RJ Howsam and Bender were initially stunned. The public heat for letting Rose leave town in 1978 had fallen on then–general manager Dick Wagner, who was all but ridden out of town on a rail. Airplanes trailed banners insulting him. Talk-show callers veritably frothed at the mouth. Wagner was the most despised man in baseball-mad Cincinnati. And the biggest reason was that he had failed to keep Pete Rose in town.

But Howsam had been the team president through the beginning of the 1978 season, and then a consultant to the club before taking over as president again in 1983. And the two men in Howsam's office that morning knew that he hadn't been any sorrier to see Rose leave town than the vilified Wagner.

A churchgoing straight arrow, Howsam—like Wagner—had a strong moralistic bent. Neither man much approved of Rose's very public adultery. Not only that, but both men had judged in 1978 that Rose had very little good baseball left in him. And now, six years later, Howsam was proposing making Pete Rose a Red again.

"RJ and I just looked at each other after Howsam went in to shave," Bender recalls. "We talked about the condition of the franchise, and the more we talked the more it made sense to bring Pete back. We needed something to get people excited again. Howsam felt he should come back just as manager, and then later when Pete said he wanted to play, Howsam insisted that he be called a *manager-player* instead of a *player-manager*, although that phrase never took.

"We felt Pete was over the hill and couldn't help the club that much. But damned if he didn't bounce back again and get some hits. But Howsam didn't want him to play as much as he did; I guess you could say Pete misled him on how much he was going to put himself in the lineup.

"He ended up hurting the careers of a couple of our younger guys—Paul O'Neill, Kal Daniels, mostly Nick Esasky. Their playing time depended some on if the manager played, and that's a tough spot for a young guy. It wasn't fair. He cost Esasky a couple of years of his career.

"I was pulling like the devil for him to break that record. And I was hoping he would break the record quick and get out of there."

Bob Howsam says that he would have preferred that Rose return only to manage, but he knew he could not get him back to Cincinnati on that basis.

"His career was clearly coming to an end," Howsam, now retired, said from his home in Arizona. "I had done some research, called people who had been with Pete in Philadelphia, and they believed that he could be a good manager. And that's what I wanted him as—a manager. But he wanted that record, and I understood that. Yes, he played himself more than I thought he would. But Pete's a very determined fellow. I wasn't surprised."

Pete Rose's return to Cincinnati in 1984 brought front-page, banner headlines in both the city's daily newspapers. Television stations cut into their regular programming to announce his return. It seemed that within hours people were walking around downtown with "Pete's Back" T-shirts. A couple hundred members of the media packed a sweaty, shoulder-to-shoulder press conference on August 16, the day he landed back in Cincinnati. The new manager was, for him, measured in his remarks.

Nobody should think he was returning to be a messiah, he said. They had found out in Montreal that one man can't make all the difference. The Reds were twenty games out of first place. They had some talented young players. Pete Rose intended to teach them how to work hard, how to win. That was all he could do.

He wouldn't put the pursuit of Cobb above the interests of the team, and he wouldn't play himself every day. The team already had a regular first baseman—his name was Nick Esasky—and that was the way it was going to stay. "Nick Esasky is the first baseman," Rose said that day. "But I can spell him on day-night schedules or during doubleheaders."

One other thing Rose said that day was that he would be especially mindful of the feelings of young players. "Because of the treatment I received when I broke into the majors, I've always said that I'll never let any young player feel that he doesn't belong," he said.

The day of the press conference was an off-day for the Reds. The next night some thirty thousand fans showed up at Riverfront, which most of the summer had been empty and dreary. They had turned out for one reason, to see Pete Rose play.

The manager heeded the call. He put himself in the lineup at first base. His first time up he smacked a line-drive single to center field, which was misplayed in the outfield and rolled to the wall. Although there was no throw, Rose went headfirst into third base, causing a cloud of dust to drift toward the third-base box seats and a swell of applause to ring out from every level of Riverfront Stadium.

The river rat was back in town.

In his last at bat he added an RBI double. He finished the evening 2-for-4, with a run scored and 2 runs batted in. "It was exciting, very exciting," says Reds assistant publicity director Jon Braude. "That first game was one of the most electric moments I've ever seen at any baseball stadium."

*　　*　　*

Nick Esasky at that time was twenty-four years old. He was then, and will remain, a minor figure in the continuum of baseball history as compared to Rose.

Esasky was 6'3", 210 pounds, soft-spoken, strong, and in possession of a looping home-run hitter's uppercut. He was never going to be a .300 hitter, but any seasoned baseball man could tell that given enough at bats, Esasky would produce 20 to 30 home runs a season, with the potential to hit even more. (Esasky was also a noticeably handsome man, but he carried that around in the same way he did his considerable baseball talent: He gave the impression he was not fully cognizant of it.)

Power hitting being in short supply all over baseball, Esasky was the type of player most teams would have found difficult to keep out of the lineup. But the promise to play him at first base, his best position, was quickly forgotten.

After Rose took over as manager on August 17, Esasky started just four more games in 1984 at first base. Rose did not once start him two games in a row there. The next season, with his manager hot in pursuit of Cobb, Esasky was exiled to the outfield, where he had never played before. Rose played most of the games at first base that season, although he did sit down against left-handed pitching to make room for Tony Perez.

With Rose still playing in 1986, and still *wanting* to play in 1987, Esasky had no regular position. Eventually, it became clear to him that his manager was determined to prevent his career from flourishing. How would it look if the young player whose career Pete Rose had postponed for his own purposes went on to become a star?

"After a while Pete didn't try to hide the fact that he didn't like me," Esasky says. "He would say things to reporters like, 'He's too easygoing, I don't know if he cares, I don't know how much Nick really wants it,' you know, all that stuff. But I cared plenty. I just didn't show it in the same way a Pete Rose does. Everybody's got their own style.

"When I look back on it, I don't think that's what it was all about, anyway. What it came down to was, any time I was playing first base, Pete wanted to be there instead. He wasn't really pulling for me. I think any player will tell you that it's mighty tough to play if you feel your manager's pulling against you."

Rose didn't try to conceal how he felt about Esasky. In 1987,

Esasky was hit by a pitch in a game against the Mets and broke his left wrist. Manager Rose was asked about it after the game. "It could have been worse," he cracked. "It could've been Dave Parker that got hit."

Esasky finally got out from under Rose in 1989, when he was traded to the Boston Red Sox, where he played every day. Relaxed and confident for the first time in his major-league career, he responded by hitting .277, with 30 home runs and 108 runs batted in. He even got some votes in the balloting for American League MVP.

Pete Rose gave himself 405 at bats in 1985, and performed, actually, somewhat better than he had the previous two seasons, although any other first baseman with his numbers would have ended up on the bench, if not released. He hit .264 with 2 home runs, his first round-trippers since the 1982 season, scored 64 runs, and knocked in 46. But he still managed only 16 extra-base hits.

Hanging on until he passed Cobb was certainly good for Pete Rose.

He became a true national celebrity, even beyond the realm of sports. He also, as player-manager, kept his $1 million annual salary, and the excitement thrown off by the Cobb chase allowed him to market Pete Rose posters, key chains, limited-edition silver and gold coins, and lithographs.

The Cobb chase was good for the industry of baseball; anything that attracts the attention of casual fans, and even nonfans, is.

And it was good for the business of the Cincinnati Reds. Rose did precisely what Howsam had hoped for: He invigorated the franchise, ended the era of bitterness, and brought the fans back. Home attendance in 1985 shot up 600,000, not all the way back to the numbers reached in the Big Red Machine years, but back to 1.8 million.

Cincinnati newspapers devoted thousands of column inches to Rose in the summer of 1985, and sold thousands more papers because of him. He was on the cover of *Sports Illustrated, Time,* and *Newsweek,* and the hundreds of media people traveling with him in the final weeks reported his every hit and his every quip back to their readers around the nation. The day after he broke the record, he appeared live on all three network morning news shows. Hit number 4,192 was a glorious event—"a piece of Americana," proclaimed baseball commissioner Peter Ueberroth. "People from age four to eighty-four are going to be paying attention and remember the moment for the rest of their lives."

There were only a few dissenting voices, barely audible above the euphoric din. Former teammate Johnny Bench, quoted by *The Cincinnati Post* in September 1985, pointed out that if Rose were not writing himself into the lineup, no one else would. "Pete's got luck on his side," said Bench. "If the Reds hadn't needed a manager, he wouldn't even be close" to the record.

Bench also echoed Morgan's comments from several years before. "You soon learn you can only play so long, then you've got to live the other half of your life," he said. "But with Pete, you wonder if he could do anything outside of baseball and be happy. Pete needs baseball. It's his biggest love. It's the biggest thing in his life. If it were up to Pete, he'd try to get a five-year contract."

Washington Post columnist Thomas Boswell was one of the few sportswriters to paint Rose's quest as pathetic and selfish, not heroic. "There's something ugly in Rose's passion to hang on and creep past Cobb," Boswell wrote in 1984. "At least Hank Aaron was still a credible slugger when he broke Babe Ruth's career home run record."

Long after the record-breaking hit, baseball historian and statistician Craig Wright, in the 1989 book *The Diamond Appraised* (written with former major-league pitcher Tom House before the gambling scandal), argued that by 1984 Rose had become "a carnival attraction."

"This is where a new game began," he wrote,

> an ugly game separate from baseball, a game in which the participant chases a record to the exclusion of all else, while cheered on by fans not so much of baseball but of a queer new game—call it "recordball."
>
> . . . The respect we have for baseball records, particularly the career achievements, is based on the assumption, *the trust*, that they are the result of performance and durability in the context of the game. That is, they came out of a winning effort.
>
> Rose betrayed the trust and was allowed to tarnish the special regard held for these records.

How seriously you take this depends on whether you care about the "integrity" of baseball records. The fact is, many fans do.

More so than other sports, baseball, as it's played on the field, is closely connected to its history and the body of statistics that have been built over the years. Very few people spend hours poring over basketball box scores or football game summaries the way baseball fans linger over box scores.

In baseball, the numbers matter, which is what made Cobb's hit record so cherished—and Rose's pursuit of it so selfish.

Pete Rose shared some striking similarities with Ty Cobb, who was born in 1886 in Narrows, Georgia, and played in the majors from 1905 to 1928.

Both men were the products of domineering fathers.

W. H. Cobb was an intellectual, a school principal, and something of an aristocrat, although not as much as he made himself out to be. In his definitive biography of Cobb, Charles C. Alexander writes that W. H. Cobb was really "potato patch kin" of a more illustrious Cobb clan in Virginia. Nevertheless, Cobb's father drilled into his son the notion that being a Cobb set him apart. Alexander writes that Cobb's father spoke in terms of "how a Cobb" acts and "how a Cobb" feels.

Even though Cobb's father wanted him to be a doctor and not a ballplayer, the message was similar to what Pete Rose heard from his father: A Rose does not fall in with the crowd. He does things his own way. He does not fit in just for the sake of fitting in. A Rose is *different*.

For both men, approval from their fathers mattered more than approval from their peers. It was like oxygen, water, food. They couldn't live without it. According to Alexander, Cobb spent his life trying to live up to his father, who "awed, intimidated and frustrated him."

Both Cobb and Rose were mercilessly hazed and ostracized as rookies, Cobb even more so than Rose. At one point during his rookie season, the veterans on Cobb's Tiger team sawed his bats in half.

Neither man ever mixed well with his teammates, although Cobb, who had a frighteningly violent temper and may well have been clinically psychotic, was more universally despised. In 1910, he was locked in a close race for batting title with Nap Lajoie, who took advantage of the complicity of the St. Louis Browns to go 8 for his last 9 at bats. When Lajoie appeared to have nipped

Cobb for the title, he got a congratulatory telegram from eight of Cobb's Tiger teammates. A recalculation actually gave the title back to Cobb.

"It was too bad," former Cobb teammate Davy Jones told Lawrence S. Ritter in *The Glory of Their Times.* "He was one of the greatest ballplayers who ever lived and yet he had so few friends. I always felt sorry for him."

Cobb, like Rose, courted the press, even before he got to the big leagues. While playing semipro baseball in Alabama, he sent letters to Grantland Rice, then the sports editor of the Atlanta *Journal*, telling of the prowess of a young player named Cobb. He varied the writing style and signed them with different last names. One of the letters told of "a young fellow named Cobb who seems to be showing an unusual amount of talent." He kept sending the letters until Rice finally wrote a column about him.

Later in his professional career, Cobb, like Rose, was exceedingly record-conscious, which was unusual for the time because baseball, in Cobb's era, had a much shorter history. Players sometimes broke records and were not aware of it at the time. Late in his career a reporter threw out the cliché to Cobb that "records are made to be broken," suggesting that his, too, would surely fall one day.

"I disagree," said Cobb. "I didn't make mine to be broken."

Cobb even had a gambling scandal of his own that broke after the 1926 season but related to a regular-season game during the 1919 season, the year of the fixed World Series between the Chicago White Sox and the Cincinnati Reds. The allegation, lodged by former major-league pitcher Dutch Leonard, was that Cobb, Tris Speaker, and Joe Wood were involved in a betting consortium to fix the September 25 Detroit-Cleveland game in Detroit's favor. The bet was to be placed by an intermediary, a ballpark attendant named Fred West. Cobb was to contribute the biggest stake, $2,000, according to Leonard.

Dutch Leonard, who had played under Cobb, was the Paul Janszen of this case. He had a letter written by Cobb which, after first trying and failing to sell it to the press, he brought to the attention of American League president Ban Johnson. In the letter, Cobb wrote to Leonard that "Wood and myself were considerably disappointed in our business proposition," a reference, apparently, to the fact that West had been able to get only a small part of the money down with a bookie.

Leonard also had a letter written to him from Joe Wood, who was by this time out of professional baseball and coaching the college team at Yale. "If we ever get another chance like this we will know to try to get down early," Wood wrote in the letter.

Leonard made no secret of the fact that he felt vindictive toward Cobb, the Tigers' player-manager, who had burned out his arm, he felt, by pitching him too much. He also harbored bitter feelings for Speaker, the Indians' player-manager and his former teammate, because Speaker had not seen fit to bring him onto his pitching staff.

American League president Johnson bought the damaging letters for $20,000, kept the matter hush-hush, and then, in a secret meeting with Cobb and Speaker, demanded that they resign as managers. They did, after which their teams released them as players.

It was at this point that baseball commissioner Kenesaw Mountain Landis injected himself into the case. Landis, who had shown no mercy to the players caught up in the 1919 "Black Sox" scandal, may have had a different agenda this time around.

To begin with, the Cobb-Speaker case was a public relations nightmare. Landis was supposed to have "cleaned up" the game with his banishment of the Black Sox culprits. Now, seven years after the scandal that had nearly ruined the game, the last thing baseball needed was another gambling fiasco, this one involving two of its greatest names.

The other factor was Landis's power struggle with Johnson for control of the game. Some baseball historians who have studied the case believe that whatever the American League president decided, Landis may have been predisposed to reverse.

"As for Landis, the hard-bitten commissioner had his own game to play," Alexander writes in *Ty Cobb*. "Landis' contest for supremacy with Ban Johnson had been going on ever since he became commissioner and was only incidentally related to the Cobb-Speaker affair. . . . By releasing all the evidence in his possession, Landis could both embarrass Johnson, who thought he had everything tidied up, and put himself in effective control of the situation. Having been just re-elected to a new seven-year term by the club presidents, who had upped his salary from $50,000 to $65,000 a year, Landis could afford to bide his time, watch Johnson become steadily less credible and more vulnerable, and eventually decide the fates of Johnson and Speaker on his own."

Cobb's posture in 1926 when faced with the gambling charges was almost identical to the posture Rose would adopt some six decades later. He acknowledged errors in judgment, admitted some of the allegations, but vehemently denied the most serious charge. And Cobb, like Rose, went outside the game to try to seek relief.

Cobb told Landis that he had written the letter to Leonard, and also that he had acted as an intermediary among Wood, Leonard, and the ballpark attendant West, whom he had suggested as someone who could place a bet. Cobb and Speaker both insisted that the game, which was won by the Tigers 9–5, had been square. Cobb, playing for the team in whose favor the game was supposedly fixed, went just 1 for 5. Speaker banged out 2 triples.

Cobb denied to Landis that he had bet any money on the game, which was the key allegation. He said the only time he had ever bet on baseball was during the fixed 1919 World Series, when he had lost $150 by putting his money on the powerful but crooked White Sox.

In the meantime, word of the allegations against Cobb and Speaker and the forced nature of their resignations had leaked out. In Augusta, Georgia, where Cobb lived, five hundred people rallied in his support in front of a flag-draped Confederate monument. The town's mayor and a federal judge attended, and a banner was hung that read, "Ty Is Still Our Idol and the Idol of America."

Cobb also traveled to Washington, D.C., where he had powerful friends, including numerous Southern senators and congressmen, to try to get them to apply pressure on Landis. Speaker and Cobb both retained prominent lawyers.

Finally, on January 27, 1927, Landis released a statement exonerating them. "These players have not been, nor are they now, found guilty of fixing a ball game," the statement read. "By no decent system of justice could such a finding be made."

Cobb signed with Connie Mack's Philadelphia A's for the 1927 season, where he hit .357. The next year he hit .323, and he retired after that season at the age of forty-one.

Landis had almost certainly allowed Cobb and Speaker back for reasons unrelated to the facts of the case, which were damning. Even if they had not bet, they had been involved in a wager in which at least one player had probably bet against his own team. But Cobb didn't see it that way.

Not long before his death in 1961, Cobb said the decision had gone his way because Landis knew that otherwise he was prepared to "tear baseball apart."

Ever the student of baseball history, Rose was well versed in Cobb the player and Cobb the man.

"Do you think he's up there looking down at you?" a reporter asked him in the summer of 1985.

"From what I know about the guy, he may not be up there. He may be down there," Rose replied.

Rose was referring to Cobb's notorious temper, which erupted violently from time to time throughout his life. The most famous incident occurred during a game in New York, when Cobb entered the stands and inflicted a savage beating on a fan who had been heckling him. The man turned out to be handicapped; because of an industrial accident, he was missing one hand and three fingers on his other. When someone screamed out during the beating that the man had no hands, Cobb was said to respond: "I don't care if he has no feet."

If Rose knew of Cobb's gambling scandal, he never had much to say about it. And by the time he broke the record, he seemed to have had a change of heart about the ultimate goodness of Cobb; he said he had seen him *up* there, along with Harry Rose, looking down on him.

Rose's comments on Cobb the player are instructive about his true feelings on his own standing among baseball's greats.

"I don't like to knock old-time ballplayers. When they played, they were the best," Rose said during one of his many press conferences as he edged closer to Cobb's hit total. "It's better off not comparing players from different eras."

But at other times he could not resist. On at least one occasion he knocked Cobb.

"How good a defensive player was Cobb?" *New York Times* columnist Ira Berkow quotes Rose as saying in 1985. "He made the most errors of any outfielder in history. Nobody ever talks about that. He won the Triple Crown one year and hit only six homers." Cobb, despite the errors, was considered an above-average defensive outfielder. And Rose did not mention that the year Cobb won the Triple Crown was 1909, during the dead-ball era, when the top slugger often hit fewer than 10 homers. (Cobb in that season actually had 9 home runs, not 6.)

To *Sports Illustrated* writer Rick Reilly in 1985, Rose began by begging off any comparisons between himself and Cobb, but again veered off course.

"I never said I was going to be the greatest hitter of all time," he said. "I just said I was going to have the most hits. Cobb's .367 average, that's untouchable. That's great. But if he was playing today, he'd hit .315, no doubt in my mind. Think about it. They never had any relief pitching back then. We get a fresh arm throwing against us every two innings sometimes. How tough could the pitching have been? You tell me how a guy is going to win 511 games. And did you ever see the gloves they used? They were about the size of a guy's hand. They had no padding at all. How many diving catches you think they made? I'm not saying Cobb was not a great player. I just think you're better off if you don't compare eras, ok?"

But comparing Rose and Cobb is really not that difficult.

Cobb was simply the best player of his generation. He won the batting title twelve times, and at one point finished first or second in fifteen of sixteen seasons. In the estimation of Craig Wright, Cobb was the best player in his league in five different seasons and was a close second three other times. (There was no Most Valuable Player award in his era.)

Pete Rose, by contrast, is an odd kind of baseball immortal. Unlike so many of the others, the Ruths, Gehrigs, Mayses, Mantles, and Aarons—unlike even his old teammates Johnny Bench, Joe Morgan, and Mike Schmidt—Rose did not dominate seasons, or even many games.

The basis of his records was his durability. His fame owed more to his staying power, his colorful personality, and his popularity with the fans and the press than it did to his on-field accomplishments.

Rose won one Most Valuable Player award, in 1973, and a good case can be made that Morgan, or Bobby Bonds of the San Francisco Giants, would have been a more deserving choice. Rose hit .338 that season to lead the league, but Morgan and Bonds had comparable on-base percentages and hit more home runs and had more runs batted in. Bonds also led the league in runs scored with 131, a figure that Rose never reached in any of his twenty-four seasons.

Pittsburgh slugger Willie Stargell was the runner-up in the balloting, and he wouldn't have been a bad choice either; he led the National League in 1973 with 44 home runs and 119 RBIs.

The baseball author Leonard Koppett, in an article for *The Sporting News* in 1984, wrote, "Rose is great, super, terrific, a sure Hall of Famer, one of the wonders of the world, a perpetual delight to lovers of baseball and a marvelous baseball player." But Koppett's bottom line was that Rose's greatness did not compare to Cobb's.

Says Wright, in *The Diamond Appraised:* "One could conceivably replace Rose's statistical contributions by finding two minor star players and placing their careers back to back."

To look at Rose's career accomplishments in relation to Cobb is to ignore a much more telling comparison, the one between Rose and his contemporaries. The fact is that Rose, who yearned to become "the first $100,000 singles hitter," was not, by a long shot, even the best singles hitter of his generation. Others who played in the 1960s, 1970s, and 1980s were far better.

Three times in his career, Rose hit for the highest average in his league. In only one of those years, 1973, did Rose far outdistance his closest competition. These are the years Rose won batting championships, his average, and the average of the runner-up:

1968: Rose, .335; Matty Alou, .332
1969: Rose, .348; Roberto Clemente, .345
1973: Rose, .338; Cesar Cedeno, .320

Compare Rose with Rod Carew, a soft-spoken native of Panama who played nineteen major-league seasons between 1967 and 1985. He won *seven* American League batting championships, in all but two cases by huge margins. These are Carew's league-leading years and margins over the runner-up:

1969: Carew, .332; Reggie Smith, .309
1972: Carew, .318; Lou Piniella, .312
1973: Carew, .350; George Scott, .306
1974: Carew, .364; Jorge Orta, .316
1975: Carew, .359; Fred Lynn, .331

1977: Carew, .388; Lyman Bostock, .336
1978: Carew, .333; Al Oliver, .324

Rose and Carew had about equal home-run power. Rose walked a little more often, but not much. Carew was a much better base stealer (although not necessarily a better base runner), and was also the last major leaguer who was accomplished at stealing home. Along with the Kansas City Royals' George Brett, Carew is the only major leaguer since Ted Williams to make a serious run at hitting .400: Carew hit .388 in 1977, Brett .390 in 1980. Rose's best average was .348.

What made Rose a better offensive player than the less-heralded Carew? Nothing did. He wasn't.

A comparison between Rose and Wade Boggs of the Boston Red Sox is even more one-sided. In his first eight major-league seasons, the still-active Boggs won five batting championships. Like Carew, he won most of them by huge margins.

In the same year that Pete Rose said that Ty Cobb, in the modern era, would hit no better than .315 because of the better relief pitching and bigger fielding gloves, Boggs hit .368. If Rose's argument is accepted, what on earth would Boggs have hit in Cobb's era?

Boggs's .352 career average after eight seasons would place him fourth on the all-time career average list, after Cobb (.367), Rogers Hornsby (.358), and Joe Jackson (.356). Of the retired players on that list, the next one after Boggs who shared any significant time in the majors with Rose is Carew, all the way down at .328. The list is dominated by players from earlier eras, when averages were higher.

Rose, after his last playing season, was 117th on the list, with a .303 lifetime average. Among those with higher averages was Hank Aaron, who managed a .305 lifetime average along with his 755 home runs, and twice led the National League in batting average. Aaron was also a dangerous base stealer, a not-much-remembered facet of his game. In six seasons he stole 20 or more bases. Rose accomplished that just once.

An argument could be made that Rose did not win more batting titles because in his prime he played with so many great hitters, more great hitters than Boggs and Carew competed with in the American League. But in Rose's own league, Bill Madlock, who is not generally considered among the game's greats and is no sure thing for the Hall of Fame, won four batting crowns between 1975 and 1983, one more than Rose.

Baseball history will show that during Rose's career, 1963–1986, some of the most remarkable hitters in the game's history played; Boggs, Carew, Aaron, Mays, Clemente, Mantle, George Brett, Don Mattingly, Frank Robinson, Mike Schmidt, Joe Morgan.

Rose cannot be ranked among those great hitters. He was a very good hitter who collected a great number of hits.

Sheldon "Chief" Bender, craggy-faced with a mop of reddish-yellowish hair, has been the Reds' director of player personnel since 1967. The former minor-league pitcher (he briefly reached the Triple A level) has survived changes in ownership and the reigns of a half-dozen different general managers through sheer competence. He knows how to run a minor-league system and he knows talent.

What he says will surprise many of Rose's die-hard fans, and more casual fans of baseball, who may believe that Rose was the vital cog on the great Big Red Machine teams of the 1970s.

If Bender had to start a new ballclub, and could choose from among all the Reds players he has seen in his nearly quarter-century in Cincinnati, how would he draft?

"The first pick would have to be Bench," he says. "I would want to start with a catcher, and besides, Bench is the best all-around anything I've ever seen here. Then I would go with Morgan, Eric Davis, Concepcion, and then Pete.

"The guys ahead of Pete could all do more offensively, with the exception of Concepcion, and he played a more important position. Hell, no question, two hundred hits, on base all the time, you would want Pete Rose on your team and he's deserved all the acclaim and money. But what people don't understand is he's played with guys who were better players and more important to the overall scheme of things."

Sparky Anderson says much the same thing. Bench and Morgan were more valuable to the team, Anderson says, although no one matched Rose as a salesman and ambassador for the game.

"Pete Rose was the best player on that team for baseball," he explains. "I say *for* baseball. He was the best player in the game for baseball, because of his great feeling for the fans. He knew how to sell the game. He knew how to make it fun for people who came to the ballpark. But he wasn't the most important player on those teams."

And if he wasn't even the most important player on his own team, what puts him in the pantheon with the game's greatest players of all time?

6

PLAYING THE PRESS

I love the media.

—Pete Rose, March 1989

EARL Lawson, as usual, was poking around for a story. On this early December day in 1962, the writer whom the players called "Scoops" had a pretty good idea of what he needed. A feature piece, an upbeat dispatch from Florida to warm the home folks back in wintry Cincinnati. Nothing too analytical.

Lawson squinted through his haze of cigarette smoke toward a ballfield where a couple dozen Reds Instructional League prospects played catch. One of these kids was going to be his story. As he scanned the field, someone came up and tapped him on the shoulder. It was Pete Rose, the ballplayer with the unerring instinct for being in the right place at the right time. Rose got right to the point.

"You gonna write a story about me?" he inquired.

Pete Rose made dozens of sportswriter friends over the years— friends and partners.

Over the course of his quarter-century in the big leagues, they helped him construct the Pete Rose Story: Harry and Pete, father and son; the scrappy kid from the wrong part of town; the relentless drive that sent him chasing Cobb and baseball immortality.

The sportswriters gave him thousands of column inches of fawning coverage. They voted him awards that others deserved more. By the sheer weight of the attention they paid to him, he became a more famous player than he was a great one.

Earl Lawson, the first of Pete Rose's friends in the press, would be many things to the young ballplayer: confidante, second father, disapproving parent, occasional running mate on the road, even de facto agent.

Mostly, he would be Rose's teacher and model for all his future relationships with writers.

Lawson knew by the time he was thirteen that he wanted to be a newspaperman, but when he graduated high school the best work he could find was stocking shelves in a grocery store. Every Wednesday, on his day off, he showed up in the city room of the *Cincinnati Times-Star* to beg for a job as a copyboy. After six months, the city editor finally gave him one.

His main task was to shuttle copy between the news desk and the composing room. Off deadline, he ran out for coffee and sandwiches and picked up reporters' laundry. Whatever anyone asked him to do, he did. The salary was meager but he supplemented it with tips.

Some reporters slipped him pocket change for writing obituaries, a job they didn't much like. Lawson completed them well enough that no one knew the difference. The sports editor paid him a buck a day to call golf courses to find out who had turned in a particularly good round or if there had been any holes in one. (Sometimes on slow days, even a *near* hole in one made the paper.) He also compiled the marriage licenses for publication.

Lawson hung around after his shift looking for the odd job or pitching the story no one else had thought to write. He was the Charlie Hustle of the newsroom, and after two years he was rewarded with a staff job as a reporter on the news side.

But just as it was getting started, Lawson's newspaper career got interrupted by World War II, which in a roundabout way is what got him into baseball writing. Several weeks after making the assault on Okinawa as a corporal with the Ninety-sixth Infantry Division, he ran into the *Times-Star*'s sports editor, who was working overseas as a combat correspondent. "He was a very patriotic man," recalls Lawson, "and seeing me in uniform impressed him. He told me right then that when the war was over he wanted me to work for him."

By 1951, Lawson, twenty-eight, had become the Reds beat man

for the afternoon *Times-Star*, a dream job for a young man enamored of baseball and newspapering. Although the Reds of this era were a mediocre, faceless club, Lawson, from his seat on press row, witnessed the great players of the National League: the young Willie Mays, Stan Musial, Jackie Robinson, Gil Hodges, Duke Snider. He covered the searing pennant race that season between the Dodgers and the Giants, and the subway series matching Leo Durocher's Giants against Casey Stengel's Yankees.

He traveled at his newspaper's expense; in his off-hours he dined in fine restaurants, drank with players and other writers, attended Broadway plays. Lawson sometimes felt as if he was stealing his paycheck, and he genuinely believed he had the greatest job in America.

In the press boxes, he sat alongside such giants as Red Smith, Shirley Povich, and Jimmy Cannon, although in truth he also rubbed shoulders with a great many hacks. If there was ever such a thing as a golden age of baseball writing, it had not yet dawned.

An ex-pitcher named Stan Baumgartner, who covered the Phillies, watched the games from press level while wearing his Phillies cap. Lawson's counterpart on Cincinnati's morning paper went home from the ballpark many nights toting a bag stuffed full of free hot dogs, hot dog rolls, whiskey, and other goodies, courtesy of the Crosley Field concessionaire, who feared that otherwise the writer might comment unfavorably on the quality of the food.

Many other baseball writers, while they may have been ethically pure, had problems in the area of grammar and syntax; the inability to write an intelligible sentence was not necessarily an impediment to landing a job on a sports page.

Lawson, over his thirty-four years on the baseball beat, would straddle two generations and two different traditions of sportswriting. He was not among the literary greats but neither was he one of the hacks. His work was good enough to be published regularly in *The Saturday Evening Post*. And he was no shill for the ballclub or apologist for the players, as were so many of his colleagues. If a man was not playing well or giving his best, Lawson wrote it. If the player didn't like it, Lawson never backed down, and on three occasions he exchanged punches with Reds players—once with Johnny Temple, twice with Vada Pinson. As a writer covering the team, Lawson considered himself an integral part of the baseball scene, and if need be, he defended his turf physically.

The closeness that Lawson would develop with Pete Rose was hardly unprecedented in the history of baseball. Babe Ruth had writers who went to Hot Springs, Arkansas, with him in the winter to "boil out." In Jerome Holtzman's wonderful oral history of sportswriting, *No Cheering in the Press Box*, former Yankees beat man Dan Daniel boasts of having "signed" Ruth to his 1930 contract. "I signed Babe Ruth for eighty thousand dollars. I made the deal with him," Daniel said, by which he meant that in the era before agents, he had acted as a conduit between Ruth and the Yankees' management to find a salary both could agree on. (Another writer, Marshall Hunt, told Holtzman that he had signed the Babe's name to baseballs, which should be of interest to anyone who thinks Rose invented the practice of having others forge his name on baseball memorabilia.)

Jimmy Cannon and Joe DiMaggio also had a close friendship. They lived in the same Manhattan hotel, frequently dined together, and even vacationed together. "It's one of the great boasts of all journalists, and especially baseball writers, that they are not influenced by their relationships with people off the field," Cannon told Holtzman not long before his death in 1973. "This is absolute myth. I always considered myself a fair and neutral man, but how could I not be for Joe DiMaggio . . . ?"

Some of the old-timers prided themselves on being newspapermen who just happened to be working sports-side. Cannon and Damon Runyon occasionally departed their sports beats to cover sensational criminal trials.

"The guy I admire most in the world is a good reporter," Red Smith said. "I respect a good reporter, and I'd like to be called that."

But there were many other sportswriters who took equal pride in *not* writing what they knew by virtue of their closeness with players—not the incidental gossip, but legitimate news. Richards Vidmer, who wrote about baseball in New York for the *Times* and *Herald Tribune*, boasted that he knew of Lou Gehrig's illness but didn't print it. "I'm the only writer who knows what's the matter with Lou. But I didn't write it," he says in *No Cheering in the Press Box*. "And why the hell should I? 'The public has to be informed,' my ass!"

*   *   *

On that day in 1962 when Pete Rose tapped him on the shoulder, Lawson was beginning his twelfth season on the Reds beat, although he was still younger than most of his colleagues. Baseball writing then was the plum job on any sports staff, and as such it was an old man's game. The typical beat man was well into his career when he landed the baseball post, and he clung to it until retirement or death, whichever came first.

A few of these old-line writers still wrote their stories in the style of theater review—all observation, no quotes. But other writers, Lawson included, now bolted out of their seats just as the last out was made to join the mad dash for the press elevator, which led to the players' clubhouses. The press box at this moment, with so many chairs being pushed out from the writing desk in unison, sounded like a schoolroom at the afternoon dismissal bell. This was the future of sportswriting: hustling for quotes, liberally sprinkling them into game stories.

The players talk to the fans through me, Lawson liked to think. But at other times, he wondered if all the quoting was such a good idea. "I saw a lot of players come and go," he says, "and damn few of them had anything interesting to say. Very few were good quotes, and even fewer were consistently good quotes."

This new style of sportswriting created the need for a writer to search out partners among the players, men who "could fill up a notebook," as it was said in the trade.

It was too early to tell for sure, but Pete Rose showed obvious promise on this count. Lawson liked him right away. He was forward and brash, probably too much so for his own good. But the game already had enough slow-talking country boys, with their *yessirs* and *no sirs* and whole dictionaries of one-word answers, and here was this rough-edged city kid who talked a blue streak and didn't even know enough to let a writer pick his own story.

Rose was a little less impressive as a player. "He played third base," Lawson recalls of that long-ago Instructional League game. "Tommy Harper was down there. So was Chico Ruiz. Chico pointed to Rose and said, 'He's got a base-hit bat.' He made a couple of errors. He also had two or three hits. What I remember most is he played with his head in the stands. He was looking at me constantly to see if I was taking notes."

Lawson was. His story the next day was all about Pete Rose, the local lad from Cincinnati's West Side with the base-hit bat. It was just the kind of story he had been looking for. A light feature. Nothing too analytical.

Pete Rose was an excellent prospect indeed, naturally gifted at press relations.

When Rose joined the Reds the next season he went to school with Lawson. Press Relations 101. He was a fast learner, a much more gifted student than he had been back at Western Hills High. In later years, other baseball writers who marveled at Rose's unfailing cooperativeness and quotability would occasionally refer to him as "having come up with Lawson."

Professor Lawson taught many lessons, but he hammered away at one theme in particular: Help the press and you help yourself. The road to riches and fame leads through the daily sports page.

Rose would remember this lesson long after changes in baseball and journalism had rendered it obsolete. That's the way Rose was—once something penetrated him, if he accepted it as fact then he never stopped believing in it.

Lawson also showed Rose examples of what could happen to players who weren't sufficiently respectful of the writing press. "I remember one day Sammy Ellis, a Reds pitcher, threw a shutout," says Lawson, "and instead of talking to the writers, he went on the radio and collected his twenty-five bucks or whatever. And in my story the next day, I wrote that his unwillingness to talk to the press was as unlikely as his shutout, because normally he was a gabby guy. This was 1963 or '64. And I said to Pete after the story appeared, 'Don't ever forget this. You'll find out in the long run that being friends with the newspaper people will make you a lot more than the twenty-five bucks you can pick up occasionally.' He said, 'I never will,' and he didn't.

"Everybody knows Pete was great copy. He was available after games, and he always had something funny or insightful to say about the game. Pete was always damn smart about baseball and you could use him to help you interpret the game.

"But sometimes he was too clever for my liking. He was smart enough to realize that if he said something and you laughed, it was a good line and he would pass it on to other reporters. And then everybody would have it in their stories, and I didn't like that. After a while, I didn't react if he got off a good line, because

I knew if I did he would go blab it to everybody. I would keep a
straight face, and then I would put it in my story.

"Pete also had a good nose for news. If he overheard a ballplayer
say something quotable, he would pass it along to me."

Lawson advised Rose on matters both personal and professional. After his rookie season, he came to Lawson upset because
he had been offered a "split" contract—one salary if he stayed in
the big leagues and another if he went down to the minors.

"Sign it," Lawson told him. "Do you really think you're not
going to make the team?" Again in 1970, when Rose was holding
out, Lawson played a role in getting him signed. "I was talking to
him from Florida—he was still up in Cincinnati holding out—and
he said, 'Earl, I'll come down for a five-thousand-dollar raise.' And
I said, 'OK, stay home, stay by the phone, I think I can get that for
you.' " Within a day Rose was signed, although as it turned out it
was for only a $2,500 raise.

One time Lawson slept in Rose's hotel room because Rose's
road roomie, Tommy Helms, had met a woman—Helms claimed
she was Miss Florida—and wanted the privacy of Lawson's single
room. Rose joked with Lawson that he'd never again allow the
arrangement. "You snore too much, Earl," he complained.

When Rose was overly candid in an interview and a writer
printed things he had intended to remain private, Lawson coun-
seled him to be more careful about which writers he could trust.
"Pete, when are you ever gonna learn who you can talk to and
who you can't talk to?" he chided him. "Aren't you ever gonna
learn it?"

Early on, with the veterans shunning the young Rose, Lawson
served as his sounding board. When the writer judged that the
young player was lonely, he would take him out to dinner.

He also introduced Rose to people around Cincinnati and
pointed him toward some of the better downtown restaurants.
When Rose got married after the 1963 season, it was Lawson who
arranged for him to have the honeymoon suite, for free, at the
downtown Netherland Plaza hotel. Occasionally he would worry
about Rose.

"The company Pete kept and the places he frequented, even
early on, were never the best," says Lawson. "One time in Los
Angeles he asked me to meet him at a place in Los Angeles called
Ronny's. 'You need a tie in there?' I asked him. 'Nah,' he said.

And as soon as I walked in the place, I said to myself, 'Tie, shit. You don't need a tie in here. You need a damn gun.' It was a strip joint in a very rough part of town."

Later in Rose's career, Lawson listened to him give a forty-five-minute address to a Reds fan club, and he beamed with pride at Rose's polish and speaking ability. "I couldn't believe it. You know, he was good, and if he made some grammatical errors, they were no longer so flagrant. Later he said to me, 'Earl, you forget, I've changed a lot.' "

Through much of his time on the baseball beat, Lawson was either unhappily married, separated, or, at the end, divorced. He's remarried now and living in a spacious log cabin in Tennessee with his second wife, Benita. They spend their time reading novels, cooking, and working their large vegetable garden. Lawson, who in 1986 was enshrined in the writers' wing of the Baseball Hall of Fame at Cooperstown, keeps in touch with the game and continues to write a weekly column for *The Cincinnati Post*. On Sundays he and Benita attend church. It is, to say the least, a new life-style for him.

"I was crazy back in those days," he says. "One day in St. Louis some girl told me she wanted to meet Pete. I said, "OK," and I took her back to the hotel, and I called Pete and told him I had this gal that wanted to meet him. And he said, 'OK, bring her up.' And I went to his room and opened the door and threw her right on the bed."

When Lawson retired after the 1984 season, Rose presented him with a 14-karat-gold Omega watch with a gold bracelet band. Rose enclosed insurance papers with the gift; he liked the recipients of his occasional generosity to know how much he had spent. The papers said the watch and band were worth $2,000. Rose had the watch inscribed: *Scoops, thanks for all your great baseball years and your friendship.*

Lawson, having begun on the beat in the era of train travel and manual typewriters, at the end was traveling by jet and writing and transmitting his stories on a portable computer. Nothing in his time, however, transformed baseball writing as much as the changes in the way writers and players related.

Television, the huge disparity in their salaries, and the modern newspaper ethos that frowned on closeness between reporters and news sources had driven ballplayers and writers apart. They were less often friends, more often adversaries.

Typically, Rose was the exception to all of this.

It was said that he played like an old-timer. He was also *covered* like one—by Lawson, who came from the DiMaggio-Cannon tradition, and, more surprisingly, by the whole new generation of younger baseball writers and sports columnists.

The modern baseball writer has the most demanding beat on his newspaper. He writes nearly every day from mid-February to late October, often more than one story a day.

He literally lives with the subjects of his stories; if he rips someone in print, he's likely to wake up the next morning and see him in the hotel coffee shop. Maybe the only other beat on a newspaper that offers such intensive access, the kind where you can't get away from the people you're covering, is traveling with a presidential campaign. "I don't even think that's tougher," says Jerome Holtzman, who is the national baseball writer for the *Chicago Tribune.* "They don't have late games on the West Coast that got into extra innings."

The writer's off-season is taken up with the coverage of free-agent signings, salary arbitrations, and labor disputes. There's no more traveling south to take mineral baths with flabby ballplayers.

The monetary rewards are now much greater: The beat men on big-city papers easily earn $50,000 a year and it's possible to make close to $100,000. But the status is no longer what it was, and most sports editors find that the baseball job is the toughest of all their beats to fill.

The baseball writer's standing in the clubhouse has taken an even more dramatic downturn. Few players any longer consider the sportswriter essential to their livelihoods. A player can make millions in endorsements without ever uttering a civil word to a writer. In baseball clubhouses, some players now refer to the writers as "flies"—pests.

In this atmosphere, it does not take much to charm a writer. The player who shows the simple courtesy of addressing him by name scores points.

Rose knew the names of the beat men who covered him, the out-of-town scribes who saw him just a few times a year, the radio reporters from the farthest-out podunk towns. He liked talking baseball, liked to befriend writers, liked their company—even more than he liked his teammates' company. The gratitude he won for such flattery cannot be underestimated.

"As a young, first-year guy on the beat, you would walk up to Willie Mays, and he would whine, and duck you," recalls Bill Conlin, the longtime baseball writer for the *Philadelphia Daily News*. "He was very suspicious, very difficult to get any kind of coherent answer out of at all, especially if you didn't know him. And then you would walk up to Bob Gibson, and he would say, 'What kind of dumb fucking question is that?' And you would get buffeted by all these temperamental superstars, which happens to every young guy while he's establishing his contacts.

"And then all of a sudden you walk up to Pete Rose, and ne says, 'How ya doin'?' Like you're one of the guys. And he's probably got you for life right there."

Tim Sullivan, a sports columnist for *The Cincinnati Enquirer*, was in 1981 just starting out as beat writer covering the Reds and did not know Rose, who was then playing for the Phillies. As Rose had done with Lawson and so many other writers over the years, he introduced himself to Sullivan and invited himself into his next day's story.

"We were in Philadelphia and I was standing in the Reds dugout," Sullivan recalls. "Rose came over and said, 'Which guy is Sullivan?' I said I was, and he said 'Why can't I get my name in my hometown newspaper anymore?' I ended up writing a Pete Rose story for the next day, and for the next eight years he was the most consistently compelling story I've had in sports."

Rose, a lifelong devotee of the sports pages, understood the writer's job, which in itself was a rarity. Unbelievable as it may seem, there are veteran players who never even learn where the press box is located. The little men with the pads and pens materialize at their locker stalls after the game, but where they came from remains a mystery.

Rose knew enough to be mindful of deadline pressure, which for many writers is a nightly struggle, often an excruciating one. With fewer afternoon papers, and earlier deadlines brought on by the long distances that trucks must travel to deliver papers to suburban readers, writers work under seemingly impossible time constraints. They write *during* the game, which means that someone who takes the baseball beat because he loves baseball finds that he really doesn't see the game in the way he anticipated.

In the late innings, the writer has his head buried in his word processor. If he hears a cheer or a groan from the crowd he looks up. Some writers are better than others at dividing their attention between their stories and the game action, but even the best of the deadline (morning newspaper) writers cannot watch the game as closely as many fans do, although they'll never mention this in their stories.

From the sixth inning on, the most frequently asked question in a baseball press box is: *What happened?* Many writers make sure to get seats in the press box near the television monitors, so they can see on instant replay what they've missed live.

After the game, the beat writers (and columnists, too) need the players. It is a physical imperative. They *need* them to be there, in front of their locker stalls, to give the quotes that they can run back up to the press box and insert in their stories. The writer often has ten minutes or even less to get the quotes.

But nowadays, it's not unusual for a writer to find that twenty-two of the players on the twenty-five man roster are crammed into the trainer's room, players' lounge, or some other area that is off-limits to the press. Or they may be seated at the long picnic table in the center of the clubhouse, eating the postgame spread that has been set out for them. They're not technically off-limits, but the response to questions often is, "Can you wait till I'm done eating?" This sort of behavior is most common after a tough loss or at times when the club is warring with its press corps.

Lawson says the increasing hostility in the clubhouse helped drive him into retirement in 1984. "That's one reason I had to quit. You think I could stand outside that lounge like a little boy? It hurt me. Those little assholes, those snotty-nosed kids, and they're treating you like that."

The player who hides out engenders something on the order of real hatred. The player who is always there engenders love. What a writer thinks of a player, and what he writes of him, largely depends on his availability after games.

Rose never hid out. Win or lose, good game or bad, he stayed and answered questions until the last one was asked. His postgame comments were crisp, witty, sometimes clichéd but always tailored to fit into a game story. A fastball pitcher who had shut his team out "could've thrown the ball through a car wash without getting it wet." Trying to hit in the late-afternoon shadows had been like "trying to swat flies with a string of spaghetti." His teammate Davey Concepcion was "the best Venezuelan import since oil."

Rose knew precisely what writers needed and he gave it to them. If there had been a complicated or controversial play, Rose could go back through it better than any television color commentator. He also had the ability to cite statistics that the baseball writers, who were themselves stat-mongers, could use for their stories. "You know," he might muse, "that's the ninth straight Wednesday game we've won." The writer who checked his scorebook would invariably find that Rose was correct, and the ballplayer's contribution was inserted as a paragraph in his story.

Rose reveled in his press coverage. After his fight with Bud Harrelson in the 1973 playoffs, he remarked, "I'm probably the only guy who can knock the Arab-Israeli war off the front page in New York." (He only talked about events outside the world of baseball if he could in some way relate them back to himself.)

"The reason Pete had so many friends among the writers is he made covering him so easy," says Murray Chass, the longtime baseball writer for *The New York Times.* "There aren't too many guys in baseball who are like that. He was an easy guy. The quotes flowed. It's legitimate to wonder how much of a factor that was in what *wasn't* written about him over the years.

"Pete was particularly good for columnists. A columnist could spend fifteen minutes with him before a game, and he was done working for the day. He had everything he needed."

Dick Schaap, a sports reporter for ABC News and a former editor of *Sport* magazine, used to visit with Rose regularly when he came into New York. "If the Reds were in town and they were staying at the Americana at Fifty-second Street and Seventh Avenue, I knew at lunchtime if I went over to the Stage Delicatessen I could find him there. He would be sitting on a stool, eating a sandwich and being Pete Rose. And he was very good at that role. We'd talk baseball. He'd give you some very good insights, some baseball gossip. He'd give you a lot of stuff you could never print. One of his favorite lines was: 'You know why I get all the women? Because I always go in headfirst.'

"I had first gotten to know him well the year we gave him the

Sport Player of the Year award. And he came to the banquet and he stood up there and said, 'This is the sixth time I've been on the cover of *Sport* magazine. That ain't bad for a white guy.' That was accurate, it was funny, it was a little dumb to say. He was not a racist, but it was something that made you wince, but you loved him for being true to himself.

"Pete knew how easy it was to play writers. He worked at it. He was one of the very few modern players who understood how much writers could do for you, and how easy it was to play them. You didn't need to be a great intellect. You didn't need to reveal your innermost thoughts. All you needed to do was give them something to write about. Wisecrack. Get off some good one-liners, which he always did, and act like you didn't think they were shit.

"Writers desperately wanted to be loved. Pete was very good at loving them and acting like he enjoyed them."

A writer or columnist did not have to be from New York or be nationally known to command Rose's attention. Nor did the writer have to be male. In marked contrast to many baseball people, Rose was usually respectful of women sportswriters and sportscasters. Many players and managers turn instantly uncooperative, sarcastic, or even raunchy in the presence of women interviewers. Former Cardinals manager Whitey Herzog was probably the most notorious for this.

Rose was bluntly honest about his interest in courting the media. If the writers didn't write flattering things about him, he reasoned, then he would not have been on the cover of *Sports Illustrated* seventeen times. And if he wasn't on magazine covers, then companies would not have paid him to endorse Aqua Velva, Grecian Formula, Swanson pizza, Mountain Dew, Zenith TV sets and other products.

If someone wanted his time, he gave it. Who knows what the payoff might be somewhere down the line? Wasn't that what Lawson had preached?

In 1988 during spring training, a columnist for a Florida newspaper took Rose aside and asked him if he had any special recollections of Fort Myers. *Fort Myers?* Rose had played there once a spring, at most, when his team visited the camp of the Kansas City Royals. Nothing significant, as far as anyone knew, had ever happened to him there. It was the kind of question that most ballplayers or managers would have laughed off.

Rose thought for a moment, then answered. Thirty minutes later he was still answering.

Let's see, he began, Fort Myers had an Astroturf practice field, and that had been a big help in 1975, when he moved to third base from the outfield. Taking all those ground balls in Fort Myers, that was one memory.

And also, it was always very hot in Fort Myers, and it was enjoyable going down there to work hard, especially if there were a few extra pounds to be sweated off.

Another interesting story about Fort Myers: After a game down there one season, the entire Reds team walked into a restaurant in their uniforms. For some reason they hadn't used the visiting dressing room to change. What a scene that was! A major-league ballclub, in full uniform, walking into this local joint to eat.

And then there was the bus trip itself. Very long. Once Rose had counted how many railroad crossings there were between Tampa and Fort Myers. It was a boring trip. You had to do something to occupy your mind. He still remembered the number of railroad crossings. Fourteen.

By the time Rose was done talking, the columnist, Bob Rathgeber, had his column. And Rose had hundreds—who knows, thousands?—of new fans in Fort Myers.

Rathgeber had worked in the 1970s as an assistant in the Reds publicity office, but he doesn't think knowing Rose mattered. "Pete knew me from when I was with the Reds, but I don't think that made a bit of difference," he says. "If you were carrying a notebook or a tape recorder, you were automatically Pete's friend, unless you did something to prove otherwise."

One splendid Gulf Coast day in 1987, with a light breeze blowing and the temperature near eighty degrees, veteran baseball writer Peter Pascarelli sunned himself along the right-field line of the spring training ballpark in Clearwater, Florida, and complained to his colleagues: "Three days into this and I already hate everybody on this fucking team. There's not one fucking guy I want to talk to."

These were the words of a grumpier than normal but otherwise typical baseball beat man.

On the outside, the baseball writer is leather-tough, battle-weary, sarcastic, jaded. On the inside, a thin layer beneath the facade, dwells a little boy who believes in heroes and still searches for them on the athletic field.

Is the word *hero* used anywhere else in American society with the frequency it is on the sports pages? Do people in business, in academia, working on assembly lines, expect to find heroes in their midst—or the hero's close cousin, the "role model"?

The baseball writer cherishes the game. He knows its history, upholds its traditions and values. The writers, along with the managers, coaches, team executives, and scouts, consider themselves the game's custodians. They are the constants, the players mere transients. ("You hear guys in the press boxes arguing whether it's good for baseball, or bad for baseball, as if they owned the damn thing," Jimmy Cannon observed in *No Cheering in the Press Box*.)

The writers, chafing at the disrespect shown to them by the players, add to this another resentment: The players do not respect the game itself. Do they know who the hell Lou Gehrig was? How many could name the team he played for?

"Writers like to talk baseball," says Sullivan, the *Cincinnati Enquirer* columnist. "Ballplayers don't like to talk baseball. They're not *interested* in baseball. They don't know anything about the history of baseball."

For the sportswriter, the search for a hero is the search to find meaning in his work. If none of the players are worthy of the game's great heritage, if none of them play hard, then what is the point of writing about sports?

But so many of the players dishonor the game. They play as if baseball were pure drudgery. Where's their joy? They sleepwalk through the season. They shrug off bad performances. They don't take extra batting practice even when they obviously need it. Nearly every player is rewarded with a huge raise at season's end, whether he's played well or not.

Most writers dreamed of being ballplayers themselves. They imagine themselves in the place of the big leaguers. The writer knows he would show up at the ballpark early, with a wide smile. He would bust his ass on every play, sign every autograph. He would love and honor the game, give thanks for every moment he wore a big-league uniform. In other words, he would act like Pete Rose.

The increasingly sour tone of the sports page worked to Rose's advantage. He was the antidote to all that was wrong, the foil for

all the bums and louts who loafed to first base, hid out from
writers, put white powder up their noses.

So many players were undeserving of their fame and riches. But
to make that point, someone had to be held out as deserving, and
that was Pete Rose.

The Sporting News named Pete Rose its Player of the Decade
for the 1970s, over such other candidates as Lou Brock, who had
set new career and season stolen-base records that decade, and
Johnny Bench, who had established himself as baseball's all-time
greatest catcher. The award might also have gone to Rod Carew,
who in the seventies won six batting titles, or Reggie Jackson,
dominant slugger on five World Championship teams.

Five years later, the so-called baseball bible honored Rose again.
In naming him its Man of the Year for 1985, *The Sporting News*
noted that his breaking of Cobb's record had been a shining moment in a season otherwise sullied by a brief strike and a cocaine
trial in Pittsburgh involving several ballplayers.

"Peter Edward Rose, a 44-year-old breath of fresh air whose
exploits on the baseball field last season helped blow away some
of the stench of what happened off the diamond, is *The Sporting
News* Man of the Year for 1985," the weekly newspaper intoned
in a cover piece on January 6, 1986. Richard Waters, the *Sporting
News* president, noted that the sports weekly had been the official publisher of Rose's diary of the 1985 season. "Through his
innermost thoughts, we became deeply involved in the personality of this individual, whose outstanding traits have led to this
honor," he said.

Baseball's bible seemed wholly oblivious to the irony that Pete
Rose was being held out as a breath of fresh air as compared to a
drug trial involving ballplayers as witnesses, just five years after
Rose's name had surfaced in relation to the amphetamine trial in
Pennsylvania. And unlike Keith Hernandez or Dave Parker, who
owned up to their drug use in court, Rose and the other Phillies
players were widely perceived to have been evasive on the stand
("What's a greenie?").

The Sporting News chose not to mention this, which was typical of much of the press coverage of Pete Rose. Even as his personality darkened, the myth was perpetuated.

Charlie Hustle was older and grayer (well, without the Grecian
Formula), but basically unchanged. The way he played, what he

was, still spoke of an earlier time in baseball and America, a better time.

Rose courted the baseball beat men who covered him on a daily basis as aggressively a he did the national writers. From his close relationships with the local writers, he gained the same favorable coverage—and dependable allies in his contract negotiations.

Bob Hertzel, who is one year younger than Rose, covered him for a dozen years as the beat man for *The Cincinnati Enquirer*, through the Big Red Machine years in the 1970s. During that time, Hertzel coauthored two books with Rose. (Daily sportswriters writing books with the athletes they cover is a common, although questionable, practice. It is essentially a business deal, and a similar arrangement on the news side of a newspaper—the city hall reporter sharing book profits with the mayor, for instance—would likely be frowned upon as an obvious conflict of interest. Such deals raise the question: How do you objectively cover someone who is your business partner?)

Hertzel covered Rose's 1977 contract dispute with the Reds, one of several bitter negotiations he had over the years. Rose seethed at the contracts being granted his teammates, and Hertzel, in print, seethed along with him. Rose thought the Reds wanted to drive him out of town, and so did Hertzel, although neither writer nor ballplayer explained why the organization would want to be less than fair with such a fine player, a gate attraction, a hometown boy, a baseball legend in progress.

In print, Hertzel described Rose as "tough" and "determined" in his contract demands. Joe Morgan, coming off consecutive MVP seasons, was also trying to win more money from the Reds, who were a notoriously cheap organization. Hertzel wrote that Morgan was "holding a gun to the club's head."

Hertzel quoted Rose as saying, "Frankly, some of these guys want too much. Some of these guys want as much as they're paying me. I worked 14 years to get where I am and they want it in two or three. Our guys need to be realistic about this. It's always been my understanding that you get paid for years of service to the club, consistency and your fan appeal." Hertzel never pointed out how extraordinary it was for a player to inject himself into his teammates' contract negotiations, or the possible negative impact that could have on team harmony.

In other stories, Rose was especially critical of Dave Concepcion. "That's a lot of money for a shortstop," he said of Concepcion's bid for a three-year, million-dollar contract.

After Concepcion signed his big contract, Hertzel ripped him for making a couple of errors in a meaningless Florida exhibition game, calling him "the world's only million-dollar shortstop," and writing that a missed tag at second base was "a dime-store play by a million-dollar shortstop."

As for Rose, Hertzel wrote:

> Pride, not greed, is what drives him. . . . It does not always come through, but there is a Pete Rose that does not drive around in a Rolls Royce. He is the man who spent a great part of Friday making a free television commercial for baseball.
>
> There is no telling how many free speeches he's given, free appearances he has made during his career. Yet he is the whipping boy of a system which allows Larry Bowa to sign a five-year contract starting at $170,000 and finishing with two years at $200,000 and leaves Pete Rose in a battle with management.
>
> So what is the answer? There is only one which is realistic. The Reds must sign Rose. It would not hurt one bit to give him everything he asks. He has earned that with 14 years of service.

When spring workouts began, Hertzel duly noted that Rose showed up early with the pitchers and catchers but some of his teammates did not:

> Remember one thing. Saturday at the first workout of the spring, Pete was there when he didn't have to be. Joe Morgan wasn't there. Neither was George Foster, who just happened to get his chance at stardom because Rose agreed to move to third base, and could play there well enough to make the switch successfully.

Tim Sullivan, who in 1977 was a reporter on the *Enquirer's* sports page, believes that Rose benefited by his relationships with the writers covering the team. "He was close with Earl, and when Earl retired he gave him the engraved watch. And he and Hertzel were very close. They ran together a lot. They went to the dog track together. [During the contract dispute] Hertzel was not talking to the front office at all. All his stories reflected Pete's point of view. It was very one-sided."

In early April of 1977, with Rose still unsigned, the Reds organization took the extraordinary measure of purchasing a half-page advertisement in *The Cincinnati Enquirer* and the *Dayton Daily News* to explain its side of the Rose contract squabble, because it did not believe it was getting a fair shake in the newspapers. "Some newspaper stories have tended to state the half-truth and misrepresent our endeavors, so we feel we must alter our usual approach and speak out on some points," the ad stated.

(Hertzel declined to be interviewed for this book. "There's nothing I could say that would help him, and I would like to help him," he said. "If I can't help him I'm not talking.")

In the battle for public opinion, the Reds management was no match for Rose. The general manager, Dick Wagner, was an insular man who by nature was distrustful of most writers. "Wagner always felt that Pete could get anything in the paper he wanted through Hertzel," says Bob Rathgeber, who at that time worked for the Reds' GM. "And if Pete had something to say, people in Cincinnati would believe him. They would take his word over anyone else's, because he was one of their own. I don't know if Dick resented Pete's ease with the media, but he may have envied it. Dick himself had no talent for that."

On the eve of opening day, Rose finally signed for a two-year deal that made him the third-highest-paid player on the club behind Morgan and Bench.

Like most sportswriters, Hertzel, in person, was unsentimental and irreverent. But the day after Rose signed, he was, in print, downright mushy.

"Nighttime is still dark. Stars still twinkle in the sky. Spring still means love," he wrote.

"And Pete Rose is still a Cincinnati Red."

When Rose signed with the Phillies in 1979, he struck up another close friendship with a writer, Hal Bodley, who was then the Phillies writer for the *News Journal* in Wilmington, Delaware, and later became the lead baseball writer for *USA Today*.

Like Hertzel, Bodley was of a generation of newspaper journalists more often criticized for tearing down public figures than building them up. But if hero worship had gone out of vogue on the news side of newspapers, it never did on the sports side. The sportswriters themselves refer to their part of the newspaper as "the toy department."

Bodley and Rose shared a beachside condominium near the Phillies camp at Clearwater, Florida, during two spring trainings. The condo was rented by Bodley and paid for by Bodley's newspaper. Bodley's friend and colleague, Bill Conlin of the *Philadelphia Daily News*, once asked Bodley if Rose contributed anything to the rent.

"I asked him, 'Are you just banging your newspaper for this whole amount, and you've got this high-salaried ballplayer living off the Wilmington *News Journal?*' And he said 'You know, he's got all these contacts, he brings home all the meat.' And he did. Rose would bring home this meat at a tremendous discount from this butcher in Tampa.

"Rose would show up. He had the worst diet of any major athlete I had ever seen, nothing but red meat, and they would cook, and the grease would be splaying. You would walk down the beach and see the grease from the barbecue. Fifty hamburgers."

Bodley is a quiet man, bordering on sullen, not the life of any party. But the condo he shared with Rose, according to Conlin, was often a buzzing place, filled with Philadelphia Eagles cheerleaders, airline stewardesses, and ballplayers attracted by the women.

The only member of Rose's family to spend time at the condo would be Pete junior; Bodley often ended up staying with him at night while Rose went to the dog track. "Pete would say 'Hey, Bods, how 'bout taking Petey out for ice cream?,' and Bodley of course would complianty go, and Rose would be off to the dog track," says Conlin.

"Bodley is basically a wimp who felt thrilled that a great athlete like Pete Rose would deign to be his friend. These are power relationships [between athlete and reporter]. Bodley was basically one rung up from Tommy Gioiosa [Rose's longtime errand-boy.]"

At Bodley's second marriage in 1981, Rose was his best man and Carol Woliung, who would become Rose's second wife, was the maid of honor. She and Bodley's new bride had been Eagles cheerleaders together and had once shared a house.

Bodley, by virtue of his role with *USA Today*, is one of the best-read baseball writers in America. Like so many other journalists, he did not confine himself to writing about Pete Rose the ballplayer. He went beyond the boundaries of the playing field to comment on Rose's decency, integrity, and generosity.

The problem was, after a while Bodley no longer believed what he was writing. He had come to know a different, less attractive Pete Rose, whom he never shared with his readers.

Bodley wrote a column about Rose's problems on April 6, 1989, which was preceded by an editor's note telling of Bodley's friendship with Rose. It was the first time such a disclaimer had run, although Bodley had written about Rose many times over the years.

The column began:

> Pete Rose, my friend, is knee-deep in a multi-pronged investigation that threatens his reputation, not to mention his tenure as Cincinnati manager.
> A gambler? Yes.
> A heavy gambler? Yes.
> A gambler who bet on major league games, possibly his own? He's told me emphatically he never has.

Bodley's column also touched on the peculiar nature of a friendship with Rose.

> He can be as crude as he is charming, can be as mean as he is loving, he can get angry with you, then flash his little smile and all is forgiven. He'd run over his mother to break up a double play.
> . . . There's one thing about a relationship with Pete Rose. No matter how much dirt he kicks in your face, you cannot stay angry at him for long.

The column never does say what exactly made it worthwhile being Rose's friend. And as it turned out, not long after it was written, Bodley decided the friendship *wasn't* worth it anymore. That was after Bodley on his Saturday Cable News Network baseball show stated that Rose was considering going to Japan to play and manage. Rose then embarrassed him by denying the report.

Bodley shared some thoughts on Rose in a short telephone conversation in the fall of 1989. (He declined a longer interview.) One of Bodley's grievances with Rose is that Bodley believed he would write Rose's official autobiography, which was instead contracted to Roger Kahn. Bodley was given what he calls "a crumb," the diary of Rose's 1985 season, titled *Countdown to Cobb* and published in book form by *The Sporting News.*

"If I said what was in my heart it wouldn't be very good for Pete," Bodley said. "It wouldn't reflect well on him and I don't know if I want to do that. We were very close, almost inseparable for a long time. We lived together; our wives lived together before we were married. This will be the first Thanksgiving in a dozen years we're not spending together.

"Pete's just not a very good human being. He wasn't a very good friend. Pete did me dirty. He said I would write his book. He threw me a crumb, the *Sporting News* book. But he wouldn't promote it, wouldn't go out on tour. And we wondered what was going on. Then I found out he had already signed with Kahn to do another book.

"A young journalist should never let happen what happened to me. When we started being friends, I was just a guy writing for a small paper nobody read. Now I'm on the most-read paper in the country. What Pete didn't understand was that I have a job to do. I got two exclusive stories [from Pete], and he denied them both. That made things uncomfortable for me, hurt my credibility.

"Reuven Katz [Rose's lawyer] told me this would happen right in the beginning. He told me Pete has had many friends over the years, respectable people, but only the undesirable ones lasted."

Despite feeling double-crossed by the book deal between Kahn and Rose, which was signed back in 1986, Bodley remained friends with Rose. And as late as the April 1989 column, he was still glorifying him in print.

If Bodley really believed that Rose was "not a very good human being," why did he attempt to give his readers the opposite impressions? And if he felt that his friend had lied to him in the past, why did he write of Rose's denying he had bet on baseball without also writing that he had reason to doubt Rose's credibility?

Instead, Bodley wrote:

> Rose, flaws and all, is one of this country's greatest resources and I'm not talking about baseball.

He ended the column by passing along an anecdote of Rose's generosity at a restaurant he had frequented during spring training:

Last Friday morning, his last at BuddyFreddy's, as discreetly as possible, Pete slipped each of the five waitresses who had served him during the spring a $100 bill.

As he was leaving, a waitress came up with tears in her eyes. "Mr. Rose, my rent is past due and I didn't know how I was going to pay it. God bless you."

Pete kissed her on the cheek, walked out the door and said, "See you later, I've got to go face the music."

But as Bodley knew, cash was easier for Rose to give than loyalty.

After parts of the Rose gambling scandal began to break in the spring of 1989, a great many writers from around the country wrote as if they had known part of the story all along.

When Rose was first summoned to New York by then-commissioner Peter Ueberroth during spring training 1989, the purpose of the meeting was not disclosed publicly by either side. But Murray Chass, in the next day's *New York Times*, wrote that the issue discussed was Rose's gambling and added, "Rose, in his sixth season as the Reds manager, readily acknowledges his fondness for betting. He is known to be a frequent bettor, particularly on horses, dogs and college basketball games. He has said he does not bet on baseball games. From time to time last season, he remarked to reporters, 'I'm not supposed to gamble. They talked to me about that.' "

Later that spring, other writers chimed in with their past knowledge of Rose's sports gambling proclivities.

Thomas Boswell of *The Washington Post*: "The devil sent him cable TV. And Rose gambled on what he watched. He always admitted that."

Steve Jacobson of *Newsday*: "Rose made no secret of his love for the racetrack and his betting on sports events. He talked about betting football and basketball. If he couldn't play, he could prove he knew more about sports than the bookmakers. And what about the game he knew best?"

Tom Callahan of *Time*, writing about the initial meeting with Ueberroth: "Reporters who knew Rose guessed gambling."

All of this was written after the fact. Why, with all the literally millions of words written about Rose over the previous three decades, had no one ever addressed head-on the issue of his sports gambling? At the very least it would have made for interesting reading; so much else of what was written about Rose was repetitive—the same stories about his father and his rugged childhood rehashed and recycled.

Beyond that, every sportswriter knew about baseball's strict rules against gambling by players. They were barred from betting on baseball, and also from "associating" with known gamblers. The only way to bet legally on sports events was to go to Las Vegas to place wagers. The other option, and the one Rose was obviously taking as a habitual sports gambler, was to place bets through bookies. And that would be a violation of baseball's rules against gambling associations.

But none of the writers who knew of Rose's sports gambling raised this issue in print before 1989. They would not have had to write that Rose was necessarily wrong or evil to pick up a phone and place a bet; they could even have written, as some did later, that baseball's rules are antiquated, that millions of Americans gamble through bookies, so why can't Pete Rose?

Couldn't America's baseball writers and sports columnists have found some angle, some way to raise the issue that one of baseball's greatest stars appeared to be a flagrant violator of the game's prohibition against gambling associations? Instead, there was only the occasional sly hint, as when Mark Whicker of the *Philadelphia Daily News* wrote in August 1985, "The latest toy arrived at the ballpark yesterday. Now Pete Rose has a phone in his Porsche, the better to call for updated scores."

Why didn't any of them write about the bookie betting before 1989—even if they had no inkling it included baseball betting?

Chass says the issue of betting through bookies did not much concern him, and he believes it did not much concern baseball either; to the extent that nonbaseball sports betting was part of baseball's probe of Rose, Chass says, it was only as a way of getting at the real concern, the baseball betting.

"I suppose I didn't consider the possibility of a guy betting and losing so much on other sports that he then goes and bets on baseball," Chass said. "Maybe that was naive on my part.

"But I have trouble with double standards. If baseball allows owners to own racetracks, and there's no problem with a player going to the racetrack to bet, and it's certainly legal to bet OTB [Off-Track Betting] in New York State, then how do you draw the distinction of betting with a bookie?"

Lawson speaks for many sportswriters when he says that his rule was never to stray too far from the beat. If a ballplayer's off-field life did not affect his play on the field, Lawson tried not to write it. If it didn't show up on the police blotter, he often told players, he could keep it out of the paper.

A baseball writer's primary job is to write baseball. It's a big job that doesn't leave much time for idle investigating. If he doesn't keep his eye on the ball, he doesn't get the job done. If he prints stories about nonbaseball matters that anger the players or the manager, he may lose access to his sources.

Lawson says the extent of his knowledge of Rose's wagering was that Rose liked to play the horses. He didn't know if Rose bet through bookies, but he would not have been surprised. If he knew it for sure, it's unlikely he would have written it.

Occasionally, Lawson says, news-side reporters would ask him why he didn't write what really went on around the Cincinnati Reds—what it was really like.

"They'd say, 'Why don't you tell it like it is?' And I'd say 'Hey, I know plenty about this city that I never read in the newspaper. I know which politician is a drunk, which corporate leader is whoring around. Why don't you ever write about that?' Well, they didn't like to hear that, so after that, they'd shut up."

But this was no ordinary piccadillo. This was baseball's biggest star treading on its most sensitive prohibition.

Of all the sportswriters who covered Rose—the ones who knew him best like Lawson, Hertzel, and Bodley, as well as the national writers who covered him over the decades—none has acknowledged knowing absolutely that Rose bet through bookmakers. They suspected it, that's all.

At the very least, on the issue of Rose's gambling there was an appalling lack of interest by the sports press in a very large story.

Pete Rose's split from his first wife in 1979 made national news. So did a paternity suit filed against him the same year. Neither had anything to do with Rose the ballplayer, but because he was a public figure, both events were of interest.

His gambling through bookmakers had everything to do with Rose the ballplayer. As a violation of baseball rules, it imperiled his continued status in the game. What could be a more important Pete Rose story? It could not be construed as nonnews. But it was.

No baseball writer chose to do more reporting into what seemed obvious, that Rose was in violation of baseball rules. With the leeway afforded to sportswriters, and especially columnists, questions about his gambling probably could have been raised in print even without more digging.

Why's Pete so interested in point spreads? Who are all the lackeys hanging out with him in the home clubhouse and on the road? Pete Rose seems to be treading on dangerous ground. Maybe he'd better watch himself.

If one of Rose's friends in the press had written such a column early enough, he might have even been doing him a favor.

I spent a spring, a summer, and part of an autumn with Pete Rose. A baseball season. It was 1987, and I was the Reds beat writer for *The Cincinnati Post.*

I came to baseball writing from a different place from most of my colleagues in the press box. I had been a news reporter most of my professional career, covering the general run of events in Philadelphia—politics, racial tension, crime, a couple of mob trials. For a brief period I reported from Beirut, Lebanon. I had done a fair amount of investigative reporting, and at one point I spent the better part of a year piecing out a complicated oil-drilling investment scam.

I liked covering baseball. To use one of Pete Rose's favorite words, it was *enjoyable.*

Mostly, I liked watching a ball game every night. The year I covered the Reds, Eric Davis had a magnificent season. I thought he played center field like a Julius Erving in baseball spikes, and I considered it a privilege to watch him. My newspaper had no Sunday edition, so I wasn't required to be at the ballpark on Saturdays, but I usually went anyway.

I admired and respected the players for their talent, and I thought most of them played with pride. I didn't much like interviewing them after the games. Very few were eloquent or insightful even about their own performances, and their quotes rarely added much to a story. I wouldn't have minded covering baseball in the era when writers stayed in the press box after games, and called down to the clubhouse by telephone if they had a factual question about a play or strategy.

I usually talked with Pete Rose twice a day, once before the game and once after. Occasionally we would talk one-on-one, but generally there were other writers around. Our conversations were mostly of the type that beat writers and managers have: *Why'd you leave the starting pitcher in so long? Wasn't that a spot you'd go with a lefty? How's Parker's knee?*

The season I covered Rose was his first as a nonplayer. I watched him struggle with the issue of whether to play again. I watched him as he tried to relate to players twenty years younger than he, and I thought he envied them their youth. I watched him supervise as others played. For Rose, it was a new phase of life, and I don't believe a happy one.

I don't think I wrote anything that glorified Rose that season. He was a manager, and not a particularly good one, and that's how I covered him.

My relationship with him was strictly business. I asked questions. He answered. (Usually.) I did not get to know him as Lawson, Bodley, or Hertzel did, or even as well as some of the national writers and columnists who have covered him for many years. I never accompanied Rose to the track or shared a meal with him. (Once in his office I did taste some cabbage soup off his spoon, after he offered it with assurance, "I don't have no diseases.")

Despite my distance from Rose, I saw things that I should have picked up on. For instance, why did he always have those non-baseball cronies in his office? Why did he sometimes take them on the road with him?

Paul Janszen was his constant companion that season. I saw him all the time (at 6'3" and a muscular 300 pounds or so, he was hard to miss), and so did the other beat writers who traveled with the team, Greg Hoard of *The Cincinnati Enquirer* and Hal McCoy of the *Dayton Daily News*. I knew Janszen was a bodybuilder and a buddy of Rose's. I did not know or suspect then that he was involved in the sale of steroids and cocaine or that he was booking Rose's bets.

But Janszen was part of a larger entourage that included Mike Bertolini, a memorabilia dealer; Mario "the Cuban" Nunez, the maître d' in the dining room at a Florida thoroughbred track; and a changing cast of others, including some unsavory-looking people whose names I never learned.

Once, in his office at the visiting clubhouse at Shea Stadium, Rose was visited by several bodybuilding types whom I assumed Janszen had brought around, including a huge man with a blond ponytail, cowboy boots, and a menacing scowl. If I had seen this man walking toward me on the street, I would have crossed to the other side.

I did not write any of this for *The Cincinnati Post*. I should have. I should have questioned in print who these people were. Other major-league players have entourages, too; the money they make enables them to bring friends out on the road with them, and sometimes these people are not so respectable-looking either.

But this was Pete Rose. Charlie Hustle. He didn't look "all baseball" to me, and I should have conveyed that to my readers. They would have been interested. The people of Cincinnati would have read that story, passed it to friends, and talked about it. It would have had a shelf life of several days, even a week. That's a good newspaper story.

I didn't know much for sure about Rose's gambling. I knew he watched every sporting event on television and talked a lot about the point spreads. Once I heard him on his office telephone discussing what I took to be a point spread.

My background and training as a news reporter were such that I should have gone to my editors and said, "I need time off the beat. I think there may be a story in Pete Rose's associations, his gambling, and I would like to investigate it."

I didn't do that. I should have.

But I was a baseball writer that season, and I kept my eye on the ball.

Rose's gambling problems became news in the spring of 1989 through a combination of baseball's own probe of him, a federal criminal probe, and the reporting of *Sports Illustrated*, which was the first publication on the story.

Not one writer in the baseball-writing fraternity did much damage to Rose. As the journalists who knew him best, they might have been expected to add something to the news coverage of the scandal. But they didn't. They stayed on the sideline and backed as far away from the actual reporting of the case as possible. "Covering this story has about as much appeal as doing time," the *New York Post*'s Lyle Spencer wrote in March 1989, typifying the prevailing attitude.

The disclosures came mostly out of the investigation led by John Dowd, the Washington lawyer who was baseball's special counsel on the Rose probe. What was uncovered independently

by newspapers was the work of news-side reporters and not baseball writers, with the one notable exception of Murray Chass of
The New York Times, a baseball writer who covered the case
aggressively throughout and was the first to report that the FBI
had betting slips with what appeared to be Rose's fingerprints on
them.

"Most of us are not comfortable with covering things like the
Rose scandal and do not like it," says Bill Conlin of the *Philadelphia Daily News*. "The reason a lot of us went into sports in the
first place is so we didn't have to deal with bullshit like that."

In a May 1989 column, Conlin acknowledged how skillfully
Rose had played his writer friends: "The media is an orchestra
that Pete Rose has conducted for 26 years with a deft baton," he
wrote. "We relay his gruff, earthy blend of raunch and reason—a
jock opera—to the public with eager precision, grateful that such
a famous athlete treats us with neither condescension, contempt
nor impatience."

There were a few writers who remained shameless apologists
for Rose.

The Sporting News's Dave Nightingale got a long interview
with him and wrote it up in a cover piece on April 24, 1989. Rose
complained in the piece about how much misinformation was
being printed about him, which led to this bizarre aside:

"Next thing you'll probably read about me is that I had some
homosexual friend who I sat behind in the 11th grade," the story
quotes Rose.

"Well, I'll tell you right now, before that story 'breaks,' I've
done a lot of things in my life but never anything like that."

The writer then interjects: "And, once again, laughter cut
through the somber silence—with the blatantly heterosexual
manager leading the guffaws."

Aside from the irrelevance of the above passage, it illustrates
yet another link that Rose had with many of the writers who
covered him. He was the ultimate locker-room male, and his
relationship with the media could be a case study in male bond-
ing. (What does *blatantly heterosexual* mean?) He was no better-
looking than most of the sportswriters who covered him, and he
was crass. But he still got the girls, the busty, thin-waisted ones.
And he loved to regale the writers with stories of his numerous
sexual conquests.

"I think there's a lot of that still in sportswriting," says Sullivan. "A lot of people in the profession have grown up with the notion that you're privileged to be on the inside of things and you're going to see things that are off-limits that you can't repeat. The writers liked to hear Pete's stories."

And Pete Rose made each of them feel like one of the guys.

Rose's most ardent defender in the media was Roger Kahn, author of *The Boys of Summer*.

Before that lyrical work on the old Brooklyn Dodgers, the great majority of sports books had drawn athletes with all the subtlety and texture of the illustrations in old high school health texts. Kahn proved that you could portray athletes in all their dimensions and that the writing could be both intelligent and perceptive.

But his book on Rose, *Pete Rose: My Story*, on which they collaborated and shared in the advance, probably set back his reputation as a journalist as far as *The Boys of Summer* advanced it. He defended Rose and was loyal to him at great personal cost. The book, which was begun well before the gambling scandal, was an unconvincing, off-key defense of Rose.

In Kahn's view, Rose made mistakes but he was not the one most responsible for his undoing. He wrote that Rose was victimized—by the convicted felons who testified against him; by A. Bartlett Giamatti, who in Kahn's view understood the *beau ideal* of baseball but not the reality; by the media; and even by his own advisers, who orchestrated a "public relations disaster" that made Rose a "whipping boy for media moralists."

Kahn accepts Rose's explanation that his gambling was simply a way to fill his off-hours, and was a natural extension of his competitiveness.

"Gambling is enjoyment for me," Kahn quotes Rose as saying. "It fills free time. I go to the racetrack and I sit with the owner of the track. I like that. I like the company of the people with money and I'm competitive. I like to win on the ballfield. No, I didn't have the most natural ability in the world, but there's nobody who ever wanted to win baseball games more than I did. More than I do."

This was vintage Rose, again taking his license. Somehow, being a tough competitor, excelling without an abundance of natural talent, explained all sorts of aberrant behavior. Kahn didn't question the reasoning.

Nor did he question why, if Rose had free time on his hands, he didn't spend it with his family. Managing a baseball team is a big job. In addition, Rose devoted part of his off-season to zipping around the country signing autographs for pay. Why, instead of gambling, didn't he spend what time was left over with his wife and young son?

The author did analyze the report by John Dowd, the Washington lawyer retained by baseball to investigate Rose, and found it analogous to a cheap suit—easy to unravel. Like Rose, he was incensed that most of the information was provided by convicted felons, "warbling felons," as Kahn called them.

Rose's lawyers offered up some of their evidence to Kahn, which they told him would eventually be used to discredit the Dowd report. Kahn gave some samples of it in his book, including an interview with, yes, a convicted felon, who told of a supposed plot to frame Rose. Kahn did not know it, but the man was also, by his own admission, a habitual liar, and had been convicted in a consumer fraud case after he claimed to have swallowed a straight pin in a hostess Ding Dong cake.

Rose laid out for Kahn his relationship with Paul Janszen, his chief accuser, and the author was aghast that a baseball great could be taken down by such a low-quality person. When Rose told Kahn he didn't bet on baseball, Kahn found him convincing.

"I took a beat," Kahn writes.

> I took a breath. And many more. To appreciate how convincing Rose is one-on-one you have to see the fire in his eye, the set of his shoulder, the pain on the Mount Rushmore face. One-on-one, he is a most convincing witness.
>
> Caught in the moment, I blurted: Pete, this is the most amazing thing. The greatest baseball player of our time put out of the baseball business by some fucking bum.

It would be reasonable to assume that Rose was grateful to Kahn for sticking by him, but he hasn't come off that way.

Rose's publicist, Barbara Pinzka, told me that Rose considered Kahn's book a great disappointment. "Where were the Phillies years?" she groused. "They were barely covered. It's like Pete didn't even exist from 1979 on. The book wasn't what we thought it was going to be." She described the post publication relationship between Kahn and Rose as "a hornet's nest."

For his part, Kahn says his relationship with Rose and his advisers began to fall apart when his suggestions on how to handle Rose's public relations problems were ignored. He advised that Rose hire public relations consultant Vic Gold, who once worked for George Bush and was Spiro Agnew's vice-presidential press secretary.

"I had a sense that this thing [Rose's problems] should be handled in a national way," Kahn says. "It was more important what Dan Rather or Ted Koppel said than what was in *The Cincinnati Post*, but they never understood that. I was hurt that nobody seemed to take any of this seriously.

"Where they [Katz and Rose's other advisers] got furious with the book is that they wanted it to be a public relations pamphlet to get Pete into the Hall of Fame. There were too many fucks in the book for it to be that. Literally."

What got Kahn angry at Rose was the same thing that had irritated Bodley: He felt Rose didn't do enough to promote the book they had written together. "I wrote to Reuven Katz. I said 'You've got to understand, the role of the most famous celebrity in a collaboration is to push books,' " he says. "But Pete wouldn't do it. We're talking money. He cost me, I don't know, a hundred thousand dollars. He cost me a lot of money."

Pinzka takes issue with Kahn's contention that Rose didn't do what he promised to promote the book. "He's been saying things that are total fabrications," she told me.

Kahn, interviewed in May 1990, said he had not heard from Rose since the book was released the previous fall. "Why wouldn't he call me or send me a thank-you note?" he wonders. "Why wouldn't any of them? I think they're all users."

Kahn is less sure than he was that Rose did not bet on baseball. After being persuaded by the fire in Rose's eyes and his Mount Rushmore face, he now says, "I don't even know anymore. I'm less convinced than I was."

The last time I talked to Pete Rose was at the visitors' clubhouse in Philadelphia on July 3, 1989. I had written him a letter in May 1989 seeking to interview him for this book, to which he did not reply.

In the clubhouse, I asked him if he would agree, at some later point, to sit down for a series of interviews.

"I don't think so, Mike," he replied. "I'm writing a book with Roger Kahn. And besides, I don't think you have authorization from my people."

When I told him that I did not need "authorization" from anyone, he replied, "If I talk to you, you'll make more money, and since I ain't gonna get any of it, I'm not gonna do it."

Pete Rose still remembered Earl Lawson's lesson. Talking to the press is essentially a business proposition.

Give a little, get a little. Fame and fortune follows.

7

MR. CLEAN'S CITY

I'd like to be in Cincinnati when the world ends, because it will happen ten years later there.

—A quote widely attributed to but possibly never spoken
by Mark Twain

To understand Pete Rose, one must first know something about
the city of Cincinnati. Al Schavel is a good person to start with.
He is the ghost of the city's wide-open past, of when downtown
Cincinnati was a lively place of burlesque houses, legitimate the-
aters, beer joints, taverns, and gambling halls.

On a late-summer afternoon, he stands by the front door of his
restaurant, as he has six days a week for the past fifty years, and
places a menu in the hand of each person who enters.

He is a tiny, gaunt man, eighty-nine years old, who wears a gray
toupee with a wave crimped into it and a baggy checked sport
coat that hangs straight down from his narrow shoulders.

Schavel's restaurant, the Rib Pit Barn, is now just eight tables
and a small bar, but at one time it included a nightclub and took
up most of a city block. In the years after World War II, Schavel
brought in the very best jazz and swing bands, and his "book"—
which took bets on any horse race being run at any track in the
U.S.—was said to be the biggest in downtown Cincinnati.

Over the years, Cincinnati would become more buttoned-down,
corporate, respectable. But enough of the wide-open city would remain to swallow up a native son named Peter Edward Rose.

*   *   *

The city of Al Schavel, Pete Rose, and the giant Procter & Gamble company—makers of Comet, Spic and Span, and Mr. Clean—began as a straightforward business proposition.

John Cleves Symmes, a Revolutionary War veteran, purchased the land along a gentle bend of the Ohio River from the federal government in 1797 and resold it much in the manner of plots in a modern subdivision. The original settlers literally bought into the city, and the successful mix of light manufacturing concerns they established attracted new immigration to Cincinnati from other parts of the U.S., and later from Europe. By 1860 it was the sixth largest of all American cities and the most populous city west of the Alleghenies.

But after this impressively fast start, Cincinnati quickly began to lose ground, in both population and relative importance. By 1890 it had fallen to ninth among U.S. cities, and by 1930 it was all the way down to seventeenth.

Even more pronounced was Cincinnati's plummeting self-image.

The early settlers and their descendants, the city's aristocracy, had largely moved up onto the hillsides, and the original city, which lay in the basin along the river, became a lawless, unruly place, even by the standards of turn-of-the-century urban America.

Prostitution was rampant and open; madams had their names posted right on the front doors of their houses. Dice games took place in the city's main public park at the foot of an Abraham Lincoln statue. Poker and craps were played in the back rooms of drugstores, saloons, and cigar shops, and many of these establishments also featured crude versions of slot machines.

Toward the end of the nineteenth century, stabbings and street rumbles were common occurrences, and the three-hundred-member police force was overpowered and outgunned by the street toughs and criminals. Cincinnati historian Zane Miller, in his book *Boss Cox's Cincinnati*, called the period from 1884 to 1894 the city's "decade of crisis." During this time, extortion rings preyed on merchants, who paid protection money in order not to be harassed, and for several years Cincinnati had the highest murder rate of any city in the nation. "Not a thoroughfare in its limits has not been stained with human blood," *The Cincinnati Enquirer* observed in 1894.

The WPA's *Guide to Cincinnati,* published in 1935, described early Cincinnati as a savage place. "The city grew fast on a steamboat boom and the river spewed all kinds of human debris into the city," the guide's editor, Harry Graf, wrote in the introduction. ". . . Loose women—white, mulatto and colored—made the rounds of the whisky places; and gamblers, card sharks, and escaped convicts mingled along the waterfront."

In 1895, William Howard Taft referred to Cincinnati as "this Sodom of ours." A clergyman called it "a place of horrors, an urban desert." In 1905, Lincoln Steffens gave this succinct view of Cincinnati: "It is terrible," he wrote. "The city is all one great graft."

Steffens had hit on what was all too obvious to Cincinnati's better citizens: The community's problems were directly related to the city government, which was corrupt, boss-ridden, and so bumbling that it could not even erect proper street signs.

The public statements of Cincinnati's elite began to take on a tone of despair. Born of such promise, the Queen City of the Seven Hills (so named for the seven hills ringing the basin) had tumbled from its place of prominence, and by the turn of the century it held no more status than nearby Louisville.

"In the race of American cities Cincinnati has been a laggard, due to the fact that it has run the race handicapped and out of condition," a Cincinnati industrialist lamented in a speech at the Literary Club in 1911.

The movement to clean up Cincinnati, soon to begin, was intertwined with concern for the city's sagging prestige. How could it move forward and take its rightful place among the nation's great cities if hooligans and racketeers ruled its streets?

But cleansing the place was a big job, and it would take a long time before Cincinnati could ascend to its present reputation: stolid, conservative, successful, a paragon of municipal efficiency and good government.

Eventually, the most glaring examples of vice and lawlessness would be eradicated. But not the gambling. That was only shunted to more out-of-the way corners, where it would no longer be a civic embarrassment.

With the proximity of Kentucky's horse country (and also of Newport, Kentucky, which into the late 1940s boasted casinos to rival any in Las Vegas), gambling would remain very much a part of the fabric of Cincinnati life.

By 1941, the year of Pete Rose's birth, Cincinnati was no longer the Sodom that Taft had referred to, but like most American cities it was a place you could get a bet down without too much trouble. The bookmakers were an accepted part of the city's landscape.

When Earl Lawson got married for the first time in 1949, two years before he took over the Reds beat, a consortium of downtown bookies threw his bachelor party. "The books just wanted to do it for me," recalls Lawson. "They promised me, they said, 'Earl, we'll guarantee your first year's rent.'

"They were going to hold the party at the Variety Club below the Metropolitan Hotel. But then they thought it might get raided there. So my best man suggested this tavern out in Reading [beyond the city's northern border], and that's where we had it. All the high rollers in Cincinnati were there. They had a craps game, and three poker tables. I got the house cut. I got about eight hundred dollars out of it.

"They did it because they liked me. I knew everybody in Cincinnati. My editor was amazed at the people I knew."

At this time, there was a "book" in virtually every downtown tavern, chili parlor, tie shop, and cigar store, and some gas stations on the city's outskirts still had slot machines. Across the river in Newport, and also in some of the grittier suburban towns on the Ohio side, the calls of horse races were piped into taverns by "the Service," which was organized crime's horse racing wire.

Authorities in Cincinnati drew the line on their downtown bookmakers by prohibiting loudspeakers in the taverns, but bartenders listened to the race calls over the telephone and barked out dramatic re-creations for their patrons.

That was how Al Schavel did it. After he had seated his lunch crowd, he moved over to the telephone at the corner of his bar and dialed up the Service. "You heard the call over the phone, and then you repeated it for everybody else," he explains. "That's how it had to be done because the police here would never allow the loudspeakers."

An occasional lunch patron at Schavel's restaurant in those days was Harry Francis Rose, the racetrack habitué, who worked just a couple of blocks away at the Fifth-Third Bank. "He would sit down by himself and eat his roast beef sandwich," Schavel says. "I don't ever remember him making a bet."

In later years, Schavel served lunch to another Rose, Harry's son Pete. This was in the 1960s, during Rose's early years with the Reds. And by then, Cincinnati was a changed place.

"We weren't calling out the race results anymore," says Schavel. "I don't think any place downtown would have been doing that. Everything changed after the Kefauver Commission." (Senator Estes Kefauver's televised hearings on illegal gambling, crime syndicates, and their political connections brought about new laws and tougher enforcement that made life more difficult for bookmakers in Cincinnati and all across the U.S.)

Another example of the transformation of downtown Cincinnati: One of the dealers at Lawson's 1949 bachelor party was an ex-prizefighter well known for his brothel on wheels. For many years, his big yellow Buick with the spacious backseat, disguised (thinly) as a taxicab, was part of the city's after-hours scene. Some of the downtown regulars called it "the rolling whorehouse."

In present-day Cincinnati, you can no longer hail that sort of cab. In fact, you can't hail *any* cab at all; by city ordinance, the taxis are no longer permitted to cruise. They wait for fares by the hotels or at a handful of designated cabstands, and exist almost exclusively to ferry business travelers to and from the airport.

No one really needs a cab to get around Cincinnati's bloodless downtown. A mid-1970s redesign kept it intentionally small to replicate, as much as possible, a suburban shopping mall. The idea was that visitors could park once and everything would be within walking distance. They could even avoid the city streets altogether, and the vagaries of urban life, by taking the overhead "Skywalk" that links some of the bigger office buildings, hotels, and department stores, including a Saks Fifth Avenue that was lured away from the suburban malls by the new downtown design. The Rib Pit Barn is not on the Skywalk route.

The remarkable thing about Cincinnati is not how corrupt or vice-ridden it once was. In its day, it may have been no more so than New York, Philadelphia, Chicago, Cleveland, or any number of other American cities. No, what's remarkable is how completely Cincinnati came clean, or seemed to. On the surface, at least, it is no longer Al Schavel's city.

"Cincinnati became very adept at keeping its sin, its vice, however you want to describe it, out of the public eye and, if possible, beyond the corporate limits of the city," observes Alfred Tuchfarber, director of the Institute for Policy Research at the University of Cincinnati. "Newport was always a flourishing den of iniquity. Everyone knew that generations of Cincinnatians went over there to gamble, to drink, to go to the strip joints.

"Yet Cincinnati has held itself out as this conservative den, this hotbed of conservative radicals. I don't know if it's more conservative than other places. It may be that it's more hypocritical."

In recent years, Cincinnati has become the most aggressive city in the nation at fighting what certain segments of the community consider pornography. A production of the play *Equus* was reviewed by police before it opened in 1988. Two years later, the opening of a controversial exhibition of photographs by Robert Mapplethorpe, featuring some pictures with explicit depictions of homosexual sex, raised a thunderous civic howl. The exhibit had earlier been canceled at the Corcoran Gallery in Washington, D.C., after pressure from Senator Jesse Helms, but was displayed without incident in several other cities.

Police chief Lawrence Whalen threatened to seize any photographs considered obscene, saying, "These photographs are just not welcome in this community. The people in this community do not cater to what others depict as art."

Cincinnati has no adult bookstores, no peep shows, and no massage parlors, and adult movies cannot be rented in its video stores.

In Cincinnati, the First Amendment seems to guarantee less in the way of free speech and expression than it does elsewhere in America. Even at the ballpark. Banners at Riverfront Stadium expressing opinions critical of team management are routinely confiscated by stadium security. One of the remarkable things is that people in the stadium do not boo or protest when this happens.

There's a long history of censoring the paying customers, stretching back to when the Reds played at Crosley Field. In 1964, when Pete Rose slumped and was briefly benched, a friend of his stretched a banner across the bleachers that said, "A Rose Cannot Bloom on the Bench."

"The cops ripped it down and then started inquiring as to who put it up," recalls the friend who erected the sign. "I said 'Hey, fellows, didn't you ever hear of the First Amendment?' "

But one activity that still gets a wink and a nod in present-day Cincinnati is bookmaking, even large-scale bookmaking.

In 1981 the city's vice squad busted a two-state sports betting ring that booked tens of thousands of dollars in bets each week. The probe took several months and involved wiretaps and a great expense of time and money by the police. A Cincinnati judge found the ringleaders guilty, but imposed as a sentence just $29 in court costs. For the defendants, the judge remarked, the endeavor seemed to be "just a side thing, nothing to get so upset about."

The city of Cincinnati is split down the middle by the marshy Mill Creek Valley, whose tangle of railroad tracks, factories, and freight terminals forms a no-man's-land between the lace-curtain East Side and the blue-collar, bare-knuckles West Side.

For many years, until the construction of new freeways, there was not even a convenient way to travel between the neighborhoods on either side of the valley. And there was no great clamoring for easier access. The new highways connected Cincinnati with other cities, and with its own suburbs, but only incidentally with itself.

"If you're born in the West, then you live in the West and die in the West," says Glenn Sample, an assistant athletic director at the University of Cincinnati. "It's the same thing with the East. It's two different cities, really."

The East Side is home to Cincinnati's corporate leaders, doctors, and lawyers, to its old-line Wasps and to the descendants of the wealthy German Jews who founded Reform Judaism in the U.S. The board members of the ballet, the symphony, the opera, and the zoo live on the East Side, as do the members of the blue-blood Cincinnatus Society.

Most of Cincinnati's money, and all of its status, reside on the East Side.

Pete Rose is a West Sider.

His part of town is sausage and knockwurst, corner bars and Saturday-morning tackle football, a keg of dark beer to the winners. And baseball.

"The West Side has always been a baseball-playing area," says Joe Kaiser, another of Rose's boyhood pals. "I don't know if anybody could say for sure why that is. But part of it is you want to follow the guys ahead of you. If there's good players from your area, then you grow up and you play the sport they played.

"It's a little like basketball is in the ghetto. Being a baseball player has always been one way to have success on the West Side. I wouldn't say it's a way of 'getting out' of the West Side, because I don't think many of us really thought that way. We liked it there."

One of the few families on the West Side during Rose's childhood that had any cachet from something other than athletics was the Zimmer clan. Don Zimmer's uncle, William H. Zimmer, was president of the power company, and the Zimmer Nuclear Power Station (which never opened because of safety defects) bore his name. Zimmer's father, a successful wholesale produce dealer, was also a legendary local gambler, and Don Zimmer himself is known around baseball as a horse- and dog-track aficionado and an occasional high roller at casinos.

The combination of do-gooding reform politics, conservative Republicanism, and upright German Protestantism that sanitized downtown Cincinnati had little impact on the West Side, which was cleaned up last—and least.

"I remember when we were in high school, this would have been around 1958, and I walked into some chili parlor with a friend of mine," recalls Ralph Griesser, Pete Rose's high school football teammate. "But for some reason we decided to go in the back way. I think we figured we would be entering through the kitchen.

"When we walked in, we saw this big tote board, with a bunch of different horse races up there. It was great, we just looked up and there it was. There were a bunch of guys sitting in there, and they said, 'What the hell are you doing in here? Get the hell out of here.' But that was the way things were. People on the West Side gambled. They did then. They do now. It's a way of life."

Harold Mills, the retired commander of the Cincinnati Police vice squad, is himself a West Sider. "The West Side is a different class of people, a rougher area," he explains. "When the reformers came in, it was the last part of the city to get cleaned up. But to say it's really cleaned up now is a mistake. Now it's just different. You can't go into a bar and have them take your bet if they don't know you. But if you are known, there's still plenty of places to put a bet down."

*   *   *

In some segments of proper Cincinnati, the West Side is considered hillbilly country. And especially Rose's part of the West Side, along the river, where much of the population has Appalachian roots.

But greater Cincinnati is not without its own image problems.

The city that emerged from the era of lawlessness projected an image of plodding efficiency, conservatism, and prudishness. If it was prosperous and squeaky clean, it was also utterly lacking in pizzazz.

The city's historic industries—shoes and boots, soap, tobacco products, small electronics products—had hardly left a legacy of romance. Cincinnati was not the City of the Big Shoulders, the Big Apple, or even Steel City. But what was it?

For a time during the last century, it was known as "Porkopolis" because of its numerous pork-packing plants. In 1988, an outdoor art installation commissioned to commemorate the city's bicentennial included two bronze, winged pigs, which caused great outrage in the city council and the city at large. True, the artwork celebrated part of the city's heritage, but was this how Cincinnati wanted to be viewed by the rest of the nation?

An Associated Press story about the flap noted that the pigs seemed in conflict with modern Cincinnati. "Now known as the Queen City, Cincinnati boasts a clean-cut image," the story said. "Its baseball team prohibits players from growing beards or mustaches. Its voters favor Republicans and law-and-order candidates, and it is home to a national anti-pornography organization."

A city councilman named Steve Chabot convened hearings to consider whether the pig sculptures should be displayed. "It comes down to: Is this going to become a symbol for Cincinnati?" he asked. "That's one of the problems. I've got nothing against the pigs, but I don't think it's really an appropriate symbol for Cincinnati to be tied into."

Another councilman disagreed: "If we're the major-league town we think we are, we need to be able to be a little more self-assured about ourselves and our place in history, and be able to laugh at ourselves," said councilman Arn Bortz, who wore a pig snout hat as he delivered his remarks.

Apart from the obvious humor, the great debate over the two little pigs demonstrated something deeper about Cincinnati: It is not a place entirely comfortable with its past, or secure about its present.

It has a malady fairly common to second-tier cities—a municipal inferiority complex. Did anyone outside of Cincinnati know or care what went on there? Could the bronze pigs, which finally were displayed, really make Cincinnati "the laughingstock of the country," as one city resident predicted they would?

Could the city's stock really be that low?

The flap over the Mapplethorpe pictures provoked the same kind of concerns. A great number of Cincinnatians were appalled and embarrassed at the sight of uniformed police officers entering an art gallery to videotape the pictures for use as evidence. Protesters on Fountain Square at the center of downtown wore bags over their heads and carried signs saying, "The Whole World Is Laughing."

As Pete Rose became famous, embarked on hitting streaks, took on Cobb, he became everything Cincinnati wasn't—interesting to the rest of the nation, confident, bold, a little naughty. He wasn't stuffy at all. He said whatever the hell came to his mind. When the president called the clubhouse to talk to him, Rose answered, "Yeah, how ya doin'?" He didn't stop to consider what people would think. He just said it.

Rose gave Cincinnati a rallying point. An identity.

"Cincinnati people are like everyone else who is not from New York or L.A.," says Jerry Springer, a former mayor turned television anchorman. "They ask, 'Why don't people recognize our city? We're really the best, but nobody knows it.'

"This is a very successful city, with a highly skilled labor force, which is why we tend not to have the great dips and severe economic downturns that other cities do. And we don't have the density of poverty of most of the other big cities. It's also a very pretty city, with great restaurants, successful cultural institutions.

"But none of this put Cincinnati on the map the way Pete Rose did. When he got that hit to pass Cobb, that was a very emotional moment in this city. It was 'Look at us. We've got the best, the very best in history, right here in Cincinnati.' "

According to Alfred Tuchfarber, the University of Cincinnati professor, Rose's appeal was not just his success, but the way he succeeded.

"Pete Rose walked on water in this town," says Tuchfarber.

"He was the whole package. This city, first of all, values hard work, application of skills, and success. In that way, Pete was very much in the city's self-image. The people here do not consider Cincinnati to be blessed with great natural resources. They believe it succeeds through their hard work, just like Pete did. He wasn't just a good player stopping through town. He was *from* Cincinnati, and his success seemed to confirm so many good things about the city."

Rose, the proverbial big fish in a small pond, was bigger in Cincinnati, proportionately, than he would have been elsewhere. He was bigger than Magic in L.A., Jordan in Chicago, Namath in New York. (After all, when "Broadway Joe" retired, New York still had Broadway.)

It seemed that every restaurant and tavern in Cincinnati gave a prominent spot to its framed, signed photograph of Rose. Doctors, lawyers, and business executives kept photographs of him in their offices. In Cincinnati, it was good business to be associated with Pete Rose. It could even help make you rich, as it did in the case of Jeff Ruby.

Ruby's ambition to own a restaurant was just an idea on a piece of paper until Rose threw some money in. Then word got around town that "Pete had a piece of the place"; ten years later Ruby was living in a huge house on a hill overlooking the Ohio River, with a fleet of classic cars in his garage.

A transplanted North Jerseyan, Ruby came to Cincinnati in the 1970s to work for Holiday Inn. He got friendly with Sparky Anderson, who never made a permanent residence in Cincinnati and was living in the hotel Ruby managed. (Anderson eventually would move twice to follow Ruby when he was transferred to other Cincinnati-area Holiday Inns.) Through Anderson, Ruby got to know Reds players, including Rose and Johnny Bench.

"My parents were in the restaurant business, and my dream always was to open a restaurant," Ruby says. "But I had no money. This was in 1981, and I had a car that was worth five thousand dollars, which I sold to show some savings. I got Pete and Johnny to back me when I was opening the Precinct [his first restaurant]. Once they backed me, I could go to other people. I got ten investors, they each had four point nine percent and I had fifty-one percent."

Ruby opened a second restaurant, the Waterfront, again with Rose and Bench among the limited partners. Like the Precinct, it was wildly popular from the moment it opened. The Waterfront is larger, fancier, and more expensive than the first venture. According to Ruby, in 1988 it was the restaurant with the twelfth-highest volume in the whole U.S.

"Once they backed me, it became a very sexy investment and a fun thing for other people to be involved in. Having Pete and Johnny brought more people to the dance. Pete especially. He's a child of Cincinnati. Johnny Bench is big in Cincinnati, but nobody could ever be as big as Pete Rose."

With all the homogeneity of American society, there remains a great variance from city to city in the tone and quality of local journalism.

There are cities that eat their own, where reporters are so eager to take a bite out of anyone who steps in the wrong place that you can almost hear their guttural growl. And there are other places, like Cincinnati, where the gathering of news is a gentler art, carried out by men and women who are less lean and hungry.

Aggressive reporting makes for better newspapers, although there's no proof that it improves a community's quality of life. Cincinnati is a pleasant place to live partly because its residents tend to dwell on what's good about the community. "People *like* living in Cincinnati. They're not embarrassed to say that," says Zane Miller, the historian and University of Cincinnati professor.

Although its newspapers and broadcast outlets are certainly capable of occasional good work, the norm is a softer, more passive style of journalism.

Before the Fourth of July, the lead story in the afternoon paper, the *Post*, concerns the rising price of meat. *Cincinnatians, those burgers and weenies on the grill this summer are going to cost you more.* On a different day, a survey showing which of the nine suburban shopping malls is the most popular also makes the *Post*'s front page.

In October 1989 the morning *Cincinnati Enquirer* crossed the line from soft to shoddy in its handling of a *New York Times* story about wrongdoing at California's huge Lincoln Savings and Loan Association, whose principal owner was Charles H. Keating, a Cincinnati native and antismut zealot who founded the first of the Queen City's pornography-fighting organizations, which he called Citizens for Decent Literature.

The *Enquirer* ran the *Times* story, but not before deleting all references to Keating, who was also the brother of the *Enquirer*'s publisher. For this, the *Columbia Journalism Review* cited the *Enquirer* for "scandalous editing," and the newspaper's business editor resigned in protest of what he said was a pattern of dishonest coverage of Charles Keating's role in the demise of his savings and loan.

This happened at Cincinnati's biggest-circulation daily. It was an example, obviously, of horrendous newspapering, but also of something more—a coziness among certain powerful people in the Queen City. Cincinnati is a city that looks out for its own and does not like to see its local heroes sullied.

Pete Rose was no Cincinnati blue-blood like Keating (perhaps he was an honorary one), but he still benefited from that coziness.

In 1985, the year he overtook Ty Cobb, law-enforcement authorities busted two Cincinnati physicians whom they considered the biggest suppliers of amphetamines in the state of Ohio. In the course of the investigation, they received information that some of the amphetamines may have been making their way into the Reds clubhouse, and they suspected that one of the recipients was Rose.

The arrest of the doctors was hailed by local law-enforcement as a major victory. The doctors had been supplying immense quantities of amphetamines over a wide swath of southern Ohio, and when they were forced to surrender their medical licenses, it caused the purchase of amphetamines by doctors in the state to decrease by almost fifty percent.

Some of the investigators who worked on the case wanted to pursue the trail of the pills into the Reds clubhouse, but they were discouraged from doing so by higher-ups. As one of the investigators recalls, "This was Mr. Baseball we were talking about, and it was never a wise thing in Cincinnati to mess with Mr. Baseball."

When Rose ran afoul of baseball authorities four years later, Cincinnatians, in the beginning, were kept remarkably uninformed by their newspapers. It was either a case of inept newspapering or a sign of civic denial.

Neither Cincinnati newspaper distinguished itself. *The Cincinnati Post* broke a couple of stories—it was the first to report a grand-jury probe into Rose's taxes—but along with the *Enquirer* it managed to ignore the Rose story for as long as possible, while *Sports Illustrated*, *The New York Times*, the *Dayton Daily News* and the Cleveland *Plain Dealer* took the lead.

The *Post*'s lead reporter on the Rose story, Al Salvato, acknowledges, "We were the last out of the chute. When Pete was first called to New York in February, we didn't send anyone there to find out why. And then we basically didn't do anything for a month. I don't think there was anything sinister about it. I think people here just didn't realize that Pete could be in big trouble."

The coverage would inspire a joke that made the rounds in Cincinnati:

Did you hear the latest about Pete Rose?

No, I haven't gotten my Cleveland paper yet.

John Dowd spent a total of a couple of weeks in and around Cincinnati during his investigation of Rose, certainly not long enough to get to know the city.

One thing that struck him was how nice people were to him, especially considering the nature of the business that brought him to town.

And Dowd came to one other conclusion about the city. It was based partly on some things he had learned about Rose's past, but also on an intuition, a feeling. What Dowd concluded was, "They've been cleaning up his messes in Cincinnati for years."

Pete Rose was the sort of local hero whom people felt they knew on a personal level. He was accessible, a common man who seemed not to set himself apart.

He rode around Cincinnati in his fancy cars, but he still honked his horn at people he knew on the sidewalk and hung out the driver's-side window to wave at them. Rose wasn't the country-club type. He popped up at bowling alleys, Little League games, and college basketball games, and he always signed autographs.

Like a good politician, he had a sharp memory for names. "I bet you don't remember me . . . ," someone was always saying to Pete Rose, and before the person could say another word, Rose had blurted out that person's name.

It was a point of pride in Cincinnati that Pete Rose remembered where he was from and that he kept so close to his old friends from the West Side. Some people were even under the impression that his neighborhood pals were the ones who had led him down the wrong path.

But all of this was an utter myth. Rose wasn't really the type who remembered where he was from, in the true sense of that expression. The West Side pals who stayed in his circle were, in a sense, ornaments. They proved how close Rose was to his roots, and he liked people to think that.

The truth was, Rose had little regard for people without money or status, although he did like the homage they paid him.

And he had no regard for friendships, old or new. When he had no more use for a friend, he tossed him away, with all the sentiment one might attach to dropping a Styrofoam coffee cup in a waste bin.

8

TEAMMATES, WIVES, AND LOVERS

He's never made a mistake. He's never bet the wrong horse. If I say 2, he don't go bet 3.

—Pete Rose, praising his friend Arnie Metz

THERE were plenty of good reasons why someone would want to spend time around Pete Rose.

He was upbeat. He could make you laugh. He was dependable; if he said he would be somewhere, he showed up. Crude as he could be, he was mannerly in some other ways. "Wherever we went, he would introduce me," says Paul Janszen. "He would say, 'This is my friend Paul Janszen.' I always appreciated that."

Rose had other charms, some of them unexpected. He was, for instance, surprisingly curious about other people's lives.

Upon meeting a new teammate or a young player from an opposing team, he'd fire away with all sorts of questions. Some were of a strictly professional nature. He would ask a rookie pitcher where he picked up his change-up, who taught it to him, how long he'd been throwing it. He'd ask a hitter about his stance. *You always hold the bat that high?* Or he might ask him for a scouting report on a minor-league pitching prospect. *You face that Drabek down there? He throw as hard as they say?*

Rose was also curious about where players were from and how they grew up, especially the foreign-born players, whom he honed right in on. *Was that a poor town? What kind of food did you eat? How many kids in your family? Did you all have to sleep in the same room? In the same bed?*

This led Rose to some theories about players from the Spanish-speaking countries. When he was a manager, he said he preferred players from the Dominican Republic. They were poorer, he believed, hungrier. On the other hand, the Venezuelans came from more money. He thought they tended to be lazy. (Longtime teammate Davey Concepcion figured prominently in this; Rose never had much respect for him.)

Rose asked his questions rapid-fire and he'd ask anybody anything.

"He always asked guys when he met them if they were married," says Larry Christenson, Rose's teammate in Philadelphia. "If the guy wasn't married, he'd say, 'Do you have a girlfriend?' If the guy was married, he'd say, 'Well, do you have a girlfriend, too? Do you mess around?' "

Rose was equally blunt with nonballplayers.

In 1987, a man named Sam Hall, who had just recently been released from a jail in Nicaragua, visited the Reds spring training complex in Tampa, Florida. Hall had been nabbed snapping pictures outside a Sandinista military installation. When Rose was introduced to him, he mentioned that he'd heard something about his case on the TV news, then he plunged right in with his first question.

"So when they caught you," he inquired, "why didn't they just shoot you?"

Another of Rose's great attractions, of course, was his sense of humor.

At a Los Angeles restaurant one night, he was seated near a party that included Toni Tennille, of the musical group Captain and Tennille. Rose approached her table and inquired, "Where's the Captain?"

"He's not here tonight," she replied.

"Well, I'm a captain," said Rose, who was then captain of the Reds. "Why don't you come along with me?"

Rose's wit could be as quick as his bat. In the Cincinnati clubhouse, a writer approached him after a game as he was getting dressed. He prefaced his question, "I'm from San Francisco . . ." Rose, who was nude, feigned alarm and quickly jumped up and pulled a towel around his midsection. That was typical Rose: He could make you laugh, even when you didn't want to.

His humor could also be cruel. When he was managing the Reds, a boy of about twelve approached him in the lobby of a Pittsburgh hotel. He was clutching an old Wheaties box with Rose's picture on it, which he wanted him to autograph. Rose waved him away. "No thanks," he said, "I already ate breakfast."

Another time, Rose was said to have told a blind man who sought his autograph in a restaurant, "I'll sign anything you want. Just get that fucking dog away from me."

Rose's barbed humor did not desert him even in times of trouble. In spring training of 1989, not long after the disclosure of baseball's investigation of him, a writer seeking an angle for his season-opening story attempted to get him to talk about "the great tradition" of opening day in Cincinnati.

"And I'll tell you another great American tradition," Rose shot back: "Innocent until proven guilty."

On occasion, Rose could even direct his humor in such a way as to help others through difficult times. Jeff Ruby, the Cincinnati restaurant owner, suffered life-threatening neurological injuries in 1987 after a bizarre incident in which he tumbled from the passenger seat of his car as it was being driven by his wife. "I went through a depression after that, and by May of 1988 I had hit rock bottom," says Ruby. "Other than my doctor, Pete was the most therapeutic guy I could have around.

"We never talked about it, but my wife told him that I needed a lift. He started coming around more, and we took a road trip with the team to the West Coast. He's not a sentimental guy, so he never would say, 'Jeff, let's talk.' He's just fun to be around and that helped. One day he was coming to the Waterfront to see me. And we had a multimillion-dollar addition going on. And he sees me, and I'm up on a construction ledge, very high up, and he yells, 'Jeff, don't jump!'

"That was as close to saying anything as he did. But it was great. I laughed. I hadn't laughed for days. That made it a good day. I realized then what a good friend he was, what a true friend."

Pete Rose made some friends in baseball.

Tommy Helms was certainly one. They were teammates on the 1962 Macon Peaches, roommates at a fifty-cents-a-night YMCA, and fellow insomniacs on spooky, all-night road trips through the rural South. They were fellow pranksters, too. The Peaches traveled in station wagons, and once, with Helms goading him, Rose climbed out the back of one and slithered across the roof and down the windshield, nearly causing the coach who was driving to veer off the dark highway.

Rose preceded his friend to the major leagues, and when Helms came up to the Reds for a brief stretch in 1964, he lived in a spare bedroom in Rose's house. Karolyn Rose painted a big 19 on the door, Helms's uniform number. When Helms returned to the Reds the next season, the bedroom, with the number still on the door, was waiting for him.

In their early years together with the Reds, Rose and Helms were road roommates, and Helms still knotted Rose's ties for him. (Despite his terrific hand-eye coordination, Rose had a devilish time executing a Windsor knot.)

In 1970, when Rose was twenty-nine years old, a newspaper columnist asked him what he'd like to do when he was done playing. "I'm going to manage the Reds," he replied, "and Tommy Helms is going to be one of my coaches."

As it turned out, when Rose became manager in 1984, Helms, who had retired after playing fourteen big-league seasons, was already a Reds coach. They still called each other friends, and people who didn't know better assumed they were close.

But they never went out together after games. Not once in five years. Nor did Rose socialize with any of his other coaches. None of them even spent time in his office before or after games, unless there was a formal meeting in progress.

"I didn't feel comfortable in his office, to be quite honest," Helms says. "He had his other friends in there, people who weren't involved in baseball. I didn't know them. I didn't care to know them. We were over in the coaches' room, and Pete was in the manager's office. Pete came over and gave us the lineups, and that was about it."

Bill Plummer was another friend of Rose's. As the backup catcher to Johnny Bench from 1970 to 1978, Plummer was perhaps the least-known (and least-paid) member of the Big Red Machine.

During spring trainings, which served as warm-weather vacations for many baseball families, the Plummers and the Roses spent quite a bit of time together, but often without Pete Rose being present. "More often than not, it was me and the two wives and the kids," Plummer recalls now. "Sometimes Karolyn would have the Rolls, and we would just ride around Tampa, go to a K mart or something. Pete wouldn't be with us. He was at the track."

The Reds, as the game's oldest franchise, always opened the baseball season at home. By Rose's birthday, April 14, the club invariably was on the road. "Atlanta, for some reason," Plummer says. "That was usually where we were. I always took him out for a nice dinner. That was a little tradition we had."

Years later, Rose would have sweet memories of those out-of-town birthdays. It was better than being home, he reasoned, because it gave him the rare opportunity to drink in the applause of fans from another city. After the PA man announced that it was his birthday, they would cheer for him. Sometimes they'd even get on their feet. It was a remarkable tribute, just about the only time non-Reds fans permitted themselves to show how much they really cared for Pete Rose.

How many people are lucky enough to get a standing ovation from forty-five thousand people on their birthdays? Rose mused in Roger Kahn's authorized biography.

Rose never mentioned the birthday dinners with Bill Plummer. Maybe he didn't remember them. To Pete Rose, the love from the stands, from the press, was intoxicating, and he held it dearer than true friendship.

Plummer tried to stay in touch with Rose. He became a minor-league manager, then a coach with the American League Seattle Mariners. He left messages for Rose at home, and at his hotels on the road. They weren't returned. "I have no idea why," says Plummer. "I guess Pete got busy with other things, being a player-manager there for a while, then all his business commitments."

Rose also drifted from Art Shamsky, his Reds teammate from 1965 to 1967 and his friend from when they were teenagers with the Geneva Redlegs. Back then, Shamsky's parents used to visit and take the two of them out to dinner.

"They considered Pete for a time like another son," says Shamsky, who became a broadcaster at the end of his playing career and then the owner of a Greenwich Village restaurant. "In the minor leagues, you developed those sort of relationships. My parents would call for tickets when he came into St. Louis. After a while he didn't return the calls. I had to tell them, 'Maybe he's real busy. Maybe he didn't get the message.' Finally, I had to tell them, 'I'll get you tickets if you want tickets.'

"The last time I saw Pete was in the clubhouse at Shea in '88. And I said, 'Pete, I would like a [signed] bat for the restaurant.' Sure, it was something in the way of a favor. But it was also a tribute to him. I mean, the bats I have in there are all from great players. Well, he never sent it.

"I had his home phone number. I talked to his wife, Carol. I said, 'Carol, just ask Pete to give me a call.' And she said, 'Oh, yeah, he'll be home in a few minutes.' I had been the guy's first friend in baseball. We were good buddies for a very significant time in our careers, and it was as if I was some fan asking him for a favor. He never called me back."

Rose was not widely liked among the rank and file in the major-league clubhouses—by most of his teammates or by opposing players. Partly, this was to his credit.

He was the equivalent of the guy on the assembly line who is told by his co-workers, *Hey, man, slow down, you're making us look bad.* Rose's unrelenting work ethic set a high standard for other players and many resented him for it.

Rose played for himself. He played for money and records. And he played for the fans. He ran to first base on walks. He dove after foul balls he couldn't possibly reach. The crowd loved it. The front office loved it. Other players did not. They considered it "false hustle," their term for showy effort put forth only for effect. And they ended up getting booed by fans who couldn't understand why they didn't hustle like Pete Rose.

While other veteran players were begging out of the despised in-season exhibition games against farm clubs, or finding excuses to not even make the trips, Rose would refuse to come out of the games until he felt he had given the fans their money's worth. In Indianapolis one night against the Reds' Triple A club, Sparky Anderson tried to take him out of the game every inning from the fourth on, and Rose wouldn't let him. "These people paid their four bucks," he told Anderson. "I'm not coming out till I show 'em something."

Finally, in the seventh inning, Rose grounded a ball through the middle, kept on running and dove into second. That was precisely what they wanted to see, the headfirst slide. Rose was out by about fifteen feet, and left the field to a standing ovation.

"Yeah, guys resented Pete for that kind of thing," says Merv

Rettenmund, his former Reds teammate. "They shouldn't have, but they did. You would hope that everyone would want the fans to feel good when they leave the ballpark, but not everybody has that foremost in their minds. He saw the game as entertainment. If everybody thought like he did, the game would be a lot more exciting."

There were other reasons Rose was disliked. Many of his teammates found him too selfish in the way he played the game, too "me-me-me."

Rose would rarely hit behind a runner to move him up a base, although the truth was, a man who hit for Rose's high average almost certainly helped his team more by trying for base hits. But that didn't matter. A player who "gives himself up," sacrifices a time at bat, performs an important rite within the player's code: He shows his teammates that he puts the good of the team above his own personal goals.

Rose may at times have been a liar, but he was no hypocrite. He never pretended the hits didn't matter to him. On Reds charter flights, while his teammates drank, slept, played cards, or engaged in bull sessions, he frequently flew in the front of the cabin, attached to the shoulder of the man doing the stats. "Sometimes he dictated the box score lines to me out of the scorebook," recalls Bob Rathgeber, who used to do the Reds' statistics. "That way he could find out sooner what his average was and how it compared to everyone else's."

All players, of course, care about their own statistics. But another part of the clubhouse code is that if an individual performs well in a game but his team loses, he shouldn't look too happy.

"If the team wins and you do poorly, you're supposed to hide your disappointment," explains Tom House, who is the pitching coach for the Texas Rangers and a Ph.D. in psychology. "If the team loses and you do well, you contain your glee. No matter what happened in the game, Rose would always have a story for writers, centering on me-me-me."

House, who pitched in the major leagues from 1971 to 1978, says that Rose displayed the same personality traits as most of his peers in baseball. But in his case, they were exaggerated. "Pete was too aggressive, too single-minded, too narcissistic even for the other ballplayers," House says. "He was in a world unto himself, separate and apart from other players, and not always popular."

There were other things about Rose that annoyed his peers. One was his habit of demeaning other players. In 1981, near mid-season, he was second in the league in batting to Art Howe, a Houston Astros player who had never before hit as high as .300. Rose considered that he was in excellent position to win his fourth batting crown. "Hey, I'm second in the league," he pointed out. "You know Art Howe ain't gonna beat me out of the damn thing."

He was right; Howe wasn't in his class as a hitter. But no one appreciated hearing him say it, except the writers.

Rose was also notoriously cheap, and this grated on his team-mates. The surest way for a superstar player to be popular with his lesser teammates is to spread his money around. Take team-mates out to dinner. Buy them drinks. Rent the hotel suites for the team parties.

Rose was known for inviting young players out to dinner, then sticking them with the check. On the other hand, he did occa-sionally take a rookie under his wing. In Philadelphia, Rose all but adopted young outfielder Jeff Stone, moved him into his house, and outfitted him in an entire wardrobe of hand-me-down slacks and silk shirts, most of which he had worn just once or twice.

But despite his occasional grand gestures (giving away the Jeeps was the grandest of them all), Rose was not, as Larry Starr puts it, "a daily guy." For example, Reds management in the sixties and seventies constantly had to hound him to get him to pay his "clubhouse dues," money paid by players to the clubhouse man at the end of each home stand for the postgame food spread and other services. "He had the habit of stiffing little people," says a former Reds executive. "That was money right out of the club-house man's pocket, and you couldn't get Pete to pay it."

Rose also rejected a suggestion in 1970 that all the money re-ceived from pregame and postgame radio shows be pooled and used for team parties. The proposal didn't seem fair to him. He reasoned that he was going to be the star of the game more than anyone else, so why should he give up some of his money?

For the rest of that season, recalls former teammate Bernie Carbo, whenever Rose was on the star-of-the-game show, some of his teammates would break open rolls of pennies and sprinkle them in his locker. Rose one-upped them: He painstakingly col-lected the strewn pennies and dropped them into a big piggy bank he had bought. "The piggy bank was full by the end of the season," Carbo says. "I don't know what he ever did with it, but knowing Pete I imagine he took it home."

Rose was certainly not the first star player to be estranged from his peers. Joe DiMaggio "led the league" in room service, David Halberstam quotes ex-pitcher Eddie Lopat as saying in *Summer of '49*. DiMaggio, like Rose, had an entourage of nonbaseball friends who were referred to at the time as his "bobos." (DiMaggio must have chosen his bobos better or been nicer to them. His never turned on him, as Rose's ultimately did.)

Star players do not often turn to each other for friendship either. They are, instead, natural rivals—for fame, fan popularity, press attention, money.

At the beginning of a season during the mid-seventies, Johnny Bench took a look at what the club had planned for its various publications. "Let's see," said Bench as he scanned them to see whose face was on the covers, "you've got me taken care of on the scorebook. You've got Morgan taken care of on the yearbook. And you've got Rose taken care of on the media guide. And Perez, he just doesn't give a shit."

That pretty much summed up the clashing egos of the star players on the great Big Red Machine teams, which between 1970 and 1976 won Five National League West championships, four NL pennant flags and two World Championships. All were concerned with the prerogatives of stardom except Tony Perez, the steady, power-hitting first baseman.

For this reason, Sparky Anderson says, "Tony Perez was the key guy on those teams. I say that because he was a tremendous player, and he also kept everybody on an even keel because he had no ego. It didn't matter to him that other guys got all the publicity. Perez had a way of keeping them all together."

Rose and Bench had, at best, an uneasy relationship. "When Bench joined the team at the end of the 1967 season," says Earl Lawson, "he was considered too big for his britches. Much like Pete had been. There were three catchers then, and [manager Dave] Bristol put him right in the lineup. The next year, he was playing full-time, and hitting only a little over .100 in May, so there was a lot of talk about that. Even when he got to be a star, which was very quick—he won two MVPs by the time he was twenty-four—he didn't endear himself to the guys.

"One of the reasons had to do with these parties that the airline stewardesses used to throw for the players, especially in St. Louis, where the Ozark Air Lines ladies always had a party. Well, all the girls would go for the Bench. They would hang back until they could figure out which girl would be the lucky one, and Bench would take a long time to make up his mind. That, believe it or not, caused a lot of problems for him. There was a lot of resentment, and almost some fistfights.

"I said to Pete at that time, 'Hey, the kid needs a friend. Don't let them do to him what they did to you when you came up.' So if you look back, Bench and Rose in the very beginning were very close, although they didn't stay that way. There wasn't much open hostility, but they were not fond of each other at all."

Says Starr, the Reds' longtime trainer, "I don't think Johnny could visualize why anyone would want to play baseball for twenty-five years. To him, baseball was his job. It was his business. And Pete couldn't visualize how anyone could feel that way. They had two totally opposite approaches."

Joe Morgan, the Hall of Fame second baseman, was considered the last piece of the Big Red Machine, the added ingredient that made a good team great. He joined the club in 1972, in a trade that sent Tommy Helms, among others, to the Houston Astros.

Morgan and Rose had adjoining locker stalls, and theirs were the prevalent voices in the Reds clubhouse of the seventies—always chirping, needling each other, needling other teammates. For a time, Morgan and Rose were frequent companions after ball games, although on the surface Rose had no more in common with Morgan than with Bench.

Morgan was college-educated, well rounded, polished. He was knowledgeable about fine wines and liked to order an expensive bottle with dinner.

Rose was one-dimensional, all baseball, rough-edged. If he was out to dinner at a nice restaurant, he made the same order every time: "Gimme a steak, medium rare, baked potato, salad, iced tea," he would say, usually before the waiter had even placed the menus down. It didn't matter who else was at the table. Among the customs Rose did not observe was the one allowing women to order first. He ordered in a hurry, and ate in a hurry.

If Rose was with a woman, especially if it was someone he had just met, he would take the wine bottle and pour her glass to the top. Although he himself did not drink, he firmly believed that if you got a woman drunk, you stood a better chance of taking her to bed. (Rose was not the least bit judgmental about other people drinking, or even using drugs. When he was asked about cocaine by *Playboy*, he said, "I hope the guys I play against do it. I don't give a shit. It is just going to make my job easier.") On rare occasions, Rose poured a small portion of wine for himself, but before tasting it he took a fistful of ice from his water glass and mixed it in.

Rose's friendship with Morgan ultimately cooled. Part of the reason was what Rose had said as he was departing the Reds after the 1978 season: Some of the Reds stars would play poorly under the pressure of being on the final year of their contracts, he predicted, while others would "sulk" because they hadn't been granted the money they wanted.

Rose said he had gotten "humpbacked" carrying the Reds on his shoulders the last sixteen years, and predicted that without him his old club would surely plummet in the standings. "The Reds are going nowhere," he was quoted as saying. "They got no leadership with me and Sparky Anderson gone." (The Reds won the NL West their first year without Rose).

Morgan said at the time, "Pete ought to zip it up. He ought to just leave us alone and go out and play. Some of the guys are really upset at some of the stuff he's been saying."

This wasn't the first time Rose had demeaned his teammates in print. He did it regularly around contract time. But this time, the remaining Reds, Morgan included, lashed back.

It was part of a pattern for Rose: Whatever friendships or relationships he did make, he eventually scuttled.

Pete Rose first laid eyes on Karolyn Englehardt, his first wife, on a sunny afternoon in July of 1963 at River Downs. As he looked through his binoculars at the horses charging down the homestretch, a shapely leg, resting on the rail, came into his view. It was Karolyn's.

A fuller view revealed that she was short, extremely busty, and flashy. She wore heavy makeup and eyeliner, dangly earrings, and a ring on each finger. Her nails were long and daggerlike.

Pete Rose liked her looks and walked down and introduced himself. They began dating, and within two months had plans to marry.

Rose called home that off-season from Fort Knox, Kentucky, where he was serving his National Guard obligation, to announce his marriage plans, but he could not bear to tell his father, who he knew would be opposed.

"He said, 'I'm gonna get married, Mom. Will you tell Dad?' LaVerne Noeth recalls. "I said, 'No way, you're on your own on this one.' Big Pete wanted him to get more experience in the major leagues before he got married. He thought it would distract him. He was afraid of the sophomore jinx or whatever they called it."

Harry Rose finally got on the phone and was told personally by his son of the marriage plans. After they hung up, Pete Rose's father cried. Later, he tried to sabotage the wedding.

"My husband was so teed off he wanted to talk to her family. He went up there and tried to talk to them, but they said they've got the hall rented and everything, and they can't stop it now."

Harry Rose's next ploy was to boycott the wedding, but that didn't work either. He got a call from Phil Seghi, a Reds executive, who told him there would be reporters at the wedding, and if the parents of the newest Reds sensation were not in attendance it would be embarrassing to the family and to the team, too.

"So we went under protest," LaVerne Noeth says. "I had to rush downtown and grab something I thought I'd look good in. We weren't so happy."

On January 25, 1964, as the twenty-two-year-old Rose prepared to start down the aisle at St. Williams Catholic Church in Cincinnati, he turned to his parents, winked, and cracked, "Here goes nothing."

Eleven months into the marriage their first child, Fawn, was born. Five years later came a son, Pete junior, called "Petey."

By nature supportive and nurturing, Karolyn Rose was in many ways the classic baseball wife. She cooked at any hour of the day or night to accommodate Pete's irregular hours. She sat behind home plate with the other wives and cheered her husband's every hit. Each February, she dutifully packed up the family for their annual trek to spring training.

Karolyn and Pete liked to do jigsaw puzzles in Florida; one year she surprised him with a special one, a Pete Rose jigsaw, thousands of cardboard pieces adding up to a smiling Charlie Hustle.

But Karolyn Rose was much more than the stereotypical, deferential ballplayer's wife. She was, in some ways, her husband's twin. Raised on the same West Side streets among the same kind of people, she was, like Pete Rose, a nonstop talker, every bit as witty and on occasion just as crude.

After facing some initial resentment from the wives of her husband's first teammates, she became wildly popular in baseball circles, where she is still spoken of in reverential tones. "This is a marvelous woman," says Sparky Anderson. "I loved her. My wife loved her. I think everyone who ever came into contact with her loved her."

Karolyn Rose built a celebrity status of her own in Cincinnati, working as a DJ at a popular club and even hosting her own radio sports show. Once, in announcing the starting time of a minor-league hockey game, she said, "Puck-off time is at seven thirty-five."

Karolyn Rose even accommodated herself, for a long while, to the most difficult aspect of being married to a ballplayer—the fact that her husband screwed around.

Rose literally had a girlfriend in every city with a National League franchise. He liked what he called "hard-bellies," young women with firm bodies and no flab. He and Tommy Helms had a little routine about this.

"Hey, Petey, how do you get all those hard-bellies?" Tommy Helms would say.

"Just look at their fingers," Rose would reply, by which he meant the expensive rings he bought them.

One of Rose's girlfriends was Terry Rubio, a Tampa woman who in the late seventies used to show up at the Reds' spring training complex in a canary-yellow Triumph convertible. She had a big shock of black hair, and, like Karolyn, she was not the kind of woman you could fail to notice. Everyone knew she was Pete Rose's girlfriend, and he bragged that he had given her the sports car "for being my personal 1977 Rookie of the Year."

Rubio filed a paternity suit against Rose in 1979 for a daughter born the previous year, whom she named Morgan. The suit claimed she and Rose had had "intimate relations" during the time the baby was conceived, and she told reporters that in taking legal action she was following a lesson she learned from Rose: "He always told me, 'If you have a sure hand, don't fold. Play it to the hilt.' "

The case was settled out of court, after her lawyer said Rose had "done the manly thing."

Like a great many major-league ballplayers, Pete Rose considered his extramarital affairs a virtual fringe benefit of his profession. The difference was, he went beyond what was acceptable adulterous behavior even within baseball's mores, by having outrageously flagrant affairs, and having them even in his home city of Cincinnati, a place still small enough that everyone's business gets around.

He had no qualms, seemingly no shame, about publicly humiliating his wife. When his very public philandering threatened his first marriage, Earl Lawson was one of the many who tried to counsel him.

"After a Royals basketball game, Pete and I met at the Cock and Bull restaurant at the Cincinnati Gardens," Lawson recalls. "This is the late sixties. I said to him, 'Damn it, watch the fooling around. I know you're going to fool around on the road, but at home your wife is going to realize that she's becoming the laughingstock of the community. And she may still love you, but just to salvage her pride she's going to have to tell you to get lost.' But that didn't make it. He didn't listen. A woman has her pride. I tried to make Pete understand that. He didn't, or didn't want to.

"Pete would listen to me about some things, especially when he was younger. But even then, if it was something he didn't want to hear, he wouldn't. When I talked to him about not cheating at home, it was like telling him 'Don't eat candy.' It was like, 'But I like candy, Daddy.' Well, then, go ahead and eat it. It'll make you sick, it'll give you bad teeth, but go ahead.' He was advised, but he chose to ignore it."

Karolyn Rose talked about life with her husband in an interview with Maralyn Lois Polak of *The Philadelphia Inquirer* in 1979, not long before their marriage broke up. The Pete Rose she described was cold to the point of cruelty.

"I guess I'm strong in one way, but I just, I would like to be with my husband constantly if I could. That's how much I love him," Karolyn said.

"Pete doesn't show his love outward. He would never kiss me in public or hold my hand. No, he's very private. I would give anything to be able to hold his hand in public and kiss him after the game.

"One time I did try it. I decided I was going to get a kiss from Pete. He came out of the clubhouse. I puckered up, but he just walked right past me. Then he came back and said, 'What's the matter with your lips, Karolyn? They look all funny. C'mon. Let's go.' So I don't think I would try it again."

In that same year, Karolyn Rose wrote about her husband's infidelities in a four-part series for *The Cincinnati Post* titled "Life with a Switch-Hitter Is No Bed of Roses."

"I knew it would be tough before Pete and I were married," she wrote.

> He was on a road trip on the East Coast not long after we had a few dates. I got lonesome and called. His team roommate answered.
>
> "Is Pete there?" I asked.
>
> "Just a minute, I'll check," he said.
>
> I was dumb but not that dumb. They're staying in one room, so where is he going to check, under the beds?
>
> "No, he's not there," the guy said after a long pause. He took a message and Pete called me back in about five minutes.
>
> After we were married the problem didn't immediately go away. Our first spring training together, I was alone in King Arthur's Inn in Tampa when the phone rang and a girl asked for Pete.
>
> "This is the maid," I said. "Mr. Rose ain't here."
>
> "Tell him so and so is in Miami and if he wants to come over I can get off."
>
> I was packed for home in 10 minutes.

Karolyn Rose didn't leave. She stayed, for fifteen years. She even moved with her husband to Philadelphia, although by then their marriage was all but over and her husband had already taken up with the woman who would become his second wife.

Carol Woliung, 5'7", blond, and blue-eyed, was a former featured twirler for the Lawrenceburg (Indiana) High School marching band. She attended modeling school, and had also been a cheerleader for the Cincinnati Bengals professional football team. (The cheerleading squad was called the Ben-Gals.)

Carol Woliung's roommate in Cincinnati, where she had moved from Indiana after the breakup of her first marriage, had a poster of Pete Rose hanging over her bed—one of those shots in which Rose is diving into a bag and his face is all crinkled up in anticipation of the dirt that's about to fly up into it. One day, before she had met Pete Rose, Carol Woliung looked at the poster and said, "He looks so ugly."

Pete Rose had never seen any posters of Carol Woliung, but he had heard about her. "The clubhouse man said, 'If you want to see the prettiest butt in Cincinnati, go to Sleep Out Louie's,' " Rose told *Cincinnati Magazine.* "I had to take him up on it."

In Kahn's book, Rose gave his wife a promotion of sorts: She no longer had the most attractive rear end just in the city, but in the *whole state.* "You can write it," Kahn quotes Rose. "I heard she had the prettiest bottom in Ohio. Some scouting reports you check out personally."

Rose went to Sleep Out Louie's, where Carol was working at the time, ordered an orange juice from Carol, and checked her out from all angles. He liked what he saw. She became his girlfriend.

He was used to juggling wives and girlfriends, but occasionally he slipped up. Once, for instance, he bought Carol and Karolyn identical diamond pendant necklaces. Karolyn spied Carol with hers one night at Riverfront Stadium, punched her, and tried to rip it off her neck.

"She split my lip," Carol told *Sports Illustrated* in 1985.

As Lawson, among others, had told Rose what would happen, Karolyn Rose eventually got fed up. She moved back to Cincinnati early in the 1979 season, and before the end of the year she filed for divorce.

Long before Karolyn Rose began packing up, Carol Woliung was already installed in the Philadelphia area, where she found work as a Playboy bunny in Atlantic City and a Philadelphia Eagles cheerleader.

Pete Rose took full blame for the breakup of his first marriage. Karolyn was "a good wife, a terrific mother, a fine lover," he said. "What happened wasn't her fault. It was my fault."

Why, then, did he trade up for the newer model? He was typically unapologetic about that. "She made me feel young," he said in the same *Sports Illustrated* story that quoted Carol about the split lip. "I like to live like that. Fast cars, fast horses, a young wife. That keeps you going."

He also said he knew how to end a marriage. "Hey, just give her a million bucks and tell her to hit the road."

Pete Rose and Carol Woliung were married during the baseball season in 1984 in a small ceremony at the home of his lawyer Reuven Katz. When their son, Tyler, was born the following October, Pete Rose was in the delivery room for the birth.

In 1985, a typically fawning story in *The Cincinnati Post* described the wonderful new life of Pete Rose and his young wife. Their new split-level home in the Cincinnati suburb of Indian Hills, Rose's first home on the East Side, was set on five wooded acres. It had a horse barn and a swimming pool. Inside, the decorative color scheme of the house was purple and mauve.

Pete called Carol "foxy," the story said. They went to the track together. Like him, she did not smoke or drink. Carol told the writer that Pete was often distracted at home. "When Pete comes home he turns on the TV and watches sports. Sometimes it's like he's in a trance."

Carol got lots of diamond jewelry from Pete, the story noted, but it mentioned nothing about the scrap over the diamond necklace.

Actually, by 1985, Carol was experiencing some of the same types of problems that Karolyn had. Pete Rose still had a roving eye, among other things. One day Carol made a surprise visit to her new husband on the road and discovered another woman's clothes in his Atlanta hotel room. She collected the clothes, took them outside, and dumped them on the city street.

People who know Carol Rose say that she is a nice woman but does not have Karolyn's smarts or spunk.

"Carol is a nice, sweet, small-town girl," says Marty Brennaman, the longtime Reds broadcaster. "But I don't believe she could tell anything to Pete that would make a difference. Karolyn was a different story. She was from the same streets as Pete, almost the same person, only she was female."

Pete Rose made a new baseball friend when he came back to the Reds in 1984—Dave Parker.

A talented ballplayer with trouble in his past, Parker had won two batting crowns and a MVP trophy with the Pittsburgh Pirates in the seventies, but by the end of the decade a string of injuries had eroded his skills and he had become the target of some vile abuse by the Pittsburgh fans. One night, as he stood in right field at Three Rivers Stadium, someone from the upper deck threw a battery at him. Later, Parker admitted that he had used cocaine during his final seasons with the Pirates.

Rose was never one to let anyone else's opinion influence his own. For better and for worse, he took a man at face value.

When Rose came home to the Reds as player-manager in the middle of the 1984 season, Parker was already there, having signed as a free agent the previous winter. Rose was glad to have him.

Parker, Cincinnati-born, was experiencing a baseball rebirth of his own. Healthy for the first time in years, he was once again a feared hitter, as well as a formidable presence among his teammates. A massive man at 6'5" and 250 pounds, with barely an ounce of fat on him, Parker's booming voice careened off the cinder-block walls of the clubhouse. He was bright, garrulous, and a master of raw insult humor.

"If I had a head like yours, I'd make a motherfucking butcher-block table out of it," he once gibed Rose. (That was about the bare minimum of *motherfucks* that Parker ever put into any sentence.)

Parker was black, like so many of the people Rose had drawn close to over the course of his career. Rose often said that Joe Morgan, another black man, was the smartest teammate he had ever played with. He respected Parker's intelligence, too. That didn't prevent Rose from telling jokes that, coming from others, might have been considered racist. From Rose, nobody took offense. His jokes just sounded silly.

"You know why all the black guys are fast?" was one of his favorites. " 'Cause the lions ate all the slow ones."

"How come an African soccer team needs two planes to travel?" was another of Rose's jokes. "One plane for the players, one for the spears."

Rose, in his 1979 *Playboy* interview, explained that his success with endorsements was because he was one of the few white superstars in sports. "Look, if you owned Swanson's pizza, would you want a black guy to do the commercial on TV for you? Would you like the black guy to pick up the pizza and bite into it? Try to sell it? I mean, would you want Dave Parker selling your pizza to America for you? Or would you want Pete Rose?"

That wasn't a joke. It was, at the time, the unfortunate truth, and Rose didn't mind speaking it.

In the beginning of his managerial tenure, Rose leaned on the veteran Parker for advice and insights. "He wanted to know the personalities," Parker recalls. "I knew a lot more about our players than he did, so he sought me out."

The two of them also drew closer as friends. They traveled together, sometimes apart from the team. When the Reds traveled between New York and Philadelphia, Rose and Parker would forgo the team bus and hire a limousine to transport them.

Their families became friends, too. Parker and his wife, Kelly, visited at Pete and Carol Rose's home during the off-season. Their son, Dave junior (who was called "D2"), was about the same age as Tyler Rose. The families exchanged Christmas presents. Parker remembers a gift Carol bought for D2, "a bear telephone, and when it would ring, the mouth would move."

Parker had four big years in Cincinnati, averaging 28 home runs and 108 runs batted in. But his last year there, 1987, was a sour season for him and the Reds.

With Parker, a number of other young offensive stars, and the best bullpen in the league, the Reds had been heavily favored in 1987 to win the NL West. But after a fast start, they slumped through much of the summer and finished a disappointing second. What's worse, they gave the impression of being an uninterested, distracted ballclub. This didn't reflect well on Rose as a manager, and there was a lot of talk about how a club led by him could possibly look so listless. Couldn't he inject some of his vaunted hustle into his own ballclub? Why couldn't Pete Rose, of all people, motivate a young player?

The Reds' play didn't reflect well on Parker either, because he was perceived as the team leader. But he had some problems of his own that season. After three seasons of relatively good health, his knees had become cranky again, particularly the left one, which through the last half of the season was a grotesque sight, swollen to the size of a grapefruit. But he played anyway—153 games out of a possible 162.

Nevertheless, when September rolled around, Pete Rose began trying to shift some of the blame for the disappointing season onto Parker. He focused on one game that Parker had missed all the way back in July, the last game before the all-star break. According to Rose, Parker had told him that his back was stiff and he had to sit out, and then he went out and pitched batting practice.

"Can you tell me how a guy with a sore back can go pitch batting practice?" Rose griped. He didn't pose that rhetorical question once, but a dozen times. It became a sort of chant, which Rose raised again and again in sessions with reporters all through the last month of the season.

At baseball's annual winter meetings in December, Rose was *still* bad-mouthing Parker, who presumably was his friend.

Had the one game Parker missed cost the Reds the season? Hardly. Was Parker a player who habitually begged out of the lineup because of minor aches and pains, to the detriment of the team? That wasn't the case either. "He had the same attitude that Pete did toward injuries," says Larry Starr. "It was, 'I ain't gonna get hurt.' And if he did get hurt, he played through it. He had a very high threshold of pain."

If anything, it was a series of injuries to another player, star center fielder Eric Davis, that had doomed the Reds' season. Davis missed more than half the Reds' games in August and September. Parker believes that part of Rose's unhappiness with him was born of frustration that Parker couldn't convince Davis to go back into the lineup.

"That was Pete's thing, shifting responsibility onto other people," says Parker. "Eric was legitimately hurt. But I wanted him to play, too, if he could. I put a bug in his ear. Hey, I wanted him to go for forty-forty [forty home runs, forty steals, a feat that Davis barely missed being the first to accomplish].

"Pete thought he should play. I told him, 'If you don't think he has a legitimate injury, then go tell him. I can't baby-sit your players and play at the same time.' I told him that several times. But he never did [confront Davis], and then at the end of the year he's bitching about me, saying I engaged in 'negative leadership.' What the fuck *is* negative leadership, anyway?"

According to Paul Janszen, Rose's relationship with Parker was partly driven by his fear of him. "He was afraid of Dave Parker," Janszen says. "He was afraid of him physically, and he was afraid he could control his team." He says Rose complained incessantly about Parker's play. "He would come home after a game and say, 'How did Dave Parker *ever* hit .300? He's the worst goddamn hitter. You wanna strike him out? Bounce three balls two feet in front of the plate, and he'll swing at them all.' "

Parker was an easy target for Rose, especially in Cincinnati. He was a big black man who wore an earring, an admitted former cocaine user, and a player who had been perceived by fans in Pittsburgh, unfairly, as a bad influence on his teammates. And his on-field performance was declining.

Rose, who was so publicly proud of his lack of bigotry, took advantage of, among other things, Parker's blackness. He knew that in any public squabble between them, he was sure to come out the winner.

In Cincinnati, Parker had worked hard to rehabilitate himself from injuries. He stayed clean off the field, and helped his image by working in community antidrug efforts.

He believes Rose's bad-mouthing of him jeopardized everything, including his continued employment in baseball. "I have very little respect for the man," he says. "What he did was totally unnecessary. He could have screwed me out of getting another job in baseball. When I look back on it, maybe it was my fault for getting as close to him as I did. I'd never been that stupid before about judging someone's character."

Parker was traded to the Oakland A's after the 1987 season and was a key performer on the pennant-winning A's clubs of 1988 and 1989. He says now of Rose:

"He doesn't have friends. He has people who serve a purpose. And then when he's through with them, they're not friends anymore. Actually, they never were friends. They just didn't know it. Most of the people who have considered themselves friends of his sooner or later get stabbed in the back by him."

Marty Brennaman, the Reds' play-by-play voice since 1974, has spent hundreds of hours with Rose, around the ballpark and away from it, too. He says much the same thing as Parker.

"In my opinion, Pete has never been close to anybody," Brennaman says. "He does not have friends, in the way most people think of friends. He has business friends. And he has people who do things for him."

Rose, uninterested in having relationships with equals, made gofers, personal servants, even court jesters out of his day-to-day companions.

"If somebody made Pete laugh, he'd keep them around," explained Chuck Byersdorfer, a former Cincinnati cop who was part of Rose's entourage and did work for him around his house. "I was being [his] little errand boy, but that didn't bother me at that point in time."

Arnie Metz, a former groundskeeper at Riverfront Stadium who became a professional horse handicapper, placed Rose's bets at Cincinnati-area tracks. Rose, in his deposition to baseball's investigators in 1989, explained Metz's usefulness: "You know, if the wrong people do that, they'll go up and tell you they got shut out and your horse wins and they'll go around to the back and cash the ticket. What I'm saying is, he's honest. He's never made a mistake. He's never bet the wrong horse. If I say 2, he don't go bet 3."

Metz, fifteen years younger than Rose, idolized him. One year Rose took him to spring training and put him up at his house. Metz went to the Florida tracks with him there and took his bets to the window. Rose hated to go to the betting window himself because whenever he did he came under siege by autograph seekers.

Metz never forgot Rose's gesture of inviting him to spring training. "He did so many things for the little guy," Metz said. "I mean, like the Florida thing. I probably, if I didn't know Pete as well as I knew him, I probably wouldn't have been to Florida yet at this stage in my life."

In his testimony to John Dowd in 1989, Metz made a special point of saying that he was not Rose's gofer, or a "ten-percenter," the racetrack term for someone who signs for winning tickets for big bettors—to ease their tax burden—in return for ten percent of the winnings. "I run his bets," Metz said. "I don't like to be termed as a runner, I don't like to be termed as a gofer, and I especially despise the word ten-percenter. I am not a ten-percenter and I am not a gofer and I'm not a runner. I don't wash his cars, you know, things like that. I am a friend, but when we're at the racetrack I run his bets."

Others had no illusions about their place in Rose's life. They existed to serve him.

One of them was Mario Nunez, a Florida-born Cuban-American who was the maître d' in the clubhouse dining room at Tampa Bay Downs, and something of a ubiquitous figure in Tampa. He regularly shows up by the sides of political figures and other local notables, including New York Yankees principal owner and Tampa resident George Steinbrenner. "Mario is one of those people who knows everybody," explains Tom McKewn, the sports editor of *The Tampa Tribune*. "He gets close to important people. I don't know how. He just does."

Nunez got friendly with Rose one spring training, and Rose began taking him out on the road with the Reds. "The Cuban," as Rose called him, used to show up in visiting clubhouses with heaping platters of red beans and rice, which the whole team would devour. In 1985, he explained in a McKewn column how his friendship with Rose worked:

"All I can say is he's a helluva guy," Nunez said. "I think of him, and I am old enough to be his father, I think of him as my father, my brother, my son, my family. I am for him a good luck charm, I know that, maybe a bit of a mascot, for sure a friend. I am company and I don't ask nothing from him. He talks, I listen. I don't ask no questions.

"I don't question what he does. I go when he's ready. I go where he wants to go. I pick him up when he comes to Tampa. We go to the dog track together, bet together. Have fun. We're friends. I don't know why. And everyone in baseball knows we are friends. They all call me 'the Cuban.' I like that even though I never been to Cuba."

In 1980 Rose was invited to the White House to help promote a U.S. Savings Bond campaign. He was flown to Andrews Air Force Base in a government jet, then taken in a limousine to the White House. With him every step of the way was Nunez, whom Rose had invited as his guest.

When they were ushered into the Oval Office, Rose shook hands with President Carter, and then said, "I'd like you to meet my friend, Mario Nunez."

9

WHAT BASEBALL KNEW

I'm not a hypocrite. What I do, I do in the open.

—Pete Rose, 1980

PETE Rose's oldest friend was gambling. The friends and associates who moved in and out of his life, however briefly, were mainly people who shared his obsession or helped facilitate it.

Just as soon as he had money to spend, Rose began wagering it. Flush with his 1963 rookie-season salary of $7,500, he spent nearly every off-day at River Downs, the local thoroughbred track. Even before night games, he sometimes caught the first half of the race card before heading for the ballpark.

He learned where the tracks were around the National League. In St. Louis he became friendly with Max Yaffe, an inveterate horseplayer and handicapper and the uncle of his old minor-league teammate Art Shamsky. They gambled together at St. Louis–area tracks; in later years, if an off-day came before a trip in to play the Cardinals, Rose preceded the team there so he could hook up with Yaffe. "I credited my uncle Max with getting Pete involved in horses," says Shamsky, "although from what I know now, I guess Pete was already fond of betting before he got friendly with Max."

Rose's taste for the track, although perfectly legal and within baseball rules, worried his first Reds manager.

"Freddy Hutchinson told him not to go to the track anymore," says Jerry Scarlato, Rose's frequent companion during those early

years with the Reds. "He really got on him about it as I understand it, because he didn't think it looked good for Pete to be
there all the time. Pete did quit going for a while, but after Hutch
died he started going back."

Scarlato, Rose's high school classmate, taught business for a
couple of years at Western Hills High, then opened a downtown
bar and restaurant called Scarlato's, which became a popular
hangout for Cincinnati's pro athletes. He moved to Louisiana in
1977, where he is a purveyor of video bingo games, a legal industry there. "From 1958 to 1970, there was nobody closer to Pete
than me," he says. "Even then, he didn't like to go to the window.
I ran his [track] bets for him. We hung out together. We double-
dated. I still consider Pete a friend, we just don't see each other
very often."

Scarlato says he knew that Rose bet with bookmakers on horses
and pro sports from Rose himself, and also from his contacts in and
around Cincinnati. He also knew that Rose did not pay his debts.

"Pete's philosophy was that he gambled with his side money,
money he didn't need to pay his bills or that wasn't involved in
any of his investments," says Scarlato. "It was pocket money,
play money.

"Once he lost a certain amount, and it got beyond being side
money, say he got into a guy for forty thousand dollars, he would
only pay him half that. He would just not pay him the rest. And
he's been doing that since the early sixties. And most of them [the
bookmakers] knew it and still would take his bets. That's the cost
of doing business for them. They write it off. Pete's not the only
person not to pay his debts, and they might have still made good
money off him.

"Pete always felt, Well, I paid them enough and I'm not going
to pay them any more."

This would be Rose's method for the next two decades. He ran up
debts, didn't pay them, then moved on to another bookie, and
after that to another.

As early as 1970, not just Rose's gambling through bookmakers, which was a clear violation of baseball rules, but also his
gambling debts came to the attention of baseball authorities.
Nothing was done, which emboldened Rose and further con-

firmed for him how special, how *different* he was. Who else but
Charlie Hustle could flout the rules in such a way?

It wasn't that baseball couldn't touch Rose, but that it didn't
seem to want to.

After he completed his 1989 investigation, John Dowd would
think back on what he had learned of Rose, of his habits and his
history, and observe, "He was notoriously sloppy. My sense was
that his gambling was a problem that had been neglected. I don't
know how it could have been, but it was."

One answer to why it was neglected is that Rose himself was
owed debts of another sort.

For cooperating so freely and for flattering them, Rose was
owed by sportswriters, who repaid him with their gushing and
uncritical coverage.

For the glory that he reflected back on his hometown, he was
owed by the city of Cincinnati, which paid up in civic adulation,
most prominently symbolized by the renaming of the street in
front of Riverfront Stadium "Pete Rose Way."

And for selling the game better than anyone else, for "putting
asses in the seats," as he liked to say, Pete Rose was owed a large
debt by the game of baseball. The way baseball repaid it was by
letting him play while violating some of the game's most sacred
rules.

Putting asses in the seats counted for a lot.

Another friend from Rose's early years with the Reds, also a res-
taurateur, says that he tried without success to get the young
ballplayer to make good on his gambling debts. "I would say to
him, 'Pete, to stay in business a bookmaker needs two things: He
needs money, and he needs his honor. And you're robbing him of
both.' "

This former friend of Rose's, who spoke on condition that his
name not be used in this book, said that he met Rose at River
Downs in 1963. A gambler himself but not a bookmaker, he set
Rose up with bookies and introduced him to the gambling scene
in and around Cincinnati.

"Gambling was not frowned upon, really. This was part of our
culture here. We had small cities which adjoined Cincinnati, like
St. Bernard and Lockland, with absolute casinos in them into the
late forties—blackjack, poker, horse boards. There were unwrit-

ten rules on what you could and couldn't have. For some reason, there were no dice games on the Cincinnati side. Of course, we had Newport and Covington across the river, which was my old stomping grounds. That was one of the real gambling meccas of the world. We all got our jollies off over there.

"I was considerably older than Pete, but we became close. He was—what's the expression?—more fun than watching monkeys fuck. I saw him practically every day he was in the city. When you own a restaurant, you can run it as a social event. We had a big bunch of people who hung out here. They knew if they stayed around they would see Pete at some point during the day. He helped me. He was good for my business. He was no moocher.

"Pete and I gambled on anything that moved—if it had legs we bet on it. Horses, football, basketball, hockey. The one thing he did not bet on was baseball. He knew it was wrong and if he was caught he would be a goner.

"That World Series when they played the Oakland A's, I did ask him which way to go. And he said, 'There's no way those funny-looking guys with the mustaches are going to beat us.' So I took the Reds and I lost. And that's the only time I remember talking about a baseball bet with him. But what he did later I couldn't tell you. If he deteriorated that badly [and bet baseball], I don't know."

In the beginning, Rose's bookies came from two sources: from among his old West Side connections and from a group of Jewish friends downtown who introduced him to Jewish gambling figures in Newport and Covington. As a nonpayer, Rose always needed more than one outlet for his gambling.

The restaurant owner, who was one of Rose's Jewish friends, says their friendship ended after seven years. "I could not tolerate his dishonesty," he says. "And that's as much as I'm going to say on that subject. That facet of his life was too horrible.

"It was not just me, but a whole group of us who broke off from him around the same time. But he always had his retinue. When he closed the door on one friend, there were always twelve syco-phants standing in line wanting to be his friend. What are they called—jocksniffers?"

For many years, the bookmakers Rose bet with let him slide. His first bookies were older men, some of whom knew his father and had known the younger Pete Rose from when he was a little boy carrying the water bucket for his father's teams. They were proud of his success with the Reds, just like everybody else.

Aside from any personal considerations, there was another reason they excused his debts: Like most people who operate outside the law, bookmakers don't like the kind of attention that might be bad for business. To engage in too public a spat with Rose, or to threaten or harm him physically, was one sure way to attract unwanted attention, and with it the Cincinnati police.

Rose's nonpayment left the bookies no option: When his debt grew too large, they left him alone.

In time, after Rose ran through all the old-line bookmakers, he would begin to gamble with a rougher crowd. These were younger men with guns, drug connections, and no particular allegiance to Rose, his family, or his old neighborhood. Only then would he learn the most difficult lesson of his life—that not paying up carries its own price.

But that lesson was still years off.

Rose's affection for the fast life on the Kentucky side of the river was no secret. Even someone who didn't know Rose but was just a close reader of the newspaper could have suspected as much.

On July 9, 1965, at 4:25 A.M., police ticketed him for running a red light and driving without a license. The infraction occurred in Newport. He didn't show up for a hearing before a local judge later that day but sent a friend instead, according to an account of the incident in that day's *Cincinnati Post.* "A youth who appeared to be 20 pounds lighter and several years younger than the ballplayer showed Rose's driver's license to Judge Joseph Rolf," the paper reported. "The judge dismissed the license charge. . . . The youth identified himself to a newsman as a 'friend' of Rose's."

Rose was fined $10.00 and $3.50 court costs for running the light. That same night, he was honored at Crosley Field for being voted into the all-star game. The honor came with a gift, an RCA color TV supplied by a local retailer.

Word of Rose's debts began to filter back to the team in his rookie year, according to Jim O'Toole, his Reds teammate from 1963 to 1966: "I knew from back then that Pete always gambled and placed bets with bookies, and bookies wouldn't deal with him anymore because he wouldn't pay his debts. He thought because he was Pete Rose he didn't have to pay his bets off. We knew that then."

What Rose's teammates knew, major-league baseball also was soon to learn.

Before Rose was even halfway to Cobb's hit record, the office of baseball commissioner Bowie Kuhn had identified him as a problem gambler—and a probable violator of the game's rules against gambling "associations."

All through the 1970s, as he stroked 2,045 hits, won a batting title and his only MVP trophy—as he became the Player of the Decade and the game's biggest star—Pete Rose was the subject of an ongoing investigation by the commissioner's office.

The focus of that investigation: Rose's gambling. His associations. His debts to bookmakers.

The public never knew of this first probe while it was in progress. And when the Rose scandal broke in 1989, there was only a hint of how long baseball had been watching him. "We did run an investigation to see what his associations were, whether there was anything amiss beyond racetrack betting," Bowie Kuhn said in the spring of 1989. "But we found nothing."

It was not in Rose's nature to be careful, to cover his tracks. (The best way for a gambler to avoid being exposed is to pay his debts.) Nor was he a particularly good liar. You would not think such a high-profile player, and such a reckless man, could violate one of the game's most deeply held prohibitions—the one against associating with known gamblers—and yet manage to slip through the grasp of baseball security.

But he did. For ten years. For twenty years. For *twenty-six baseball seasons*, his entire career.

Is it any wonder that as John Dowd's investigators began to close in on him in 1989, Rose seemed surprised? Or that he seemed arrogant in his belief that baseball could not, or would not, move against him?

The story of that first investigation of Pete Rose, and why it never led anywhere, begins with Henry Fitzgibbon, a good and honorable man who loved the game of baseball. Had he loved it less, he might have done a better job investigating Rose.

Before the 1970 baseball season, then-commissioner Bowie Kuhn determined that the game needed to bolster its security efforts. Security had been handled out of baseball's legal office, but with evidence of increasing drug use among players, and the ever-present worries over gambling, Kuhn wanted a separate office and a seasoned law-enforcement professional to take charge of it.

To help him find his man, he turned to FBI director J. Edgar Hoover. The man Hoover recommended, and whom Kuhn ultimately picked, was Fitzgibbon, a G-man right out of Central Casting.

Fitzgibbon grew up on an Iowa cattle and corn farm along the Missouri River. In his youth he was a gifted student as well as a fine amateur-league baseball player. Tall and skinny, a fast runner with a good right-handed batting stroke, he was offered a Class D contract by the St. Louis Cardinals in 1938 for $30 a month and meal money. He turned it down, a decision that he would not regret but would often look back on.

"I don't know that I could have been a major leaguer," he says. "I very much doubt it. Back then they were offering minor-league contracts to nearly anyone. But if you're given the chance to play professionally and don't take them up on it, you're bound to wonder about how you would have done.

"But at the time, I had my heart set on joining the FBI. I went to Creighton University, and then enrolled in Creighton Law School for the sole purpose of joining the FBI. After my application was accepted, I later learned that they were recruiting me because I had established a reputation as a marksman with the Army Reserves. I had set some records with the Eighth Infantry Corps rifle team. And this naturally being a good thing for law enforcement, being able to handle firearms, the FBI was already looking at me."

Just two years after joining the bureau, Fitzgibbon was summoned from his position in the Philadelphia office to a post at FBI headquarters in Washington, a highly prestigious transfer for such a young agent, or so it seemed.

"I knew only the experienced men were sent to Washington," Fitzgibbon remembers. "So I rushed home and told my wife, 'I've been transferred to FBI headquarters. They're really taking notice of me right away.' I rushed down to Washington expecting to be greeted there, I guess, by Mr. Hoover, but I arrived and instead was greeted by one of his underlings. And I found out my assignment was very mundane. I was to sort through statistics on stolen automobiles.

"After this man told me what my duties were, he said to me, 'Mr. Hoover would like you to go out for the FBI baseball team.' Well, I didn't even know they had a baseball team. But I found out there was a D.C. government league, and the State Department and the Army and the Navy all had teams, and so did the FBI. And Mr. Hoover, being like he was, never wanted to lose at anything, so he had passed the word along, if we ever get any good baseball players, bring 'em back here so we can put them on the team.

"I played on the team for three or four years, and Mr. Hoover frequently attended those games, which is how he first came to know of me. My name became familiar to him from seeing it in the lineup."

Fitzgibbon progressed in the FBI. Liberated from sorting through car-theft statistics, he became part of a team that apprehended the bureau's most wanted and most dangerous criminals.

The team included a "stick man," a driver specially trained to maneuver a car through traffic at high speeds. Fitzgibbon, with his background as a marksman, was the "fast gun," the man who jumps out of the car with his gun drawn and yells: *FBI!*

"It was exciting work," says Fitzgibbon. "I enjoyed it. But after a while, the aging process sets in. You're not a fast gun anymore, so you have to move on to something else."

He moved on to a succession of investigative and administrative posts. In 1970, when Kuhn went to see Hoover, Fitzgibbon had just retired from the FBI; his last posting was as special agent in charge of the New York office.

"When Mr. Hoover recommended me to Bowie, I'm sure it's because he remembered me as a ballplayer," Fitzgibbon says. "He knew I liked baseball. That's the way his mind worked."

After landing the job as baseball's first director of security, Fitzgibbon and his late assistant, Arthur Fuss, split up the major-league cities, each taking charge of half of them. Fitzgibbon kept Cincinnati for himself, for two reasons: His wife was from a small town in northern Kentucky, about forty miles away, and he was also a Reds fan.

"We divided up the ballclubs," he says. "And then we had someone in each major-league city who we retained to do our routine investigative work. But I didn't have somebody in Cincinnati. I handled it all myself because of my interest in the Reds.

I liked to go out there myself when I could find an excuse. I picked the clubs I liked."

Fitzgibbon did establish contacts with local law-enforcement officials in Cincinnati and attempted to cultivate whatever other local sources he could, which was the procedure he and Fuss followed in all the big-league cities.

Fitzgibbon found allies everywhere. Managers and coaches tipped him off to potential problems. In some cities, members of the local business community volunteered to keep an eye out for ballplayers who appeared to be keeping bad company or getting involved in drugs. (In Cincinnati, a local car dealer was one of the people who volunteered to keep watch.) Fitzgibbon even found that many of the players were eager to help. He mentions Reggie Jackson as someone who was particularly helpful on two occasions in getting ballplayers under suspicion for drug use to come forward and seek help.

"One of the nice things I experienced was that some of the real top stars, the quality players, recognized that drug abuse, gambling, and hoodlum associations affect a player's skills and shorten his career. I got some real wonderful information from baseball players. Some leads I got came from teammates."

The idea of Fitzgibbon's network of contacts was to ensure that if a ballplayer stepped out of line, the information would be funneled to the security office and ultimately to Kuhn. "It's like setting traps, although if you use that word it makes it sound like we were trying to catch a bear," says Fitzgibbon. "What we were doing was trying to keep the game clean. Commissioner Kuhn was very strong in protecting the integrity of the game. He considered that his prime duty."

Right at the start of Fitzgibbon's tenure, Denny McLain, the Detroit Tigers pitcher, got caught up in one of the traps. Detroit law-enforcement officials tipped Fitzgibbon off that McLain might be involved in bookmaking activities, and Fitzgibbon's own investigation confirmed it. McLain was suspended for half of one season.

The next one to be caught up in baseball's investigative net was none other than Charlie Hustle, one of the stars of Fitzgibbon's favorite ballclub.

Fitzgibbon says that as early as 1970, and no later than 1971, his sources began to feed him information on Rose. "It was very early in my operation, right after the McLain case," he says. "When I got to Cincinnati the information was that he enjoyed his gambling a lot and he goes to the track all the time."

For the next decade, Fitzgibbon would suspect that Rose was betting large sums of money through bookmakers.

He would confront Rose, and when the ballplayer denied betting illegally or owing bookies, Fitzgibbon would suspect him of lying.

Until he retired in 1981, Fitzgibbon would maintain what he considered an open investigation of Rose.

Fitzgibbon was a big fan of Rose the ballplayer, but as he got to know him he drew some conclusions of a more personal nature. "I loved his style of play, his all-out style. But as a person, I thought he was devious, self-serving, and not too smart."

As it turned out, Rose was smart enough.

Fitzgibbon says the original tip on Rose came from someone in local law enforcement. "What I would do when I came into a city was talk to the city police and usually my old acquaintances in the FBI. I would tell them, 'Here's what I'm doing. Is there anyone in professional baseball you're investigating?' And someone told me to look into Rose."

Fitzgibbon's source also told him that Rose might owe money to bookies—a red flag because of the possibility that a bookmaker could use a debt as a wedge to induce a player to influence a game. But his initial investigation could not confirm that Rose owed bookies, or even that he used them.

"After I found that out [that Rose might owe bookies]," Fitzgibbon recalls, "I checked it out with Reds management, which at that time was Sparky Anderson, Dick Wagner, and Bob Howsam. Then we all sat down with Rose and outlined the dangers, and he was quite forthright and assured us he wasn't betting on baseball or betting illegally."

Fitzgibbon didn't stop there. He had found Rose to be "defensive. As an investigator, you take that as a sign that someone is covering things up."

Fitzgibbon went back to his Cincinnati law-enforcement sources. "I asked them, 'Who would be handling the bookie action for a guy like Rose?' I didn't have an allegation that any specific one was handling the action, but you know there's always certain bookies in every town who will handle big action.

"I did talk to some bookies in Cincinnati over a period of several years, I would say '71, '72, and '73. I got negative information"—denials that Rose was betting with them.

"But anything a bookie said I would take with a grain of salt. If a bookie said the sun was shining, then I would want to see some sunburn. That's why I kept the investigation open. If a person is as fond of gambling as Pete was, I knew it was only one more step to pick up the phone and call the bookie, and that's what I was afraid was happening. But I could never prove it."

Fitzgibbon says he no longer remembers the names of the bookies he interviewed. However, Al Esselman, who was convicted on federal charges of interstate gambling in 1963, says that he was interviewed by a "representative of the commissioner's office, an ex–FBI man," in the early 1970s.

Esselman, a West Sider who once owned a nightclub in Newport called the Turf Club, received a two-month prison sentence on the bookmaking rap, which at the time was referred to by his friends as a "vacation." He says he retired from bookmaking in 1975.

What Esselman says he told the ex–FBI agent jibes with what Fitzgibbon was getting from the Cincinnati bookies. "The commissioner sent a man in because of the bad paper Pete had around the city of Cincinnati," Esselman says. "He point-blank asked me if Pete owed me money. I said no, because I didn't want to get involved. Pete and I knew what was going on. Why did I need to tell this guy?"

Esselman still is not willing to tell all, at least not without being paid for it. When I reached him by telephone late in 1989, he said:

"You're talking to the right man. I could tell you stories about Pete Rose that would make your hair stand on end. Is there any money in this? I've been offered up to a hundred thousand dollars but I didn't want to do it. I would want at least twenty thousand dollars to tell all of what I know."

The offer was refused and Esselman was not paid anything. But he did provide some background on his history with Rose—and something less than a denial that he had booked the ballplayer's bets.

"Pete grew up in my neighborhood," he said. "He was a ball boy on some of the teams. I played catcher on Trolley Tavern, with Pete's dad. And I also played football with him on the Saylor Park

team. I was a tight end and played defense, too. We all played both
ways.

"His father and I were very good friends. We [Esselman and the
younger Pete Rose] were friends first. I knew him way back when
he was sitting out his senior year at Western Hills High School.
Then one thing led to another. You know how that is. But as far
as his gambling with me, I won't admit to anything."

For Henry Fitzgibbon, being in charge of baseball's security office
was a lot different from working for the FBI. It was still, in a
sense, law enforcement, but he no longer jumped out of cars with
his gun drawn, and his first mission was not to apprehend and
arrest. Now he had a whole different set of considerations.

"We tried, if possible, to avoid giving the game a black eye," he
says. "We would try to keep the players from getting in trouble.
We much preferred that. But on the other hand, if we found that
someone had broken the rules, we went after them and they were
subject to baseball's disciplinary process."

Having failed to pry loose any information about Rose in his
interviews with Esselman and other bookies, Fitzgibbon took a
different approach. He didn't press the investigation. Instead, the
ex–FBI fast gun attempted to become Pete Rose's confidant. If
Rose had anything to confess, Fitzgibbon wanted to be in a position to hear it.

"I didn't continue to get tips on Rose after the first couple of
years," he explains. "But I continued to talk with him. My idea
was to counsel him and keep him clean, and he took this in the
spirit of cooperation.

"We did this at least on an annual basis. I would talk privately
with him. We became friends over this period of time. We would
talk baseball. We would have lunch or dinner. I was 'Fitz' and he
was 'Pete.' We had that kind of association.

"I might say, 'Let's have lunch' or something. We would sit
down somewhere in the ballpark, in the office area, or arrange to
go to a restaurant. Mostly it was in baseball settings. I was at his
house twice, as I recall. It wasn't like we were going out on the
town. I wasn't that kind of friend.

"If it was to save his time and mine, we ate lunch. Don't build
into this that we were asshole buddies, because we weren't. I
didn't need him as an enemy not to trust me. I needed to have

him as someone who would come to me if he had problems, and
I would help him if I could. In a professional way, not as a personal friend. I was representing baseball, not Pete Rose."

Fitzgibbon says that if he had been able to prove Rose's contacts
with bookies, it would have been a basis for disciplinary action.
"He knew that. I held that up over his head, but in a friendly way.
I didn't say, 'Look, you son of a bitch.' I would say, 'Pete, you
can't get involved in this sort of thing.' I tried to counsel him, to
avoid him getting into trouble."

Rose, of course, was lying to Fitzgibbon.

His gambling through bookies and his debts to them were more
than enough to earn him at least a year's suspension. Others,
including Leo Durocher in 1947, had been disciplined for far less.
While baseball's director of security was telling himself that he
was engaged in keeping Rose out of trouble, Rose was already
deep in it. Knee-deep, waist-deep, had anyone cared to look more
closely.

"In the beginning, I think he was still aware that it [his gam-
bling] was something he shouldn't be so out front with," says
Scarlato. "Then the more he did it, the less and less he cared
about people knowing it."

Fitzgibbon says he kept the Reds front office informed of his investigation of Rose. But he was not telling them anything they
didn't already know. It's probable that the Reds knew more about
Rose's activities than Fitzgibbon, and did not share their knowledge.

Rose was hugely popular in Cincinnati and becoming more so
with each passing year. Why dime him out to baseball security
when he was putting paying customers in the seats? The Reds
kept their own watch on Rose, and held close what they knew.

Dick Wagner, the Reds general manager during the seventies,
had his own network of informants, made up of law-enforcement
people and others who traveled on Cincinnati's seamier side. He
knew of Rose's debts to bookies. According to a *Cincinnati Post*
story from the spring of 1989, Wagner commented to other Reds
executives in a meeting in 1978, "Pete's legs may get broken
when his playing days are over."

Wagner, who was working in the commissioner's office during
the Rose probe of 1989, would not be quoted for this book. As for
the comment attributed to him by the *Post*, he said, "I'm not

going to comment on that either way. I won't confirm it and I won't deny it."

At least early on, Rose's nonbaseball friends were not really the leg-breaking types. They might not have been the people whom the commissioner's office would choose as companions for the players, but most of them were nice folks—colorful and funny, the sort who put friendship and fun on an equal footing with work and career. If one could generalize about such a thing, they were probably much better company than the Cincinnatians who advocate sending police in to screen art exhibits and plays for possible obscenity.

None of these people were as hard-charging as Rose. They liked to drink, hang out, play the ponies, play pinball. Some of them, like Danny Gumz (pronounced "Gumps"), could tell quite an amusing story.

In the late 1960s and through the 1970s, Rose frequently ate lunch and played cards at Gumz's restaurant, the Gay 90s Cafe, which he owned along with his brothers, Bobby and Billy. Their father had run the Gumz Cafe in Riverside, which was just down the street from where Pete Rose grew up.

In 1962 the Gumz brothers sold their father's taproom along the river on the city's West Side and opened up the Gay 90s in the town of Cheviot, a hardscrabble place just outside the city limits that is really an extension of Cincinnati's West Side.

The Gay 90s features a very good hot roast beef sandwich, a convivial family atmosphere—Pete and Karolyn Rose sometimes brought their kids for dinner—comfortable vinyl-upholstered booths, and a lively card game nearly every afternoon. Rose for many years was a regular there; people driving by could tell when he was inside because they'd notice whatever luxury car he happened to be driving parked in the lot. "You couldn't help but notice it, because nobody else around here can afford cars like that," says David Voss, the Cheviot police chief.

Late one afternoon in the fall of 1989, Danny Gumz talked about his friend Pete Rose, about life in Cheviot, and about playing cards for the pure sport of it and not for money.

"Yeah, Pete would play up here," said the affable Gumz as he sat at his bar, sipping Miller from a can. "Hearts. That was his

game. There was no money involved. He loved to sit down and
play it. He would come in and sit there and play, and he loved to
play gin rummy, too. Gin rummy games.

"He'd play with my brother Bob, and Sudsy, he's an old guy,
seventy-eight years old. He's in the hospital now. Just whoever
was around Pete would play with. Just play cards and have a good
ol' rap session. He did it quite often. It was relaxing for him.
Hearts and gin rummy, that was all he ever played. Once in a
while he might play some pinochle. But not too often."

Rose could really enjoy a card game without any money changing hands? "Yeah," Gumz insisted. "There was no money involved. He'd sit in just to enjoy a day."

As for the regulars, the ones who play nearly every day, Gumz
says they never gamble either. If they get bored, they leave the
Gay 90s and walk down the street to another bar, where the
games do involve money. "They'll play cards all day in here and
there's never a dime involved, never a penny involved. It's like
amateur league here."

Gumz provides some background on Cheviot. He says the
town, as befitting the mores of its residents, has long been a
gambling haven, although, miraculously, he and his brothers have
somehow managed to keep illegal wagering from invading the
walls of their establishment.

"In the sixties, you could bet in any damn tavern in this town,"
he says. "You could find somebody to run the bet up the street,
down the street, across the street. In Cheviot today, there's one,
let's see, there's one, two, three, four places at least you could lay
down a bet. We didn't get involved. If somebody here wanted to
get involved, they would, like I say, walk out and run the bet up
the street or down the street."

Harold Mills, the commander of the Cincinnati police vice squad
from 1975 to 1986, says that on three separate occasions in the
1970s and early 1980s his investigators got tips that Rose was
betting large sums through bookmakers.

In each case, the information, which came from disgruntled
bettors trying to get back at their bookies, produced enough evidence to convict the bookies. "In gambling, when a man loses his
shirt and the bookie throws him out on his ass and won't take any

more bets, he comes to us," Mills explains. "Let's face it, that's how we bust bookies."

But the betting sheets confiscated by Mills's men contained only code names for bettors, and there was no link on paper to Rose. Even if there had been, Mills says, his squad had little interest in moving on individual bettors, so they went after the bookies and did nothing with the Rose information.

The situation was similar to the Cincinnati-area amphetamine investigation in which Rose's name surfaced: Law-enforcement authorities were primarily interested in someone else (the doctors) and did not go after Rose.

Mills says that in the gambling investigations, the courts were not even much interested in the bookmakers; of the dozens of bookies his squad arrested, "we never had one go to jail. It was just costs and probation."

Mills says that he never talked to baseball security during the time his squad was receiving information on Rose. "I talked to a man that Dowd sent around, but that was this year [1989]," he said. "That's the first time I ever met with anyone from baseball."

Henry Fitzgibbon's boss was Bowie Kuhn, the genteel Princeton graduate and corporate attorney who was baseball's fifth commissioner

On February 4, 1969, the day Kuhn took office, the baseball commissioner's job was still defined, to a remarkable degree, by the man who had first held it, Judge Kenesaw Mountain Landis.

Landis's legacy to succeeding commissioners was the nearly dictatorial powers of the job. Landis had carved those powers out, and over the years the courts had upheld them. His successors were free to rule "in the best interests of the game," to dispense discipline or mercy as they saw fit.

Hired in the wake of the Black Sox scandal, Landis dealt lifetime bans to eight of the White Sox players accused of fixing the 1919 World Series, even though they were acquitted in criminal trials, which were themselves questionable. He banned four more players over the next four years for baseball-related gambling. He even bounced New York Giants outfielder Benny Kauff in 1921 after his arrest on car-theft charges. "An indictment charging felonious misconduct by a player certainly charges conduct detrimental to the good repute of baseball," Landis said after banning Kauff.

Seven years later, Landis exonerated Cobb and Speaker, despite the strong evidence they had conspired to fix a game. That was typical of Landis's broad powers, and the potential power of all baseball commissioners. He could be merciful as well a stern, depending on what best suited his or the game's needs at the time.

The last recipient of Landis's discipline was Philadelphia Phillies president William D. Cox, who on November 23, 1943, was banned for life for making "approximately 15 or 20 bets" of "from $25 to $100 per game on Philadelphia to win." Cox was forced to sell his share of the team.

Kuhn, who followed Happy Chandler, Ford Frick, and William D. Eckert (a politician, a sportswriter, and a general) in Landis's job, had a curious reign.

On the one hand, he could come across as weak, a hired hand who buckled under to owners and refused to use his authority as commissioner of all baseball to take an assertive role in labor negotiations. One year, Kuhn also looked like a stooge of the television networks as he allowed a 1977 National League playoff game in Philadelphia to proceed through a cold, driving rain, then sat in the stands and watched it without an overcoat, as if to make the point that the weather was really fine.

But what the public may best remember Kuhn for was an act that seemed forceful: his banning of Willie Mays and Mickey Mantle from all official baseball duties, which prevented them even from working as spring training instructors. The reason was that Mays and Mantle had taken jobs in public relations with Atlantic City casinos—jobs that amounted to playing golf with high rollers.

Kuhn's action, although it was widely unpopular with fans and ultimately overturned by his successor, Peter Ueberroth, did establish him as a hard-liner on gambling—a reputation he may not have deserved.

Fitzgibbon says that he routinely submitted reports to Kuhn at the conclusion of his trips. Each of the many times he talked with Rose, he would have included it on the report.

"Oh, I mentioned to Bowie what I was doing with regard to Pete

Rose," says Fitzgibbon. "I'm confident we did have a conversation about it, probably more than one. But I never had the facts I thought could sustain a violation of baseball rules.

"We had a process in baseball which was similar to a criminal investigation. You have a complaint, you have an investigation, and you have a closing of the case—or you have an inconclusion and you just keep following it. In this case, I had an inconclusion. We didn't have the kind of information we had on McLain or we would have gone that way. We didn't have enough to indict, let alone to have a trial."

Fitzgibbon says that Kuhn never asked him to change his tactics with Rose, to use more aggressive investigative techniques. "Bowie let us do our work in whatever way we thought was best. It wasn't his way to interfere."

Like nearly everyone else at baseball's executive level, Kuhn considered Rose to be one of the game's great assets. "I'd like to have six hundred Pete Roses playing baseball," he commented in 1978 during Rose's 44-game hit streak.

(Kuhn was not available to be interviewed for this book. During the time it was being researched, the New York law firm of which Kuhn was a partner went bankrupt, and some of his former partners charged that he had gone into hiding to avoid being served with legal papers relating to the firm's demise and the debts he might personally be liable for.)

In the absence of any directives from Kuhn, or any new ideas of his own, Fitzgibbon continued on the same course. Even though he had found Rose to be deceptive and suspected he was lying—and as a matter of course he just assumed the bookies had lied to him—the ex–FBI man did not press the investigation. He did not, as was done a decade later, seek to examine Rose's telephone or financial records.

Baseball's top cop shut down his old FBI instincts and went easy on Rose. He accepted Rose's lies, and stopped pursuing new leads. Instead of investigating the ballplayer, he tried to help him. In effect, what Fitzgibbon did was counsel Rose for compulsive gambling—years before Rose acknowledged having that problem.

"I checked in with Pete on at least an annual basis," Fitzgibbon says. "I thought he was a compulsive gambler and I told him so. I told him it was going to get him in trouble and he ought to try to conquer it, or it would be his undoing. He didn't believe it. He said, 'No, I just enjoy going to the races.' "

＊   ＊   ＊

Baseball's 1989 probe of Rose did not delve into his gambling before 1984. In the course of that probe, however, Rose did let slip how long he had been a heavy sports gambler. In the deposition he gave to baseball's investigators on April 20, 1989, in Dayton, Ohio, Rose was asked by John Dowd, "Were you betting on sports in 1986?"

"Probably," Rose replied.

"And if you were betting on sports . . . ?"

"If I was betting, I bet with Tommy [Gioiosa]."

"Okay, were you betting on sports in 1985?"

"Probably. I was probably betting on sports in '75. . . . No more, no less in '85 than in '75."

This, of course, was precisely what Rose had denied to Fitzgibbon all those years—during those long talks at restaurants, at the ballpark, at his home.

How did Rose neutralize the veteran FBI man? Did he charm him? Co-opt him? Con him?

"I didn't get that impression [that I was conned]," Fitzgibbon says. "But one of the things you learn is you don't believe anybody. You hate to admit that you didn't go far enough, but in the light of Monday-morning quarterbacking, I have to admit now I should have gone farther."

A decade before his 1989 downfall, baseball had what amounted to a second chance on Rose.

It was an opportunity to rein him in before he shamed himself, before a lifetime ban was mandated, before—as likely happened—he got too deep into debt and began to gamble on what he knew best, baseball.

The opportunity was lost, for the usual reasons: Someone in a position of power liked Pete Rose too much—and, in this case, was making too much money off him.

William Yale Giles comes from what is commonly called a "baseball family." His late father was president of the Cincinnati Reds from 1937 to 1951, and then president of the National League from 1951 until 1969.

He was just about raised in old Crosley Field, and as an adult the only career he's ever had is working for ballclubs. Giles is currently president of the Philadelphia Phillies, and as a member of several key owners' committees, including the broadcasting committee, he is one of the most powerful men in the game.

Jowly and red-faced, he shows the signs of some hard living. For a time, Phillies trades were made by a committee of club executives dubbed the Gang of Five, and it was written that Jack Daniels was the sixth man in on all deals.

Giles presided over the Phillies as they fell from perennial contender to last-place club, so he is not popular with fans. But among people who know him, it's hard to find anyone who doesn't like him. He is an open, gregarious, emotional man who feels genuine sadness when he must trade or release a player he's been close to. Letting Pete Rose go after the 1983 season was one of the toughest things he's ever done. He removed himself several years ago from player personnel decisions, and one of the reasons, he said, was that he tended to let his feelings get in the way of his better judgment.

There is one other element of Giles's baseball résumé that few people know: He had his own brush with the commissioner's office over illegal gambling. It occurred in the late sixties, while he was working in promotion for the Houston Astros and his father was still National League president.

"When I was a young man in Houston, making very little money, I used to bet a couple hundred bucks a week through bookies. Not directly, but through somebody I knew who booked them through a bookie.

"I was called on the carpet for this. Commissioner Kuhn called me personally and said, 'Your name shows up on the bookie sheets in Houston, betting on football, and you better not do it anymore.' So I stopped."

(It is significant that the stern warning Kuhn issued to Giles was not a step he ever took with Rose, at least as far as Fitzgibbon knows. During the whole decade-long "open" investigation, Fitzgibbon says he is not aware of Kuhn once calling in Rose to talk to him about the allegations. Would it have made a difference? Probably not. But still, it is another sign of what was a shockingly lackadaisical approach to the Rose problem.)

It was Giles who brought Rose to Philadelphia. The deal was not driven by emotion, but by cold-blooded finance: The numbers worked.

Rose, after the 1978 season, put himself on the free-agent market and, along with his lawyer Reuven Katz, set off by private jet on a week-long tour of the seven places he was considering playing. This bizarre traveling auction of Rose's services stopped last in Wilmington, Delaware, at the estate of Ruly Carpenter, who then owned the Phillies.

"We sat down with Pete and Reuven and they had a videotape of how great Pete was. Not only as a player, but as an off-the-field guy, as far as public relations and everything," remembers Giles, who was then the team's executive vice-president. "It was all very impressive.

"Finally, Ruly says, 'What kind of money are we talking about?'

"And Reuven Katz says, 'Well, you're going to have to start with seven figures a year, because that's what we're talking about.'

"And Ruly, who's a Yale graduate, starts counting on his fingers, and then he says, 'My God, that's a million dollars a year, right? Let's just have lunch and forget about it.' And then we called a press conference later that day to announce that we were not going to be signing Pete Rose."

Giles, however, did not give up. He asked Katz to delay having Rose sign anywhere else, and the next day Giles approached the television station that broadcast the Phillies games to see how much more they would pay for the rights if Rose was signed. "I met with them, and I said, 'Now, if we sign Pete Rose, the ratings are going to go up, you can charge more for your advertising, so why don't you pay us an extra six hundred thousand dollars a year?' And they agreed to do it."

Within a week, armed with the additional money from the television station, the Phillies signed Rose. It paid off before he ever played a game for them.

"His signing was the most exciting and dramatically effective thing that we've ever done here, certainly in the twenty years since I've been here," Giles says. "Within two months after we announced that we signed him, we sold two point five million dollars more in season tickets than we'd ever sold before. So in two months we made back almost three times the money that we'd signed him for.

"What Pete said at the time, and I agreed with him, was that there were really only two people in the game who put extra people in the stands—himself and Dave Parker. This was in the late seventies, and in my judgment Pete put a lot more people in the seats than Parker."

Giles was acquainted with Rose before he signed in Philadelphia, although he really may have known Karolyn Rose better. In her role as Earth Mother to the baseball world, Karolyn visited Giles's father daily as he lay dying in a Cincinnati hospital.

But Giles did know Pete Rose well enough, and he retained good enough contacts in Cincinnati, to know that the Reds had nonbaseball reasons for wanting to rid themselves of their hometown star. "I knew the Reds people well, and I knew the reason. It was because of the personal things. It was unbelievable to me that they didn't want to sign him. And I don't know whether it was the women-chasing or the gambling. I never did know."

Not long after Rose arrived in Philadelphia, Giles learned firsthand of Rose's football and basketball betting. "I knew he was using bookies," Giles says. "I mean, not directly, but through friends. I knew of friends of his that I had met who were not bookies, who would call the bookies for him. At least, I suspected that at the time. Because he would talk to people and say, 'Go out and bet five hundred dollars on the Eagles today,' or something like that.

"I didn't think it was that big a deal, to be honest about it. If I had an inkling that he was betting on baseball, that would have concerned me more. But betting on other things, my personal opinion is a little more liberal than if I'd been the commissioner. When you're commissioner, you have to do things a little bit differently than when you're a marketing guy for a club, which I was at the time."

A limited partnership, with Giles as the managing partner, bought the Phillies from Carpenter on October 29, 1981. He was an owner of the club and its president during Rose's last two years with the Phillies. During that time, Giles says, there was another player on the team, whom he refuses to name, who he also believed was betting through bookmakers. The player was suspected of placing calls from a pay phone near the clubhouse—which was then removed—and also occasionally from phones in Phillies' offices.

"We had another player that we suspected was using it [the clubhouse pay phone] a lot. He used to also come in the office and use the phones. I thought he was using bookies too, and I reported it to the commissioner's office, but he was never called on the carpet, to my knowledge."

If Giles reported another player for dealing with bookies, why did he not report Rose?

"Oh, looking back on it," he says, "it was probably that I loved and respected him so much. I didn't really think it was my place to do it. Baseball has a very large security operation.

"And, you know, he was our bread and butter."

10

THE FRIENDS OF PETE ROSE

I try to create a relaxed atmosphere in the clubhouse
so everybody can have fun.

—Pete Rose, 1985

WITH his gambling unchecked by major-league baseball or anyone else, Pete Rose by the early 1980s was becoming simulta-
neously more famous and more desperate.

On the trail of the all-time hit record, he let the press into his
surburban Cincinnati home, where he was photographed with his
wife, Carol, and their young son, Tyler, who was named in honor
of the object of his chase, Tyrus Raymond Cobb.

He showed off his trophies and plaques, which had become so
numerous that they spilled out of the den and into every part of
the house. He led his visitors around his five acres and out back
to the stables, where they watched him feed his horses.

It was a life to be envied. Pete Rose, at forty-four, surrounded by
plenty and still playing the game he loved.

The sports pages, filled as they are with feature stories about a
ballplayer's childhood, his relationships, and other aspects of his
personal life, convey a false sense of intimacy. The reader may
feel that he truly comes to know the subject of the story, but that
is rarely the case. It wasn't with Rose. The hundreds and hundreds of stories bolstered the myth; few shed any light on the
man.

Rose led what amounted to a double life. With all that was
written about him, it never came through. If it had, the baseball
fans of America would have felt very differently about him.

Many would still have liked him. Some would have pitied him and hoped that he would seek help. But few would have held him up as an ideal, the best of baseball or America.

Beyond the sweet domestic portrait, Rose spent his days with a creepy entourage of bodybuilders, baseball memorabilia hustlers, and drug dealers. In the very week he broke Cobb's record, he was visited in his office at Riverfront Stadium by a cocaine dealer who lent him $17,000 in cash.

Rose's life by this time was ruled by his obsession to gamble, which crowded out everything else, including baseball. He needed ever-increasing amounts of cash to feed his habit, and the friends he chose were men he thought could help him get it.

By the mid-1980s, Pete Rose was a lonely, pathetic man. He had a wife, three children by his two marriages, baseball records that were beyond comprehension, money, and the admiration of millions. But he was isolated enough to make best friends of people he had just met. All his better friends he had driven away, or they had walked away.

The new crowd around Pete Rose was more dangerous, and less forgiving of him.

Rose first met Paul Janszen in October of 1986 when a common friend, Tommy Gioiosa, brought him to Rose's house to watch a National League playoff game on television.

Since 1978, Gioiosa had served numerous roles for Rose—housemate, car-washer, beard, bet-placer. He also saw himself as Rose's baseball protégé. When he played for the University of Cincinnati baseball team in the late seventies, Gioiosa styled himself after Rose, right down to sliding headfirst, wearing number 14, and running to first base on a walk.

But Rose's introduction to Janszen coincided with his growing distaste for Gioiosa, who of late had become even more loud-mouthed and ill-tempered than usual. Gioiosa recently had caused a ruckus in a private room that was reserved for Rose and his friends at Turfway racetrack in Kentucky. Rose wasn't there that night, and until he got things straightened out with the track owner the room was closed off.

Within a month after they met, Janszen took Gioiosa's place in Rose's life. Rose began inviting him to his house without Gioiosa. He also took him around the country to baseball card shows, where Rose was paid thousands of dollars to sign autographs. One of Janszen's tasks was to count the money, which Rose normally accepted in cash from the promoters and stuffed in a brown lunch bag.

Less than four months after first visiting Rose at his home, Janszen and his girlfriend, Danita Jo Marcum, were invited to Florida to spend part of spring training with Pete and Carol Rose.

Janszen remembers the day they arrived at the Roses' rented home. "We go down to Tampa, we pull up in the taxi, to stay with him for two weeks," he said in an interview with the author in the fall of 1989. "It turned into six weeks. As soon as the cab pulled up, he comes running out, grabs me by the arm, and says, 'Paulie, look at this place.' He shows me around the game room and the swimming pool, which had these sliding boards that came twisting down like a spiral staircase. He says, 'Look at the sliding boards!' That was the part of Pete Rose that people don't get to see. That was the part I liked."

Janszen was 6'3", and by the spring of 1987, through a combination of weight lifting and steroid use, he had built himself up to nearly 300 pounds. But he didn't project a sense of great power. He came across as oafish, perhaps because he looked so unnaturally big. (Gioiosa had also bulked up with steroids, and at 5'5", he looked even stranger than Janszen, as if someone had inflated him with a bicycle pump.)

Even before he introduced him to Rose, Gioiosa told Janszen, "Pete'll want to hang around with you because he'll be impressed with the fact that you're big."

And he was.

Rose, who for most of his career had eschewed rigorous training, liked big muscles in the same way he liked fast cars and young women—they impressed him, and he figured they impressed other people, too. Sometimes, after he introduced Janszen, he would add, "He's big, ain't he?" It was as if he'd just kicked his tires.

Janszen grew up on the West Side of Cincinnati, played some football at the local Catholic high school, attended a couple of years of college, and then went to work as a salesman for the same steel barrel company that employed his father. He was sixteen years younger than Rose and had grown up watching him play on television. He certainly had never expected to become his friend, and now, not that long after meeting him, he found that he was his virtual shadow.

In Tampa, they drove together from Rose's house to Redsland, the club's training complex. Every morning they would stop for breakfast at the same pancake house, where they were sometimes joined by Bill Bergesch, the Red's general manager. Rose and Bergesch talked about what players they might trade, who would make the team, and who would be sent to the minors, all of this right in front of Janszen, who ate his breakfast and listened.

Bergesch, who is no longer with the Reds, confirms this. "As far as I was concerned, he was a friend of Pete's," he says. "We'd talk about whatever we had to talk about, and he would be there. He didn't say anything. I had no reason to think anything bad of him."

At the ballpark Janszen got to meet all the Reds players, and some of them, like Rose, were impressed by him. A few of the younger ones even sought him out for weight-lifting tips.

At night, he and Rose went to the dog track, although Janszen did not have to run his bets to the window. That was Mario Nunez's job in Tampa.

When the Reds returned to Cincinnati at the end of spring training, not only were Janszen and Rose closer than ever, but Carol Rose and Danita Marcum had also cemented their friendship.

After Reds games at Riverfront Stadium, the four of them usually met back at the Rose home. For the next several hours, until well past midnight, Rose and Janszen stayed planted in front of the large-screen television set in the Rose living room, which was surrounded by a couple of smaller sets. They watched whatever sporting events came in over Rose's satellite dish.

Rose's dish picked up just about any game that was being televised anywhere in the U.S. or Canada. When he came to the ballpark one of the things he liked to talk about was what he had watched via the dish the previous night. On the rare occasions someone asked him about a game he hadn't been able to tune in, he would say, "It wasn't up there," as if the heavens were full of free-floating ball games.

When John Dowd took his deposition in 1989, Rose joked about the dish. "I get everything," he told Dowd. "I get you walking through the airport when the monitor hits you . . . Don't carry no bombs aboard."

Janszen recalls that during those late nights at Rose's house, he sometimes marveled at where he was. "Pete had this couch, a

U-shape, kind of, and we'd just be sitting there together watching the games," he says. "It would be two, three in the morning, and sometimes we'd both fall asleep. I would wake up and look over, and he would be sleeping, and I'd think, You know, everybody in the country would want to be me. Here I am, and he's just my buddy—Pete Rose.

"And then he'd wake up and we'd whack each other with pillows or something. You know, just throw pillows at each other— stupid things that guys do."

While this was going on, Carol Rose and Danita Marcum were usually upstairs in the master bedroom. Sometimes they watched a movie on TV; more often, they spread Carol's new clothes on the bed and pawed through them.

"We looked at all the clothes she picked out on her shopping sprees," Marcum says. "I would say, 'This is nice. This is nice. Oh, this is really nice.' After a while it got boring, but I didn't want to go downstairs with them and watch the games."

Sometimes the women fell asleep upstairs while the men were sleeping downstairs. Eventually someone would wake up and they would get it all sorted out.

(In one of the few references to her in Kahn's authorized biography, Pete Rose says of his present wife, "You know Carol. You know how beautiful she is. Well, there's one other thing Carol is world-class in. That's shopping. I get some pleasure setting her loose in a mall.")

Janszen and Marcum all but moved into the Rose home. He drove Rose's cars. He put together a play set in the backyard for their son, Tyler. He bought fishing gear so Rose could fish the stream on his own property. She ran errands for Carol and babysat for Tyler.

On July 4, 1987, Janszen set off a fireworks display in the backyard of the Rose's home. Janszen has a home movie of this event, in which the Pete Rose captured on videotape could be the young Pete, transported back to Anderson Ferry and the banks of the Ohio River.

"Hey, Paulie, you're crazy," a delighted Rose chortles as another round of fireworks explodes.

"Now watch this, Smudgie," Rose instructs Tyler, calling his four-year-old son by the nickname he gave him. (Rose gave everyone nicknames. He called his first son, Pete junior, "Googly.") "See that, Smudge? See that?"

"Hey, we coulda sold seats! We're probably the only ones in the state that waited till twelve o'clock to do this."

"Hey, Paulie," he teases Janszen, "here comes the cops! Paulie, here comes the cops!"

Janszen says he and Marcum ultimately grew weary of spending so much time with the Roses. "The funny thing that happened," he says, "is that Pete started to need me around. I mean, he would get upset if I didn't go to his house at night after the Reds games. He would never say to me, 'Hey, Paul, are you coming over tonight?' That wasn't in him.

"But he would have Carol say something to Danita. Like, "Is Paul upset with Pete? Why doesn't he want to come over" And she would say something like, 'Carol, we've been over the last twenty-two nights straight. We would like to have a break.'

"And then later I'd see Pete at the stadium, and he would say to me, 'Hey, Paulie, I'll buy dinner tonight.' Because we used to stop by the Montgomery Inn or somewhere and bring ribs or something back. And I used to buy like eighty percent of the time. And that was his way of saying he wanted us to come over.

"He was lonely, that's what he was. You know, if somebody said to you, 'Pete Rose is lonely,' you would say, 'Hey, wait a minute, no he's not.' Because all you see is this tough side of him. But he is."

It was true that Rose hated to be alone. He often talked about the "working Joe in the stands," but one of Janszen's attractions was that he didn't have a job. (He did, however, have plenty of money, which Rose says never aroused his suspicion.)

One thing Rose had always looked for in a friend was someone whom he could pal around with during the day and late at night, when most working Joes are either working or sleeping.

Metz, the professional horseplayer, was available to Rose any time he wanted him, and so was Nunez, whose employment at Tampa Bay Downs was flexible enough that he could join Rose out on the road. The restaurant owners Rose had been friendly with years back were also good daytime playmates, always candidates to slip off to the track with him in the afternoon.

But Janszen, Gioiosa, and some of the other young men whom Rose had befriended at Gold's Gym, a suburban Cincinnati body-building center, had something else to offer him besides companionship, the thing that he desperately needed—ready access to large sums of cash.

What Henry Fitzgibbon had concluded years back, that Rose was a compulsive gambler, was now glaringly obvious to anyone who spent much time with him away from the ballpark.

By the time he passed Cobb's record in 1985, Rose had debts to bookmakers that he could not possibly cover out of his allowance from his lawyer Reuven Katz. In the four-year period between 1984 and 1987, Rose's income was nearly $5 million, of which a little more than $2 million went to taxes. But in the same period, he lost hundreds of thousands of dollars to bookies, possibly $1 million or more.

He dealt with bookmakers in at least five states, as well as one in Canada. And these bookies were not the friendly uncles who worked out of the taverns and candy stores on the West Side, or the Cincinnati fire fighter who once booked his bets, or the older gent who worked out of the Western Hills Country Club, who was yet another of Rose's bookies. At least some of his 1980s bookmakers had mob connections. Even Pete Rose knew he'd better pay them at least some of their money.

Of course, being Pete Rose, he didn't pay them *all* of it. He has said that his losses never threatened his daily living expenses or his investments. However, if he had paid the bookies all of what he owed them, his gambling might very well have cut into his nest egg.

All the elements were certainly in place for Rose to have a gambling problem. To begin with, his father liked to gamble, which experts on compulsive gambling say is just about a prerequisite.

"It's much like alcoholism," says Dr. Gary Glass, the director of InterPsych Associates in surburban Philadelphia, which treats compulsive gamblers, and an associate professor of psychiatry at Temple University Medical School. "If you grow up in a house where there is no liquor, it's possible you'll become an alcoholic, but it's much less likely. It's the same thing with gambling. We find that compulsive gamblers, in nearly all cases, have fathers who liked to gamble. The gambling may have been casual, perhaps just a friendly poker game on Friday nights, but it was present."

Rose's old teammate Tommy Helms has a more succinct way

of saying the same thing: "If your daddy's a fisherman, then you'll be a fisherman, too. Pete's daddy liked to gamble, so when Pete grew up, that's what he liked to do."

Rose's upbringing on Cincinnati's West Side, with its gambling culture and large population of bookmakers and bettors, certainly also played a part. "You can't bet if you don't have the opportunity," says Glass.

The final element was Rose's personality.

"The typical compulsive gambler is someone with unreasonable optimism," says Arnold Wexler, who is the executive director of the New Jersey Council on Compulsive Gambling. "These are people who believe they can accomplish anything. They are people who believe they can't lose, that they are invincible."

Glass adds to this profile: "There's a syndrome called 'big-shotism.' It applies to most pathological gamblers. They have very low self-esteem, and need to bolster it in external ways. They do it by being big shots. They flash money, fancy clothes, fancy cars. No amount of success seems to have an impact on them. These people are never comfortable with the norm. They're prone to excess in almost all areas."

(Rose loved talking about his money and possessions as much as he did about his baseball records. In *Charlie Hustle*, his diary of his 1974 season, he boasted about the home he and Karolyn had recently bought: "I've got nine rooms, four and a half baths, eight telephones and five color television sets. That's living. About $125,000 worth of living and I love every inch of it.")

Anyone who gambled as heavily as Rose was likely to be a big loser. This is because the odds, no matter what the game, always favor the house—whether the wagering is on blackjack at a casino, on sporting events with a bookmaker, or on horses at a track.

There are exceptions—gamblers who are successful, who win more than they lose.

By nature, the successful gambler is patient, disciplined. He's rarely the "big shot" who makes a show of throwing money around. He can go to the track and bet just one or two races, which he has chosen after having doped out the whole card. If the race does not go off at the odds he anticipated, he may not bet it. On an NFL Sunday this type of gambler rarely bets more than a handful of games. If the successful gambler's wagers are large, they are also well considered.

Not surprisingly, Rose did not fit this profile. By all accounts, including his own, he was a particularly inept gambler.

He understood the charts in the *Daily Racing Form*, but he didn't have the attention span to spend much time with them. His idea of handicapping was to identify people he thought were knowledgeable and let them pick his horses for him. He handicapped the handicappers, not the horses.

In his testimony to John Dowd on April 20, 1989, Rose made a telling confession. Why did he use Metz's tips, and, if their horse came in, give him a cut of the winnings?

Because, said Rose, "I don't know diddly-squat about horses."

What Rose liked about gambling, to use the gambler's term, was the "action," the excitement of having money riding on something.

"One time he asked me who I liked in the weekend football games," recalls Murray Cook, who was the Reds' general manager in 1988 and 1989. "And I told him I didn't have any opinions, because I didn't much like football. That seemed to shock Pete, and he said, 'If you don't have some money on it, how can you expect to enjoy it?' "

At the track, Rose was a scattershot bettor who liked to put several different kinds of bets down on the same race. He would also make large wagers at tracks with low "betting handles," which, in essence, amounted to betting against himself.

Under the pari-mutuel betting system used at tracks, the odds are set by the bettors; the more money put down on a horse, the lower the odds that it will win, and the lower the payout if it does. At a track with a low "handle," meaning a relatively low amount of total money being bet on each race, a wager on a horse by one big bettor can significantly drive the odds down.

An associate of Rose's, Randy Kaiser, told Dowd that Rose regularly "bet the odds down to nothing."

Stan Hochman, a *Philadelphia Daily News* columnist and longtime track aficionado, says he was occasionally around Rose at Tampa Bay Downs, a low-handle track. "He would knock a horse down from eight-to-one to five-to-one. It wouldn't trouble him. That's not something a savvy bettor does, but Pete wasn't a savvy bettor. He needed to put enough down to make it interesting for him."

Rose was capable of huge losing days at the track. In February of 1988, Janszen and Mike Bertolini, a baseball memorabilia dealer and Rose associate (Rose sometimes referred to him as his personal photographer), had a conversation about Rose's gambling. Bertolini felt that Rose owed him money—as much as $200,000, which Bertolini had fronted to New York bookies to cover Rose's debts—and he was exasperated that instead of paying him back Rose continued to gamble and lose at the track.

"We'd be sitting there, and Petey would be throwing $1,000, $1,500 a race," Bertolini told Janszen of a visit to a Florida track with Rose. "He fucking lost 10 grand. He lost, he loses 10 grand every night." (The conversation was secretly taped by Janszen; a transcript of it was part of the three-thousand-some pages of testimony and exhibits accompanying the Dowd Report, the document submitted to Commissioner Giamatti in May 1989).

According to Ron Peters, the Franklin, Ohio, bookmaker who said Rose bet baseball with him, Rose was betting as much as $30,000 a day in the summer of 1987.

Rose could be positively feverish when he gambled. He bet the way he played baseball, full bore, only his energy did not produce the same results.

Like much of the baseball community that gathers in Florida each spring, Rose loved to gamble at Derby Lane, a St. Petersburg greyhound track. But he was there more than most and his wagers were bigger.

Dennis Schrader, a greyhound owner and bettor, recalls watching the races alongside Rose from a fourth-floor lounge at Derby Lane on numerous nights in the early and mid-1980s. "One night, I remember Rose was directly beside me," says Schrader. "The little guy, Mario, would run the bets to the window for him. Pete wrote checks. He didn't use cash. He's the only one I ever saw that wrote checks.

"He'd look at the program, he'd look at the odds board, and he'd say to Mario, 'give me the one-two quiniela fifty times, the one-four twenty times, and the two-four fifty times.' That's how he'd bet, strictly quinielas. You pick two dogs, and they come in either-or.

"He would bet like that, and then he would say to Mario, 'What's that come out to?' And Mario would say, 'Five hundred fifty dollars.' And then he'd scribble the check out, and Mario would take it to the window. That night, as he was leaving, he turned to my wife with his stack of losing tickets and said, 'You want these?'

"We counted them. There were ten thousand dollars' worth of losing tickets. He did win some races that night, but I guarantee he didn't win ten thousand dollars.

"I think he loved the action. This guy has got more energy than any human I've ever seen. I don't think he needed to drink, I don't think he needed food. He needed the action."

There were people who worried for Rose and offered well-intentioned advice. Typically, he rejected it.

One of them was Hochman, the Philadelphia columnist. He and Rose liked to talk horse racing. They also had a private, small-stakes pool on the NCAA basketball tournament every March during Rose's Philadelphia seasons. "We bet every game, like a dollar a game or something," says Hochman. "He beat me for five dollars one year and he was chortling so much you would have thought it was five thousand dollars." Hochman eventually concluded that Rose's gambling had reached the level that it was "borderline sick."

"One Sunday in September, I don't know what year it was but it was near the end of his tenure with the Phillies, it became clear to me that he was keeping track of ten pro football games," Hochman says. "I forget what the evidence was, whether it was a sheet or just him asking me about all the games, but one of them was like Denver against Houston, or some meaningless game, and I'm thinking, Why does he give a shit about this game?

"And I knew enough about gambling to think it was borderline sick to be betting ten games. I had also heard a rumor the league was calling him in about his gambling. So I asked, 'Pete, the league's going to do something. You're going to get in trouble.'

"And his response was, 'Hey, everybody does it,' which was stupid. For one thing, not everybody has the bankroll to bet ten games. But what I said to him was, 'Not everybody's in your position.'

"He waved me off in disgust. I was getting too personal for him, so that's the last time I raised it."

*   *   *

Among those who spent the most time with Rose, it was a given that he had a problem.

In the 1988 conversation between Janszen and Bertolini, Janszen suggests that perhaps Rose should seek professional help, perhaps from Gamblers Anonymous. "What is that, gamble-holics?" Janszen says to Bertolini.

"What are you, [crazy]," Bertolini replies. "You know what kind of fuckin' scandal [that would cause], man. I don't think he can go, I don't think he can get help, Paulie."

The bookies, too, knew precisely what kind of gambler Rose was.

Late in the 1984 football season, Rose wanted to begin placing bets with Joseph Cambra of Somerset, Massachusetts, whom Rose had met the previous spring while training in Florida.

Cambra was involved in bookmaking operations, and on November 12, 1984, a wiretap placed by the Massachusetts State Police picked up a conversation between Cambra and his boss in the operation, a man named Manny Fernandez. They were discussing Rose.

Why was he coming to them so late in the season? Fernandez wanted to know from Cambra. Obviously, he must have run out of credit somewhere else.

"I says we haven't heard from this guy all season," Fernandez said, according to a transcript of the wiretapped conversation. "It scares me like that."

Fernandez feared Rose would stiff them, and he instructed Cambra to put a $1,000-a-game limit on him.

Cambra feared he'd done the wrong thing by taking Rose's bets. "Alright, I can call and tell him no bet if you want. I mean, you're the boss."

"No, no, no," Fernandez replied.

The two bookies then talked about what an easy mark Rose seemed, and Fernandez even relented on the $1,000 limit. As the state police transcript quotes them:

MANNY: The guy's gotta be nuts, you know.

JOE: I can see Pete Rose. He makes millions. You know what I mean?

MANNY: Yeah, but we ain't gonna get any of it.

JOE: Hey, we'll knock him out, we're gonna knock him out.

MANNY: So, let it go. If he gives you 1,000 times [dollars] take it, if he gives you, whatever he gives, take, but I mean, don't let him get ridiculous.

Rose was deposed by John Dowd and two other lawyers representing major-league baseball in two sessions, which took place on two different days in April 1989. The location, picked by Rose's legal team, was a basement room in a Catholic conference center outside of Dayton, a former monastery which had been renamed the Bergamo Center for Lifelong Learning. The center was run by Marianist priests.

The transcription of Rose's testimony runs 358 pages, but his answer to the very first substantive question put to him was typical of his answers throughout.

The answer was a lie.

That first question concerned Joseph Cambra. What did he understand his occupation to be?

"Baseball fan," Rose answered.

"Did he have any other occupation?"

"Not to my knowledge."

"Did you know that he was a bookmaker?"

"Not to my knowledge."

Rose apparently did not have much better luck betting with Cambra than he did elsewhere. Cambra ended up with one of his World Series rings as well as a $19,800 check from him.

Rose said the check was for a real-estate deal in Somerset, Massachusetts, which fell through. Cambra, while visiting him in Montreal, returned him the money in cash, Rose said.

"All right," said Dowd. "And what did you do with the cash?"

"Put it in my pocket," said Rose.

"What did you do with it after that?"

"I don't remember."

In January 1989, Paul Janszen wrote a letter to Rose's attorney Reuven Katz. The purpose of it was to seek some $34,000 that Janszen believed Rose owed him. By then they were at odds, and

the alleged debt was the main point of contention. In the letter,
Janszen urged that Rose seek psychiatric help.

"It's time for him to take some responsibility for his actions,"
he wrote to Katz, "and if need be to get some professional help
along the way before he has nothing left."

Dowd asked Rose about the letter in April 1989. "We felt that
to be kind of amusing, the stuff he said in there," was Rose's
comment.

To someone other than Pete Rose, the scene at Gold's Gym might
have been repugnant. To a healthier person, it might also have
seemed a bit comical.

The men wore very short gym shorts to show off the muscles in
their upper legs, and silken tank tops to display their barreled
upper bodies and popping biceps. But as lightly as they were
dressed, Rose's friends at the gym were weighted down by thick
gold necklaces and bracelets and $10,000 Rolex watches.

They were also in the habit of carrying thick wads of cash,
which they stuffed into their knee-high tube socks. At Gold's,
you could tell how flush a man was on any particular day by
checking out the size of the bulge on his calf.

When Rose came to the gym, he carried his money the same
way, according to Mrs. Dallas Doran, who worked at the front
desk and is the mother of Michael Fry, who was the gym's principal owner. "When Pete Rose came in, he would have his nose
up in the air and this big blob of money in his sock," she says. "I'll
tell you, it was awfully ridiculous, when I look back on it now."

The Gold's clique included, among others, Janszen, Gioiosa,
Fry, and Donald Stenger, who had invested $25,000 in the busi-
ness.

The clique was a grotesque example of what Dr. Glass calls
"bigshotism." They competed to have the biggest, the best, and
the most of everything, whether it was money, fancy cars, gold
jewelry, or big muscles.

To build their muscles, they used steroids, under the guidance
of Stenger, a former Mr. Cincinnati who was the gym's medicine
man. "You felt solid, you felt healthy, you sometimes felt a little
aggressive" is how Stenger, testifying in federal court in 1989,
described the effects of taking steroids.

At Gold's, bodybuilders were constantly ducking into offices and rest rooms to inject each other in the butt, the biceps, or the legs with steroids. Even some of the women participated.

Rose's initial link to this outlaw gym was Gioiosa, whom he had first met in 1978 in Florida, where Gioiosa had traveled with his junior college baseball team. As Rose has told the story, Gioiosa (pronounced "Gee-oh-sah"), a clean-cut youth at the time, was playing catch with Pete junior, in the parking lot of their hotel while the rest of his team was out drinking. Gioiosa didn't like to drink, which was one of the things Rose liked about him.

Rose's son brought Gioiosa back to the room to meet him, they struck up a friendship, and a few months later Gioiosa came to Cincinnati to live with Rose and his then wife, Karolyn. "He made such an impression with my little boy that I told him when the season's over if he wants to come to Cincinnati and see some games, come on and he can live with us," Rose said.

Not everyone thought Gioiosa was such a nice young man. "I didn't like him," says Rose's sister Jackie Schwier. "He strutted around with all those gold chains, and he never worked."

Gioiosa was a particular nightmare to the mothers of the young women he dated. He once got in an argument with one of his girlfriends, who was sixteen at the time (Gioiosa was twenty-two), pushed her down the stairs of his apartment, then got drunk and showed up at her parents' house to throw snowballs against her bedroom window.

At his trial in 1989 on cocaine trafficking and income-tax evasion charges, which ended in a conviction and a five-year prison sentence, a woman named Fay Cordes, the mother of another of his former girlfriends, testified about Gioiosa:

"I didn't like Tommy," she said. "I didn't like him at all. I always said he looked like a gorilla."

"How did he act?" Gioiosa's defense attorney asked her.

"Basically like a gorilla. He was very nasty, very rude, very crude. Usually every sentence started with an *F* and ended in basically the same way."

"How did you feel about Tommy going out with your daughter?"

"Like any mother, I detested it."

Gioiosa had the same sort of unpleasant effect on Mrs. Doran. "I don't know how to describe him," she says. "He was obnoxious. The loudest mouth I ever heard. He was obscene."

Stenger, Fry, and Janszen, as well as Gioiosa, were all involved

in illegal drug trafficking—cocaine as well as steroids. All have
been convicted on drug-related charges and have served or are
serving prison time. (Janszen pleaded guilty to income-tax evasion relating to unreported income from the sale of steroids. He
has acknowledged also being involved in cocaine deals.)

Rose occasionally lifted weights at Gold's Gym, although rarely
with enough vigor to break a sweat. The attraction of the place
was not its weight machines.

Gioiosa began bringing Rose to the gym in 1984, the year of the
gym's opening and the year Rose returned to the Reds. He liked
showing him off to his other friends, and he also knew that there
were people at Gold's who could front Rose the cash to pay his
gambling debts—debts Gioiosa was acutely aware of, since at the
time he was the go-between to Rose's bookies.

Michael Fry visited Rose at his Riverfront Stadium office in
September of 1985, he told Dowd, and lent him $17,000 in cash.
The visit to his office occurred about a week before Rose broke
Cobb's record.

Rose repaid him several weeks later, and Rose borrowed another $30,000 late in October, which he also repaid.

He continued borrowing from Fry over the next year. In exam-
ining Rose's financial records, baseball investigators found
$24,000 in checks that Rose in February 1986 had made out to Fry
or that had been made out to cash and endorsed by Fry.

That same year, Rose sold Stenger an M1-BMW for $75,000 in
cash in order to pay off a gambling debt. The car may have been
worth twice as much as that. He sold four more cars for cash to a
friend of Stenger's in New Jersey. In 1987, he sold a Rolex watch
to Janszen for $11,000.

Rose's new friends were using him to launder their drug profits.
Plain and simple. And Rose was using them to raise cash to pay
his gambling debts.

No one got taken advantage of. It was a square deal.

"He needed to be around people who had money, and that's
what we all had," says Janszen.

"I'm guilty of one thing in this whole mess, and that's I was a
horseshit selector of friends," Rose said in the spring of 1989,
implying that the young men at Gold's Gym were responsible for
leading him astray.

This has been one of the biggest lies perpetuated by Rose, that he somehow unknowingly fell in with a bad crowd. In truth, he walked into Gold's Gym with his eyes open. He knew what he was looking for—cash—and he found it.

A particular irony is that the parents of Janszen and Fry warned *them* to stay away from *Rose*. They didn't think the Cincinnati legend would be a good influence on their sons.

Says Janszen: "My dad said he knew some people who knew Pete years ago, and he said, 'Pete's no good, Paul, stay away from him.' "

Fry used to boast to his mother of hanging out with Rose. "He would say, 'Oh, Mom,' and he would start telling me this and that about Pete Rose. He was so proud of his friendship with him," says Mrs. Doran. "And I would say, 'Be careful of him, son.'

"You see, I've lived around Cincinnati all my life. I'm fifty-six years old. I've worked in bars, and when you work in bars you hear stuff. I admire Pete Rose for his baseball, but I didn't care for what I heard about him as a man. And then when I got to meet him, I saw that when he looks at you he looks like he's smelling shit. And I didn't care for that.

"Michael would go to Pete's house, and he'd say, 'Oh, Mom, you ought to see Pete's house.' And I'd say, 'Michael, Pete's house doesn't interest me.' "

Pete Rose often boasted that the only book he had ever read was the Pete Rose story—which one he didn't specify—and that he hadn't even read all of that, just a couple of chapters.

But he was "street smart." He was proud of that. Being street smart was part of being Charlie Hustle.

Few people who knew Rose took him for a fool. "Sparky Anderson probably said it best: He said Pete Rose probably has more street sense than anyone he ever met. I have to agree," Reuven Katz commented in 1979.

It would figure, then, that Rose would have been aware that his new friends, the sources of all that free-flowing cash, had to be involved in some sort of illegal activity. They must have been dealing drugs. What other endeavor would allow someone to buy a car for $75,000 in cash—or purchase a watch for $11,000 when he had no visible means of support?

But Rose has insisted that he was shocked to learn that some of his friends dealt cocaine. Somewhere along the line, apparently, he had become street *stupid.*

It wasn't as if any of the Gold's crowd were discreet about their wealth. Gioiosa, whom Rose knew best and with whom he had the longest association, owned at least six different cars between 1983 and 1988—two Porsche 911s, a Datsun 280Z, a BMW 323, a Chevrolet Corvette, and a Chevy Blazer. He had also become a fancier of exotic birds. In 1986, he bought a yellow-naped Amazon parrot for $950 from a store called All About Birds, then returned several weeks later and traded it in, along with more cash, for a $2,600 scarlet macaw. Why the trade? he was asked at his trial. "The macaw was bigger," he replied. He named it "Boss"— "because it was so big."

Rose did notice that Gioiosa seemed to be living well. Around 1984, when Gioiosa got involved at Gold's Gym, "the first thing he did is he bought a new Corvette and he had a Rolex watch, he had all kinds of gold, and he had a pocket full of money," Rose told Dowd.

Rose also observed that Fry looked prosperous. "He had a new Ferrari, Rolex watches, and gold everywhere."

But Rose, who thought nothing of asking a married ballplayer if he had a girlfriend, showed a remarkable lack of curiosity about the source of all these riches:

"I didn't ask them where they got their money. It wasn't none of my business."

Rose knew Janszen had no job in 1987, because Janszen spent so much time with him around Cincinnati and also joined him numerous times on the road. But Janszen, too, always had plenty of cash, and was able to plunk down the $11,000 to buy the Rolex from Rose.

But Rose didn't know about Janszen's illegal activities either. He didn't even have a suspicion.

"So you really had no clue Janszen was involved in drugs?" Roger Kahn quotes himself as asking Rose in *Pete Rose: My Story.*

"No, no," he tells Kahn.

> "I found out during spring training of 1988. Janszen asked me, he asked Reuven Katz actually, could he borrow $30,000.
> "I said, '$30,000? For what?'
> "Katz said, 'Janszen said he needed to hire a lawyer. Janszen is

going to get prosecuted for drugs. He says you're his only hope.'

"I said, 'Reuv, I can't lend anybody $30,000. That's just too much to lend. Maybe we'll lend him ten, if he pays me back.''

"So we loan him ten. That's what the $10,000 check to Janszen was for.

"I thought, 'I got to get away from this guy. He's in the drug business.'

"Janszen made some road trips with me. He must have felt he was very close. But I'm thinking, 'Janszen, take a hike. Janszen, I don't need problems with drug agents and stuff. Janszen, I got to fire you as a friend.' "

"Did you tell Janszen that directly?"

"No, I was in Florida. He was in Cincinnati. I just ducked him."

In one of Rose's endless bull sessions with reporters as the Cobb chase wound down late in the summer of 1985, the name of Al Capone somehow came into the conversation.

"I wish I could have met the big guy," Rose interjected. "Wouldn't he have to give you a tip on a horse or something?"

It was a harmless enough comment. Anyone could have said it. But in Rose's case, it was illustrative of something in his personality: He was attracted by criminality. Just the whiff of it made his heart beat faster.

The Gold's Gym crowd, it should be pointed out, was not exactly the Colombian drug cartel. They were, instead, sort of the Keystone Kops of drug-running.

One of the pieces of evidence introduced at Gioiosa's trial was a gym bag that he used to ferry cocaine back and forth from Florida. On the inside of the bag he had his name written in pen. When it wasn't being used to carry cocaine, Gioiosa used the bag to store the softballs for his Friday-night softball league.

On one occasion, Gioiosa, who failed a brief tryout in the Baltimore Orioles organization, made a delivery of cocaine in the parking lot of a Catholic church outside Cincinnati. He pulled his car up to the car of the intended recipient and attempted to throw the bag into the open driver's-side window. He missed, and had to get out of the car and pick the bag up off the ground.

Rose thought his friends were big-time. And the evidence is overwhelming that he knew precisely what they were up to.

At Gioiosa's August 1989 trial, a Cincinnati-area foreign-car dealer who sold Porsches, BMWs, and other luxury autos to the Gold's clique testified that on several occasions in 1986 Rose, Fry,

Stenger, and Gioiosa came to browse on his lot, after which they went out for breakfast at a nearby Perkins Restaurant. The car dealer, Peter Neuhmar, testified that he went along.

He was asked by the assistant U.S. attorney persecuting Gioiosa what Rose and his friends talked about.

"There was a lot of talk about gambling and drugs," said Neuhmar, who was not exactly squeaky clean himself. He acknowledged in his testimony that he once had a side business of selling smuggled Rolex watches.

Another piece of evidence introduced at Gioiosa's trial was a 1988 conversation between Gioiosa and Janszen, which was secretly taped by Janszen at the FBI's request. The conversation involved a dispute between Gioiosa and Janszen over the collection of a drug debt from a third party. The taped conversation indicates that Gioiosa had asked Rose to mediate this dispute between them, and that Rose had expressed no surprise about their involvement in cocaine dealing.

In his disjointed manner, Gioiosa explained what he had told Rose about the deal: "We, we loaded Ralph up, and then you were in on it with me with Ralph and we, you were helpin' me out. I said, I was telling Paul, Cindy that Paul had it and Paul would say I had it and then Cindy would just back off. That's exactly what I told Pete."

Rose, according to Gioiosa, had told him to be careful of Janszen, that Janszen might hurt him. "He said, you're crazy," Gioiosa says on the tape.

Rose had also warned Gioiosa that his dealing might get him in trouble, but there was no indication from Gioiosa that Rose had been surprised to learn about his drug involvement: "And then I hear Pete sayin', 'You better be careful, DEA's [the Drug Enforcement Agency] gonna nail you.' "

Most baseball fans would have expected Rose to be familiar with the acronym ERA—earned run average. Few would have expected "DEA" to roll off his tongue.

When Rose pleaded guilty in April 1990 to two felony counts of failing to report income, the government stated that it had found no evidence of his involvement in his associates' drug-dealing. The government did not comment, however, on whether he knew about it.

Janszen says that, indeed, Rose was not involved. But he does say that Rose had wanted to get involved and on several occasions volunteered to help finance cocaine deals. One reason the offer wasn't taken up was that the Gold's Connection (as it was dubbed in the Cincinnati newspapers) had plenty of cash to purchase coke; what it lacked was enough customers to unload it. Rose's money would have been of no help.

"Pete was like a little kid when it came to criminals," Janszen says. "He was fascinated by the whole thing. Even Tommy was scared at times of the way Pete was, because we would be sitting up in the room at the [Turfway] racetrack, which was just next to the press box, and Pete would say real loud, 'Hey, how are the kilos going?' Just like that. Just something stupid.

"It wasn't even drug talk. Nobody would say, 'How are the kilos coming?' They might say, 'Did you get a kilo in?'

"Gio would say, 'Fuck, Paul, what's wrong with him?' And I would say, 'Hey, you know him better than me.' And I'd have to say to Pete, 'Uh, Pete, you never know who might walk in here.' His response was, 'Ah, fuck 'em.' I mean, you could have explained to him that you can go to prison for dealing cocaine, but he would never understand that. He never thought of the consequences."

Why would he? When had he ever had to face them?

Janszen says that he was with Rose in New York in 1987 when Mike Bertolini introduced them to two men who were involved in a variety of criminal activities—a credit-card scam, cocaine dealing, and a stolen-car ring. Rose first asked about financing a cocaine shipment, Janszen says, and then became interested in possibly purchasing stolen cars.

Rose, according to Janszen, asked them. "Hey, do you ever steal Mercedes?" They said they could probably steal two of the particular model he wanted. Later that night, Janszen heard Rose tell Carol, his wife, "I just bought us two Mercedes."

Rose had another way of raising large sums of cash, apart from his associations at Gold's Gym, and that was through the baseball memorabilia business.

Even outside of Rose's involvement in it, "the hobby," as memorabilia dealers sometimes refer to their industry, is rife with counterfeiting, fraud, forged autographs, and theft. Without overstating the case, it is a cesspool.

For example, major-league baseball teams have traditionally

passed uniforms down to their minor-league affiliates after one year's use by the big-leaguers. Nowadays, many of the uniforms—particularly the ones worn by the better-known players—get "lost" in transit and end up on the memorabilia market, where they are sold for as much as $2,000.

Bats, gloves, shoes, caps, even batting gloves—any piece of equipment used or any part of a uniform worn by a major leaguer—can be sold on the market. If the item is autographed it's worth more. Much of what is bought is not genuine; several of Rose's associates, including Janszen, Fry and a clubhouse assistant, testified to forging Rose's signature on balls and other items—at Rose's behest.

"I'll give you one example," says Howard Eskin, a Philadelphia sportscaster and memorabilia collector. "Hats. A lot of what's out there is fraudulent. Somebody will try to sell you a cap that, for example, they say is a hat Darryl Strawberry wore. Well, if you know what the hell you're doing, once you've seen a legitimate hat of a certain player, you keep track of what his hat size is. And half the time, the hat somebody's trying to sell you is the wrong hat size. But people buy this shit. They don't know better, and that's a shame.

"Greedy people, dishonest people, are ruining the hobby," says Eskin, who owns numerous pieces of Rose memorabilia, including a ball from his 44-game hit streak. "It's not fun anymore."

With its low standards for honesty and fair dealing, and its large cast of shady characters, the memorabilia business was a natural for Rose, and he dove into it headfirst.

He was one of the most frequent signers at autograph shows. Blessed with a first and last name that stretched only eight letters, he could scribble better than six-hundred *Pete Roses* in an hour (never pausing to look at, let alone talk to, the autograph-seekers), and for a couple of hours' work it wasn't unusual for him to be paid $20,000 by the promoter.

He also sold, as has been widely reported, many of the items connected to his record-breaking hits. Whatever sentiment he had for them was washed over by his thirst to raise money to pay debts and keep gambling.

"What will you keep as souvenirs?" he was asked by a reporter during the final stages of the Cobb chase.

"I'll keep the ball and the bat" was Rose's response, as quoted in a United Press International story.

But Rose sold the bat and ball involved in his 4,192d hit for $129,000. He wore nine different uniform jerseys that night, and sold them all.

Rose, in pleading guilty to federal tax charges on April 20, 1990, admitted to failing to report $348,720 in earnings from baseball-card shows and memorabilia sales in the four-year period between 1984 and 1987. That was not the total of his memorabilia-related income; there were hundreds of thousands of dollars more that he *did* report and pay taxes on—as well as the possibility that there was more unreported cash the government did not discover.

In his memorabilia dealings, Rose sometimes outsmarted himself: He tried to scam someone and ended up getting scammed himself.

The best example was a transaction involving his diamond-studded Hickok Belt, which he was awarded for being named the top professional athlete of 1975. Ten years later, he sold the belt for $82,000 to an Oregon collector named Dennis Walker, who owned as much as $300,000 in Rose memorabilia.

Although Walker didn't know it, Rose removed the diamonds from the Hickok Belt before turning it over to him, and had them replaced with counterfeit diamonds according to Janszen.

Walker had a surprise of his own for Rose. His payment for the belt was in the form of a certificate of deposit from the Bank of Tonga that turned out to be worthless.

Walker, a former college professor, had a grandiose vision of his place in the memorabilia business: He wanted to be king of it. In the same year Rose sold him the belt, he was the master of ceremonies at the opening of Walker's National Sports Hall of Fame, which was located off Interstate 5 near Salem, Oregon.

Walker dropped out of sight about a year after Rose spoke at the opening of his museum. Much of his collection, valued by the FBI at as much as $7 million, vanished with him.

On July 3, 1987, police found a badly decomposed body in a Las Vegas hotel room. He had been dead about three days and had no identification on him. He had registered under the name Charles Lee from a nonexistent Phoenix address. Several weeks later, law-enforcement authorities identified the dead man as Walker.

"I've talked to Pete about this," says Eskin. "He thinks that wasn't Walker they found in the room. He thinks the guy's still alive, and selling some of the stuff on the market."

As it turns out, one of the diamonds that Rose had removed

from the Hickok Belt has also now vanished. In the spring of 1990, there was a break-in at the Roses' new home in Plant City, Florida, and the burglars took much of Carol Rose's jewelry. "One of the things taken was a very sentimental piece to Carol," explains Rose's publicity agent, Barbara Pinzka. "It was a choker with a diamond from the Hickok Belt."

Pinzka said she did not know the circumstances under which the diamond was removed from the belt, although she was aware that the payment from Walker, the Bank of Tonga certificate, did turn out to be worthless.

"Pete considers that belt to have been stolen from him," she says.

Rose's main connection to the memorabilia industry was Mike Bertolini, whom he first met in 1985 when Bertolini was sent to Florida by his employer at a Brooklyn card shop to line Rose up for an autograph show. Bertolini was nineteen at the time; he succeeded in signing Rose for a show at a Brooklyn grammar school, which he attended on the morning before a Reds-Mets game.

Within a year, Rose had taken him into his entourage. Bertolini became a merchandiser of autographed Pete Rose baseballs, bats, uniform jerseys, and photographs, and, with Rose's name behind him, a major promoter of autograph shows featuring such big names as Joe DiMaggio, Ted Williams, Willie Mays, and Mickey Mantle.

To Rose's friend Jeff Ruby, Bertolini was a "vagabond, a get-rich-quick kid."

To Charles Sotto, a Cincinnati memorabilia dealer, Bertolini was "a dreamer, unorganized, someone who will either make a million one day or end up in jail. He was typical Brooklyn—very pushy."

To Bill Hongash, who employed Bertolini at Capital Cards in Brooklyn and ran an autograph show with him in Atlantic City, Bertolini "was like the plague. Some people can remember the day Kennedy was shot. I remember the day I cut my ties with Mike Bertolini—March 31, 1989. Life's been a lot better since then."

But Pete Rose had a different view of Bertolini. "He's a young kid that knows more about the memorabilia and card show business than anybody I've ever been around," he told Dowd. "And he's going to make a lot of money in this business someday. As soon as he gets a break."

Rose noted another attribute of Bertolini's which made him want to help him out. "He's got a kind heart."

Baseball's investigators tracked an extraordinary flow of money from Rose to Bertolini. In 1986, Rose wrote twenty-one separate $8,000 checks, for a total of $168,000. Government regulations require banks to file currency reports on transactions of $10,000 or more. The checks were made out to fictitious names, but Bertolini was able to get them cashed at a newsstand in the garment district in Manhattan. (Rose seemed to have written any name that came into his head. One of the checks was made out to "Herbie Lee," which was Rose's nickname for Mike Schmidt. Rose had a boyhood friend by that name, and when he came over to the Phillies he decided that Schmidt looked like Herbie, so he began calling him that.)

In addition, between 1987 and 1989, Rose either cosigned or took out loans for Bertolini totaling $218,000. He also regularly sent him undetermined amounts of cash, usually via Federal Express.

The Dowd Report concluded that Rose was using Bertolini as a conduit to place bets through New York bookmakers, and that the money funneled to him went toward Rose's gambling debts.

Rose denied this. He said the cash was to finance Bertolini's card shows, to pay players and ex-players up front for their appearances, and to rent halls. Rose said that he took no note on the loans, and that Bertolini kept track of the repayment.

"Mikey can keep track of that. Eighty thousand dollars is very simple," he said. The money was repaid "just a little bit at a time; cash at a time."

Rose's relationship with Bertolini was perhaps the most pathetic of all his "friendships." Bertolini was no big shot. When Rose met him, he was a fat kid, about 5'8" and well over 300 pounds.

Rose called him "Fat Mike." When he was angry at him he called him "Fat Ass."

Bertolini called Rose "Skip," which is what major-league ballplayers sometimes called their manager—it's short for "Skipper"—and what Rose's own son, Pete junior, called him. Bertolini occasionally referred to Rose as "Dad."

Rose testified that Bertolini would have a difficult time ac-

counting for the uses to which he put one of the loans. "He'll
have a hard time explaining the first one to you," he said. "Because that was a period of time when he got hooked up with some
whore in Tampa and he blew the money on her. . . . Here's a guy
that went to spring training that year and he met her and he
weighed 360 pounds. And in the next year, because of that girl, he
lost 160 pounds. And he just fell in love and she put him through
the mill."

On April 4, 1988, Janszen secretly taped a conversation with
Bertolini. In it, Bertolini, who has a true gift for profanity, said
that Rose owed him and the bookmakers a total of "two, two and
a quarter"—apparently $200,000 or $225,000.

"But we're forgetting them, he's just gonna take care of me,"
Bertolini said.

"Doesn't he even give a shit?" Janszen asked.

"What are they gonna do Paulie? . . . They made enough off
him. What the fuck are they gonna do? . . . What he owes, they
already got that in previous losses. Know what I'm saying? Man,
fuck'n, they already raked the guy, fuck it man."

Bertolini said that he owed, on his own, as much as $200,000 in
gambling debts, but that the bookmakers knew which debts were
Rose's. And he said Rose had talked directly to the New York
bookmakers. "They know who did it," he said. "Because he's told
them, he's talked to them lots of times."

Bertolini vowed that he would take the secret of Rose's gambling to the grave. "I'm the only one who can prove it and man,
he's my best friend in the whole world. Know what I'm saying,
fuck that, I'd die before I'd ever get him in trouble."

In a conversation with Janszen in March 1989, Bertolini, at this
point aware that Rose and Janszen had fallen out, offered to set up
a session for the two of them to make peace. And he came up with
a novel idea to ensure that neither of them would surreptitiously
try to tape the session.

"You will be fuckin' nude when you fuckin' talk," he said,
unaware that he was being taped himself. "Both of you. I tell you,
we'll go in a fuck'n Jacuzzi or something. So if anyone's got anything on they'll be electrocuted."

Although he denied it, the underside of Pete Rose's life invaded
his baseball life. He didn't keep them separate. He was not Pete

Rose, ballplayer and manager, during the summer months and Pete Rose, addicted gambler, in the off-season.

Fry visited him at Riverfront in the final week of the Cobb pursuit to lend him $17,000 in cash. Gioiosa, Janszen, and Bertolini, among others, had the run of his office—they regularly made phone calls from his desk—and they also had the run of the Reds clubhouse.

Rose was visited on the field in Tampa in 1985 by someone collecting a gambling debt, a fact that was known to Reds executives.

Early in the 1986 season, someone came to the clubhouse door at Riverfront Stadium to collect a debt. Through a clubhouse assistant, Rose passed him an envelope stuffed with cash. This incident was known to Bill Bergesch, who was the Reds' general manager.

Rose said his job as manager of the Reds engaged him, but it did not. He was bored and unhappy—and strangely detached from his team. In particular, he was an abject failure at communicating with or inspiring his players.

"Pete was so involved with other things that he had very little communication with the players, and not that much with the coaches either," says Chief Bender, the Reds' director of player personnel. "He would always say, 'I'm at the ballpark every day at three P.M.,' and he was.

"But it didn't matter. He was there tending to other things—his friends, business stuff, signing things for Bertolini, which was sickening to see. There were so many people in his office doing various things that a player wouldn't want to come in."

Tommy Helms remembers asking Rose for guidance on how best to instruct a young player whom he had been tutoring on his infield play. Rose's response was, "I think you know what to do, that's why I hired you. Do whatever you think is right."

Helms says Rose's response made him feel good, because it reflected his confidence in him. But it also said a lot about Rose's enthusiasm for his job. Perhaps more than any living ballplayer or ex-ballplayer, he knew the intricacies of the game, but he refused to pass them along.

Other than making out the lineup cards, Pete Rose really couldn't be bothered with baseball. He was busy. Gambling wasn't an off-season diversion; it obsessed him just as much in July and August as it did in December and January.

*   *   *

In the beginning, Rose did click with a few players, principally young, white, run-through-a-brick-wall types who bore some similarity to the young Pete Rose. A couple of bullpen pitchers, John Franco and Rob Murphy, found inspiration from Rose just in the way he handed them the ball when he brought them into the game, slapped them on the backside, and said, "Go get 'em."

"I really got charged up," says Murphy. "I mean, that was *Pete Rose*, and I responded to that."

But by 1987, Rose's first season in which he did not play at all, he had abdicated the traditional manager's role of changing pitchers and assigned it to low-energy pitching coach Scott Breeden. The only time he left the dugout during a game was to argue with an umpire.

"We begged him to start coming out again," Murphy says, "but he wouldn't do it."

Murray Cook, the Reds' general manager at the time, came to believe that Rose was embarrassed to be seen on the field. "I think he felt that if he's not playing and he's not involved in the baseball action, he had no place on the field," says Cook. "He was embarrassed to be out there."

Cook, too, tried to get Rose to resume going to the mound to change pitchers. Rose did it for a while in 1988, then stopped.

Rose failed as a manager partly because he envied his own players their youth.

His last major-league at bat, a strikeout, came on August 17, 1986, when he was forty-five years old. He never officially retired as a player and never stopped believing he *could* play. No one doubted that if the front office hadn't insisted that he come off the active roster he would not have made the move himself. "The ball still looks the same to me, and I've got a sneaky suspicion that if I go up there, I am going to hit," he said in 1987, when he was contemplating a comeback as a player.

Rose was particularly jealous of an outfielder named Tracy Jones, who was so gung ho that he literally ran into walls chasing home runs that landed twenty rows into the seats. The Cincinnati newspapers liked to compare him to Rose, which Jones encouraged.

Jones's ambition was to become "the first white man to steal a hundred bases," which sounded a lot like something Rose would have said. The difference was that Rose would have gone ahead and done it. At last check, Jones's best season left him 69 steals short of his goal. Rose should have chuckled at Jones; instead, the young player made him feel insecure.

"It drove Pete crazy when people compared Tracy to him," says Janszen. "One night Tracy had a big night, he went like four-for-four, and we're talking about Tracy and the next thing you know, he says, 'Paul, do you realize, I have so many records that I should have the record for the most records.' "

When he stopped playing, Rose even quit being so fastidious about the way he wore his uniform. In fact, he no longer even *wore* a full uniform. Not even the threat of a fine in 1987 by the league could induce Rose to wear his official Reds jersey; instead, over his baseball pants, he wore a red windbreaker. Rose was at least 15 or 20 pounds over his playing weight, and the uniform top tended to accentuate the rolls in his midsection.

His old 1963 teammate, Jim Brosnan, saw him in the Reds clubhouse in 1987, when he was in town to do a piece for *Life* on Eric Davis. "He was pig fat,"says Brosnan. "That surprised me, because I always admired him for keeping in as good a physical condition as he could. He was also very brusque in his answers. That gave me cause for worry, because I had never seen Pete in quite that way."

The Reds organization has never believed much in frills, not even for Pete Rose, so his manager's office on the bottom level of Riverfront Stadium was not much to look at.

It was furnished with a standard-issue metal desk, a dented metal wardrobe, a minirefrigerator on the floor, and couple of straight-backed chairs for visitors. Except for some baseball bats propped up against one of the corners, the place looked like where you'd expect to find the foreman of the loading dock.

Spare as it was, the office did represent just about the only thing Rose had gained as he passed from being a player to being a manager—a place of his own in the stadium.

He liked bringing his buddies to work with him. There was a lot of dead time in managing, even more so than in playing.

By about 10:00 A.M. on opening day 1986, Rose had wheeled his

Porsche into the tunnel under the stadium and had parked it near the entrance to his office. With him was Gioiosa. As they approached the clubhouse door, Gioiosa was stopped by a uniformed security guard. No "nonbaseball personnel" could pass by him, the guard said, other than accredited members of the media.

This was a longtime major-league rule, which teams other than Cincinnati had enforced more stringently since 1985. The crackdown was ordered by Commissioner Peter Ueberroth after testimony in the drug trials in Pittsburgh revealed that cocaine had been bought and sold in baseball clubhouses.

Rose, of course, knew about the disclosures at the trials, and about the edict from Ueberroth. He knew everything that went on in baseball. But what did it have to do with him? He'd never used cocaine, and he had nothing to do with the Pittsburgh drug trials.

Rose cursed the guard. It was *his* office, he said, and he could let in whomever he wanted. When the guard held his ground, Rose demanded that he use his walkie-talkie to summon his boss, Doug Duennes, the director of stadium operations. Rose would straighten it out with him.

What followed, on the morning of opening day, was a thirty-minute-long shouting match in the manager's office between Rose and Duennes, with Bergesch officiating.

"It was a very serious thing. Very heated," recalls Bergesch. "Pete was going to punch Duennes. That's how upset he was."

Finally, Bergesch gave Rose his way.

He did it by splitting a hair. The manager's office wasn't technically the clubhouse, he ruled, because a door (unguarded) separated the manager's quarters from where the players dressed. Bergesch said Rose's friends could come into his office, but he did issue a warning of his own: Rose had better make sure that they never walked through the unguarded door into the player's locker room.

But Gioiosa that season moved freely about the players' clubhouse. And the following year, so did Bertolini and Janszen. In fact, Bertolini conducted a great deal of business there. He moved from locker to locker, soliciting Reds players to autograph bats, balls, and photographs. After he sold the items he was supposed to return a cut of the money to the players, but by the end of the season many were bitching that the manager's buddy was ripping them off.

"I didn't like Pete's friends hanging around either," Bergesch explains. "I agreed with Duennes. I was the one who told him to start enforcing that regulation, but then Pete got so heated. I was just trying to come up with something that would satisfy him, so he wouldn't punch Doug."

As for Rose's friends moving out into the player's quarters, he says, "That was a shame. It happened. I know it happened. But it shouldn't have."

Within a couple of weeks after Bergesch caved in by letting Gioiosa through the door on opening day 1986, Rose had the clubhouse assistant walk a cash-filled envelope out to a man waiting outside.

"Our stadium manager, Duennes, told me somebody came and wanted to see Pete," recalls Bergesch, who as the Reds' GM from 1985 through 1987 was technically Rose's boss. "I guess Pete owed him a lot of money. I really didn't know what it was about. Pete sent him some money out through one of the kids in the clubhouse.

"I didn't know the details. I didn't consider it my business. I didn't have reason to think anything odd about it. As I understood it, there wasn't any trouble about it."

Like Bill Giles in Philadelphia, Bergesch decided to turn a blind eye to Rose, who as the Reds manager was still the club's premier gate attraction. The ballclub was still "Pete Rose's Cincinnati Reds," and Rose, even as a nonplayer, was perceived as integral to the franchise's fortunes.

With Rose's well-known fondness for betting, what could the cash-filled envelope have contained but payment for a gambling debt. It should have been a cause for concern for Bergesch, but instead he ignored it.

Like Giles, and like Henry Fitzgibbon, he preferred not to assume—or see—the worst of Rose. The people Pete Rose was bringing (and attracting) into the baseball environment were precisely the types that the commissioner's office was endeavoring to keep out. At times, it took a great effort to remain so blissfully ignorant of the life Rose was leading.

It took a long time for anyone in a position of authority to own up to it, but Rose's problems were baseball's problems.

11

THE FINAL DAYS

When you're not doing nothing, why worry? People
who do something worry. People that worry jump off
bridges. I can walk across any bridge in the world.

—Pete Rose, April 25, 1989

EVEN baseball's final investigation of Pete Rose, the one that led
to his banishment, got off to a sputtering start.

It began with a tip that federal law-enforcement authorities
investigating a drug ring at a surburban Cincinnati gym had received information on Pete Rose. Baseball's all-time hits leader
was somehow mixed up with the drug dealers; it wasn't clear yet
in what way.

This got the attention of Kevin Hallinan, the former New York
City detective who in 1986 had become baseball's director of
security. (He replaced a former Secret Service agent named Harry
Gibbs, who became Henry Fitzgibbon's successor in 1981.)

Hallinan put a man on the case, a private detective in Cincinnati who had worked with baseball on other security matters.
This was early in the summer of 1988. Almost immediately, the
investigation hit a roadblock, which came in the form of a message from the feds. The message was: *Hands off.* More specifically, it was: *Hands off Paul Janszen.*

In law-enforcement parlance, Janszen had been "flipped" by the
FBI, which meant that he was now working with them to catch
others, including his associates at Gold's, in the same criminal

activities he had once participated in. He enticed people into drug deals. He secretly recorded telephone calls and wore a hidden microphone in face-to-face meetings. He did this for the reason that most people do—to save his skin, to win a lighter sentence for his own crimes.

Janszen had made a nice living selling steel barrels. He made a better one pushing steroids. Now, in his role as a federal informant, he performed with remarkable competence and great vigor. He was a self-starter, highly motivated. He even taped conversations when the FBI had not specifically requested that he do so.

If setting up his friends did not qualify Janszen as a particularly appealing person, it did make him a valuable resource for law enforcement, and, potentially, a tool for baseball—if indeed baseball had truly mustered the resolve to take on Pete Rose.

"The word that came back from the feds in 1988 was 'Let us finish our business before you talk to Janszen,' " says John Dowd. "It was not that direct. It was more unspoken, but as I understand it, that was clearly the message.

"So baseball basically took a seat in the bleachers. Joe [Joseph Daly, of the Cincinnati office of Business Risks International, an investigative firm that assisted baseball on the Rose probe] poked around a little bit, confirmed the essentials, the relationships. Information kept coming in. But baseball was just coming off the thirty-day thing with Pallone [Rose's suspension for pushing umpire Dave Pallone]. There was not a big appetite to go back after Rose.

"In the beginning of 1989, the word came back, 'If you knock on his [Janszen's] door, he's ready to talk.' "

On February 20, 1989, Rose was summoned from spring training to New York to see baseball commissioner Peter Ueberroth and his anointed succesor, Bart Giamatti. At that meeting he was given an opportunity to come clean, which no one expected he would do.

Ueberroth asked him if he bet on baseball. Rose denied it. He asked him if he owed money to bookies, and Rose denied that, too.

Following the meeting, Rose told reporters that Ueberroth and Giamatti had asked him to New York to seek his advice on some baseball matters. Then why had he brought two lawyers with him? "There were two commissioners, weren't there?" he replied.

Ueberroth was no more forthcoming. As quoted by *The New York Times*, he said, "There was nothing ominous and there won't be any follow-through." But on February 23, three days after the meeting, Ueberroth's office formally retained Dowd as special counsel on the Rose matter.

Dowd, the father of five adopted children, was a private attorney in Washington, D.C., whose work consisted mostly of defending accused white-collar criminals. He had spent a decade with the U.S. Justice Department in Washington, where he was in charge of the unit that prosecuted organized crime members. Dowd was known for not backing off tough assignments. Assigned in 1976 to investigate whether then-FBI director Clarence Kelley had improperly accepted gifts from subordinates, he recommended that Kelley be reprimanded or fired, neither of which happened.

Dowd liked baseball. He read the box scores in his morning *Washington Post*. He went to ball games when he could. But he was not consumed by the game.

"I read about it, I go to games," Dowd says. "If I'm on the road, and somebody says, 'Let's go to a ball game,' Dowd's always the first one to want to go. And I'll have my beers and two hot dogs, and thoroughly enjoy myself."

A native New Englander, Dowd grew up as a fan of Ted Williams and the Red Sox and later rooted for the Baltimore Orioles. Like nearly everyone who appreciated baseball, he enjoyed watching Pete Rose. "I admired his enormous hustle," he says.

There was one thing that Dowd didn't like about Rose. "I did not care for the hurting of Ray Fosse. I thought it was completely unnecessary."

His criticism on this point is ironic, because Dowd's reputation was that he practiced law not unlike the way Pete Rose played baseball: aggressively, with great passion and intensity. You would not want John Dowd investigating you any more than you would want Pete Rose charging at you if you were holding a baseball and standing between him and home plate.

Nor would you hire Dowd to lead an investigation you hoped would be halfhearted or a whitewash.

*   *   *

On February 24, 1989, Dowd conducted his first interview in the
Rose probe, with Janszen. Their taped sessions took place over
two days (Janszen had to stop early in the evening of the first
session to return to his halfway house) and were attended by
Janszen's girlfriend, Danita Marcum, and by Hallinan and Daly.

After a year of interrogations by agents from the FBI, IRS, and
DEA, Janszen was an old pro at this sort of thing. He had been
conditioned to hold nothing back. When he recounted events, he
droned on, moving from one incident to the next without the
benefit of a transition and seemingly without pausing for breath.
His tone may have been flat, but what he said was astounding.

Unlike some of the people Henry Fitzgibbon had talked to years
back, Janszen had no interest in protecting Rose. Fitzgibbon had
had no such source, which was an important difference between
his investigation of Rose and Dowd's.

Janszen told of placing baseball, football, and basketball bets for
Rose, and of Rose's huge debts to bookies. He told the interviewers about the criminal activities of the Gold's crowd, Rose's
knowledge of those activities, and his eagerness to become involved in cocaine deals.

He told them about the bundles of cash Rose accepted at card
shows and did not report. Nothing excited Rose like cash, Janszen
related.

Janszen gave them betting sheets he said he had lifted out of
Rose's house. He gave them a notebook he had kept of Rose's
bets. He played them tapes in which others talked of placing bets
for Rose through bookmakers.

Janszen talked of his own involvement in criminal activities.
And he also made it clear he harbored a grudge against Rose,
because he believed Rose owed him some $30,000 that he had
refused to pay.

Using Janszen's information as a starting point, Dowd's team of
two dozen lawyers and detectives would spend the spring and
most of the summer combing through Rose's life.

They tracked the phone calls made from his home, from baseball clubhouses, from the Reds' road hotels, and from his car.
They assembled his banking records, and they talked to people
who said they had booked his bets and lent him money.

What they found was what Henry Fitzgibbon had suspected almost two decades before: Rose gambled through bookmakers and heavily.

He did not spend his days as most baseball fans might have imagined or hoped he did. He was not thinking baseball, scribbling out new lineups, conferring on trades, pondering whether perhaps Bo Diaz would be more effective batting sixth rather than seventh.

Pete Rose spent his days scheming for cash in association with his strange coterie. It seemed that he did not so much choose his associates as he was *drawn* to them; could he really have set out to find a foreign-car dealer who dealt on the side in smuggled watches?

As much as any single piece of evidence, what jumped out at Dowd was Rose's arrogance. He was in flagrant violation of baseball rules and had been for many years. But his behavior was not that of a man who cared much about concealing anything.

Dowd and Giamatti were both the sort of men who formed close bonds in the course of their work, and they quickly became friends. (A photograph of Giamatti occupies a prominent spot in Dowd's office.)

Dowd remembers a conversation he had with the late commissioner in the spring of 1989. Rose had been accustomed to special treatment, he told Giamatti. When he didn't get it he would be likely to strike back. Taking him on would be unpleasant and it would come with a cost.

"I remember telling Bart, 'The reason we're gonna have a problem is nobody has ever yanked this guy up. It's been finessed. You're a straight guy, and you're gonna pay for it.'"

Dowd submitted his report to Giamatti on May 9, 1989, about two and a half months after he was retained to look into the Rose allegations. The report ran 225 pages, and was backed by some 2,000 pages of transcribed interviews and documents.

The following September, a final report and another 1,000 pages of exhibits was submitted to Fay Vincent, who had become baseball's eighth commissioner (and third in six months) after Giamatti suffered a fatal heart attack just one week after disciplining Rose.

Nowhere in any of the material that Dowd passed on to either commissioner was there a "smoking gun" on the most serious charge against Rose—the charge that he bet baseball and bet on the Reds.

There were no tape recordings of him placing baseball bets, no videotapes. There were the betting sheets, said by baseball's handwriting expert to be in Rose's hand. And bookie Ron Peters even claimed he had Rose on tape, but the tape seemed to have been misplaced. Peters thought it might be in some boxes in his ex-wife's garage, but baseball's gumshoes searched the boxes and couldn't find it.

Rose insists that he did not wager on baseball, and anyone who chooses to believe him cannot, with absolute certainty, be proved wrong. But if he did not, then Rose was the victim of an elaborate, ingenious frame-up, a hoax of monumental proportions—one involving lies by witnesses who testified that he bet on baseball; presumably forged betting sheets; fabricated betting notebooks; and telephone toll records from his home, automobiles, road hotels, and baseball clubhouses that made it look very much as if he was calling bookies in late June and early July when there was no football or basketball to bet on, just baseball. (There are horse races to bet in any month of the year, but Rose had never claimed that as an explanation for the nightly flurry of calls, most of which occurred in the early evening, just before the baseball games on the East Coast were to begin.)

To believe that Rose was framed, one must, first of all, believe Rose, despite the statement in his April 1990 press release that "compulsive gambling makes you less than honest about your life. . . . Sometimes even I didn't remember what the real story was anymore."

One must assume that Janszen lied, even though he was not caught in a lie through the whole of the Rose investigation or in his testimony in several criminal trials that led to convictions. The one mark against Janszen's veracity is that he flunked his first lie detector test. A polygraph examiner retained by major-league baseball found some of his answers to be "deceptive in nature." He passed the next two polygraphs, finishing with a .667 average.

One must assume that bookmaker Ron Peters lied—and that he and Janszen got together to get their stories straight. What makes this especially unlikely is that Peters and Janszen were hardly friends. Working with federal drug agents in July 1988, Janszen, wearing a hidden microphone, bought one ounce of cocaine from

Peters, which led to a guilty plea by Peters on drug charges and a two-year prison term. In other words, Janszen set Peters up and got him sent to federal prison.

In addition, one must assume that someone, presumably Janszen, was capable of orchestrating this conspiracy against Rose. And few people who have followed the case consider this likely.

"If Janszen's lying, if he conned everybody, he's an absolute master. He should be running the CIA," says Murray Chass, who covered Rose's downfall for *The New York Times.*

Says Dowd, "Every word out of Janszen's mouth has been corroborated."

Finally, one must believe that a commissioner of baseball, in his first months on the job, would want to treat Rose unfairly, that he would find some gain in banning for life one of the most popular players in baseball history.

And that might be the most unlikely scenario of all.

Sports Illustrated, in its issue dated March 27, 1989, was the first publication to provide detail on what deep trouble Rose was in. Knowing that the *SI* story was imminent, Ueberroth had broken the news of baseball's probe of Rose two days before the magazine hit the newsstands. For the rest of the spring and summer, *Sports Illustrated* and numerous other publications continued with what must have seemed to Rose like an unrelenting barrage of allegations and attacks.

It would turn Rose bitter toward the press, which for so long had been his ally. In an interview early in March 1990 with Peter Pascarelli of *The National,* he said, "I don't know why they had to turn on me this way. It hurts."

Kahn, his authorized biographer, wrote in *Pete Rose: My Story* that the press had responded to Rose's troubles with "orgasmic glee." Rose's bruised feelings are understandable. But Kahn's view was wildly off base.

The press in Cincinnati, after ignoring the story at the start, included plenty of voices in support of Rose. The city's top-rated news anchor, Jerry Springer, the former mayor, offered up a steady diet of emotional defenses of Rose and strong denunciations of Giamatti on the two-minute commentaries he is afforded on his nightly newscasts. He alerted his viewers early on in the Pete Rose affair that they should not expect him to be a newsman; he would, instead, be a cheerleader. And he was, right to the end.

"Sorry, I'm sitting this one out," he announced in his commentary on March 22, 1989, the day the *Sports Illustrated* piece hit the newsstands. "I don't want any part of this posse chasing Pete's scalp. This time the lynch mob will have a riderless horse—mine. And it's not because I'm above it all, but rather because I still have a memory.

"I remember what Pete's done for this town and for baseball, and for every kid who wore a 14 on his jersey, slid headfirst into second at the local schoolyard pickup game, and who saw in Pete that you didn't have to be born with superior skills to make it in this world, that sheer hustle and determination and trying your best all the time was the real ticket to the top."

Two days later, Springer complained that baseball was drawing out the investigation of Rose, leaving him "twisting in the wind." Short of evidence that he bet against the Reds, Springer argued, they should leave him alone.

"But who is this Peter Ueberroth or Bart Giamatti to tell us, from some office in New York, who we like as manager of our hometown team?" Springer said in his March 24 commentary. "If there's illegalities, let the justice system decide.

"Short of that, we'll decide. It's our team, our town, our game. And Pete's done a helluva lot more for all three than any commissioner ever did."

As the evidence of Rose's gambling and unsavory friendships mounted, Springer, a lawyer, adopted a different tone. Sure, Pete had made some mistakes, he reasoned, but wasn't that part of his birthright as a hard-charging, always-hustling athlete? Shouldn't we have expected it? "But I guess we should've known that Pete lives like he plays, always hustling, always running, with headfirst slides," Springer observed on June 22. "And in life, like in baseball, when you do that, sometimes your uniform gets dirty."

When Giamatti died a week after he banished Rose, a sudden and shocking epilogue to the Rose affair, Springer praised the commissioner as a man of great achievement who genuinely loved the game, but he still took issue with his treatment of Rose. He began his September 1 commentary: "Last week, Bart Giamatti took the heart out of Pete Rose by banishing him from the game that is his life. 'Lifetime suspension,' he ruled. Today, in the saddest of ironies, Bart Giamatti had his own heart removed— suspension from life—the fifty-one year-old commissioner of the game he loved—dead." He added: "I still think he was dead wrong on Pete. Now, he's just dead."

The lead sports columnists for both of the city's dailies, Tim Sullivan of the *Enquirer* and Paul Dougherty of the *Post*, took a tough tone on Rose. But early on, both criticized baseball for dragging out the probe, until it became apparent that it was Rose's legal team delaying the proceedings. When the columnists called on Rose to resign long before he left baseball, neither seemed to do it with much glee.

"These are the saddest of possible words: Pete Rose must go," Sullivan wrote after the Dowd Report was released publicly in late June.

Rose gained sympathy as well as criticism from the national writers and broadcasters covering his story, many of whom had known him since he was a young player. Consider some of the headlines from around the nation (none are from Cincinnati papers) on stories and columns on the Rose case:

"For Pete's Sake, and Baseball's, Say It Ain't So"

"Rose Remains a Competitor"

"It's Time to Cut a Deal for Rose"

"A Banner for Rose Still Waves"

"Before Anything Else, Rose Deserves a Fair Shake"

"For Rose, One Year Is Enough"

"Guilty or Not, Pete Is Denied His Due"

"Pete Rose Needs Help, Not 'Life' "

"Rose: All He Wants Is a Fair Opportunity"

"Rose Says Probers Set Him Up"

"Probe Shouldn't Keep Rose Out of Shrine"

"Rose Rising to Occasion"

"Rose Still Belongs in the Hall of Fame"

"Why So Long in Pete Rose Inquiry?"

"Sad Day for Baseball if Bloom Is Off Rose"

"Beleaguered, but Still in Love with Baseball"

Does that sound like *orgasmic glee?* Do they sound like headlines for stories celebrating Rose's demise?

Most of Pete Rose's friends on the sports page were genuinely saddened by his gambling scandal. Especially before the release of the Dowd Report, they strained to see his point of view.

"Until this happened it was very hard to think of Pete as having an evil side," says Dick Schaap, who covered Rose's demise for ABC News. "It was hard to think of him as an embodiment of evil. He had a crude side, a misogynous side, all of those things, sure. But what's hard to think about is that he's really done something evil, premeditated, *bad*.

Says Jerome Holtzman: "Pete being cooperative with the press won him points. It wins anybody points. If a guy's an asshole to you he doesn't win points. Do you try to be fair with everyone? Sure. Does the guy who's not an asshole win more courtesies? Sure he does. That's human nature, isn't it?"

After the report's release, many columnists called for Rose's resignation as Reds manager, pleaded with him to get help for his gambling, to come clean, to seek mercy. But Rose's tone became only more arrogant and defiant.

"It was a hatchet job, a piece of crap," Rose said of the Dowd Report on July 31. "If people think this is all bad for baseball, I want them to know: It's not my fault. I didn't start this thing. I just want a fair hearing. If I get a fair shake, I will prove everybody wrong. Believe me, I think everybody in this world, you can find a little bit of dirt on anybody—if you want to dig enough."

When he was finally banished, *Miami Herald* sports editor and columnist Edwin Pope wrote, "If you're looking for sympathy for Pete Rose, sorry, wrong station. He got exactly what he deserved." But that was only after a long, protracted ordeal in which Rose showed he was willing to undo the whole power structure of baseball to save himself. The members of the toy department finally rose up in righteous indignation. They were angry at Rose, but who among the people who had admired Rose was *not* angry at him?

It's possible that Rose, out-of-control gambler that he was, put the brakes on before he bet baseball.

It's possible that Janszen and Peters formed an unholy alliance, cooked up their stories, phonied up records of Rose's nonexistent baseball wagering, and made everything match. (How telephone records from two years previous would have been made to fit into this scheme is a more difficult puzzle.)

It's possible that Rose was framed, that he bet on no games involving the Reds, no baseball games at all.

But what is much more probable, and much more reasonable to believe, is that Pete Rose bet on baseball and the Reds—and that in denying it he clings to one last lie.

The testimony and the documentary evidence gathered in the course of the investigation demonstrates that Pete Rose bet on baseball, and in particular, on games of the Cincinnati Reds Baseball Club, during the 1985, 1986 and 1987 seasons. That conclusion, from page 3 of the Dowd Report, was based largely on:

• *The testimony of Janszen.* He said that during the first half of the 1987 baseball season he bet nearly every night on Rose's behalf, including regular wagers of $2,000 per game on the Reds.

Janszen said he placed Rose's baseball bets through three sources: Peters, the golf pro turned bookie from Franklin, Ohio; "Val," a clerk for a bookmaker in New York who later was identified by baseball investigators as Richard Troy; and Steve Chevashore, a Florida man who allegedly was a "runner" for the same New York bookmaker. Telephone toll records showed that there were calls from Rose's house and hotel rooms to all three of these men, as well as numerous calls made to them by Janszen, frequently right after or before he had talked with Rose.

Janszen turned over to baseball's investigators (and to the FBI) three pages of "betting sheets"; two of them, dated April 10 and 11 (1987), listed baseball games and results, as well as pro basketball games and what appear to be point spreads on the basketball games. A third undated sheet listed college and pro football games, with the notation "five dimes" ($5,000) next to three of the college games. A retired FBI agent and handwriting expert hired by baseball, Richard E. Casey, concluded that the sheets were written by Rose.

Janszen also turned over to baseball a notebook that he said charted the bets he made for Rose.

• *The testimony of Peters.* He testified that he took Rose's baseball bets, including bets on the Reds to win, from Gioiosa in 1985 and 1986, and from Janszen and Danita Marcum in 1987. He also, on occasion, took bets directly from Rose, who refused to use a code number Peters had given him. Instead, according to Peters, Rose would call and say, "This is Pete."

Peters's testimony on the time frame when Rose was betting with him in 1987 jibed with Janszen's account. In addition, his version was supported by telephone records, which showed that the "telephone traffic" that had been directed toward New York, when Rose was supposedly placing baseball bets with bookies there, moved to Franklin, Ohio, when Rose was said to have switched to Peters—and when the written records of both Janszen and Peters indicated he had moved his betting to Peters.

In 1986 and 1987, Peters said, he took in $1 million in wagers from Rose on baseball and other professional sports and made "good money" off him. Rose bet between $14,000 and $34,000 a day on baseball in the summer of 1987, he said. In the beginning, when Gioiosa first brought him Rose as a customer, he said Gioiosa told him, "You'll love this guy's action; all he does is lose."

"And when he bet on baseball, did he bet on the Cincinnati Reds?" Dowd asked Peters.

"Yes he did," Peters answered in his sworn testimony.

"And was this at a time when he was manager of the Cincinnati Reds?"

"Yes, sir."

"Is there any doubt in your mind?"

"Absolutely not."

• *The testimony of Danita Marcum.* On occasions when Janszen was not available, she said she called Rose in the clubhouse, took down the teams he wanted to bet, and called them in to Peters. Telephone records kept by the Reds in 1987 showed that Rose took her calls on several occasions in the hour before game time.

• *The testimony of others who said they knew of Rose's baseball betting but had no direct involvement in it.* A friend of Janszen's, Jim Proctor, testified that he heard Janszen taking Rose's baseball bets over the speakerphone in Janszen's Corvette. "And he would say, 'Give me a dime [one thousand dollars] on this and give me a dime on that,' " Proctor said he heard Rose say over the car phone. ". . . After he hung up I said, 'You've got to be kidding me. Pete Rose is betting baseball?' And Paul looked back over at me and said, 'Yes. Can you believe that?' "

Dave Morgan, who worked as a clerk in Peters's bookmaking

business, said that Peters told him in the beginning of 1987, when the Reds were on a hot streak, that he was "getting murdered" by Pete Rose on baseball betting.

• *The Janszen tapes.* His tape-recorded conversations with Bertolini and Chevashore left no doubt that Rose had used both of them as conduits to bookmakers. Chevashore, like so many others, expressed frustration that Rose would not pay his gambling debts. On one of the tapes, Chevashore speaks of money Rose owes to the New York bookies: "You know what they said to me? The guys in the office, the bosses. They said, 'This guy probably did this before with other people.' "

• *The telephone records.* From the testimony of Janszen and Peters, as well as the written records kept by each man, baseball's investigators concluded that Rose had bet with the New York bookmaker on baseball through "Val" (Richard Troy, who got his nickname because he used to be a valet parker) and Steve Chevashore in April and the first half of May 1987, then moved to Peters beginning on May 17, 1987, when the New York bookie refused his action because he owed too much.

The Dowd Report tracked the calls, day by day, from April 17, 1987 to July 5, 1987. Some examples from the report:

April 27, 1987 was an off day for the Reds. Telephone records indicate Janszen called Chevashore at 4:23 p.m. The call lasted two minutes. Janszen called Val at 5:16 p.m. The call lasted two minutes. A call was placed from Pete Rose's home to Chevashore at 6:37 p.m. The call lasted four minutes. A call was placed from Pete Rose's home to Chevashore at 6:44 p.m. The call lasted two minutes. A call was placed from Pete Rose's home to Chevashore at 6:53 p.m. The call lasted five minutes.

On April 28, 1987, the Reds played the Braves in Cincinnati at 7:35 p.m. and lost 7–3. Telephone records indicate Janszen called Chevashore at 5:59 p.m. The call lasted one minute. Janszen called Chevashore at 6:16 p.m. The call lasted five minutes. Janszen called Pete Rose at the Reds clubhouse from his car phone at 6:43 p.m. The call lasted two minutes. Janszen called Pete Rose at the Reds clubhouse from his car phone at 6:52 p.m. The call lasted one minute. The Reds clubhouse records indicate that Janszen called Pete Rose twice, once at 6:45 p.m. and again at 6:55 p.m., from a number which has been determined to be

Janszen's car phone. Janszen called Chevashore at 6:57 p.m. The call lasted five minutes.

Beginning on May 17, the Dowd Report states, the "records show a pattern of telephone traffic prior to the beginning of each Reds game—home or away, night or day—between Janszen, Marcum, Rose and Peters." More examples:

On May 17, 1987, the Reds played the Cardinals in St. Louis at 2:15 p.m. and lost 10–2. Janszen was in St. Louis. [Janszen stayed in the team hotels when he traveled with Rose. He told Dowd the Reds paid for his rooms.] The phone traffic with Peters began on this day. Telephone records indicate Janszen called Peters from St. Louis at 10:38 a.m. The call lasted two minutes. Janszen called Peters from St. Louis at 10:54 a.m. The call lasted one minute. . . .

May 18, 1987 was an off day for the Reds. Telephone records indicate Janszen called Ron Peters from the Westin Hotel in Chicago at 11:27 a.m. The call lasted one minute. Janszen called Peters from the Westin Hotel at 6:08 p.m. The call lasted seven minutes. A call was placed from Pete Rose's room at the Westin Hotel in Chicago to Peters. A call was placed from Pete Rose's room at the Westin Hotel in Chicago to Janszen. [The hotel could not place the time of calls that were not made on credit cards.]

On May 19, 1987, the Reds played the Cubs in Chicago at 2:20 p.m. and lost 9–2. Telephone records indicate Janszen called Peters from the Westin Hotel in Chicago at 5:54 p.m. The call lasted two minutes. Janszen called Peters from the Westin Hotel in Chicago at 6:03 p.m. The call lasted six minutes. Janszen called Peters from Chicago at 6:16 p.m. The call lasted one minute. Two calls were placed from Pete Rose's room at the Westin Hotel in Chicago to Janszen's home. Fourteen calls were placed from Pete Rose's hotel room in Chicago to the sports line.

On June 20, 1987, the Reds played the Braves in Atlanta at 1:20 p.m. [Janszen was not on this trip.] Telephone records indicate a call was placed from Pete Rose's home to Atlanta Fulton County Stadium at 12:58 p.m. The call lasted three minutes. Three calls were placed from Pete Rose's home to Peters at 1:13 p.m., 1:16 p.m. and 1:18 p.m. Each call lasted one minute. A call was placed from Pete Rose's home at 1:17 p.m. to the golf course in Franklin, Ohio that Peters frequented. The call lasted one minute. Two more calls were placed from Pete Rose's home to

Peters at 7:21 p.m. and 7:46 p.m. The calls lasted two minutes and one minute. . . .

June 29, 1987 was an off day for the Reds. Telephone records indicate Janszen called Peters at 4:41 p.m. and 4:48 p.m. The calls lasted one minute each. . . . Calls were placed from Pete Rose's home to Peters at 6:28 p.m., 6:33 p.m. and 7:09 p.m. The calls lasted two minutes, one minute, one minute and five minutes.

On June 30, 1987, the Reds played the Astros in Cincinnati at 7:35 p.m. and won 5–4 in ten innings. Telephone records indicate Marcum called Pete Rose at the Reds clubhouse at 6:40 p.m.

The banking records. At the very least, the checks to fictitious signees (twenty-one of them to Bertolini in one year alone, for $8,000 each), the checks to Mike Fry, and the numerous checks for cash established that Rose owed large amounts of money. So did the sale of his memorabilia, including such cherished items as the bat and ball involved in the record-breaking 4,192d hit. Coupled with the gambling evidence, his debts were almost certainly to bookies.

Rose also acknowledged that he took $109,000 in a satchel to spring training with him in 1989. That was his share of a January 1989 Pik Six wager at Turfway. (For a short stretch he kept the money in his refrigerator, and would tell visitors, "If you wanna see some cold cash, open the fridge.")

Even with all the unpaid debts to bookies, the bruised feelings, and the friendships gone bad, the testimony most damaging to Pete Rose was not given by someone who was out to hurt him. The testimony that doomed him was his own.

Rose did not grasp that a score was being kept, that he needed to tell the truth. Or he may just have been incapable of it. Either way, much of what he said in that basement conference room of the Bergamo Center for Lifelong Learning was not even remotely credible.

Rose claimed that he had never used Janszen to place his bets with bookies. Not baseball bets, not bets of any kind.

Why then did Janszen call you so often at the ballpark, Dowd asked, sometimes, two, three, or even four times in the hour leading up to the game? "He called me a lot in the clubhouse,"

Rose acknowledged. "Every time he wanted tickets to the game."

The toll records showed numerous calls to Peters, Troy, and Chevashore, all of whom Rose denied betting with, made from Rose's home. Some were made during the time he was at the ballpark, so Janszen was obviously at his house without him. But dozens of them were made on Reds' off-days and late at night after home games, when Rose was presumably at home. And then there were the calls to them made from Rose's hotel rooms. Could Rose shed light on any of these calls?

None, Rose told Dowd. He couldn't explain them, except to venture a guess that Janszen was gambling on his own, and using his phones and his name to place the bets.

With all the hours he spent with him on the road and at home, on the couch with him late at night watching ball games, Rose must have known plenty about Janszen's habits. Dowd asked Rose: If all of Janszen's calls to bookies were made on his own behalf—including the ones charged to Rose's home phone and hotel rooms—had he known that Janszen liked to gamble?

No, Rose replied, he had no idea. "He's a big boy. Real big," Rose added, implying that he didn't involve himself or have any knowledge of Janszen's business.

Apparently, when Janszen was making the calls to bookies late at night from Rose's house, or from Rose's hotel room, Rose never overheard him or asked what the calls were about.

He showed a similar lack of curiosity with regard to Gioiosa, who was the only person through whom he acknowledged placing bets—but just bets on basketball and football. "Well, what I'm telling you is the only guy I ever bet with is Tommy Gioiosa," he told Dowd.

He did admit to traveling once with Gioiosa to Jonathan's Cafe in Frankin, Ohio, which was the luncheonette owned by Ron Peters and one of the places he conducted his bookmaking operation. Both Mike Fry and Peters testified that Fry had gone along. Rose at first seemed unsure if Fry was with them, and then vehemently denied it. Finally, he decided he'd never been with Fry except at Gold's Gym.

"Okay, was Mike Fry with you on that day?" Dowd asked.

"I don't think so," Rose replied.

"Are you sure?"

"No, I'm not sure. . . ."

"Could have been?"

"He could have been. I mean, I can't—the reason I'm hesitating—I'm trying to think what car we took. Because if we took his car, there's only two seats in the damn thing. And my car was a Porsche then and there's only two seats there. I think there was only two of us. . . . Like I said a minute ago, and I'll repeat it, okay? To my knowledge I've never seen Mike Fry outside of Gold's Gym. Except in the parking lot when he's leaving."

Peters testified that the purpose of Rose's trip to his restaurant was for Rose to collect his gambling winnings for the week. Normally, Gioiosa (and later Janszen) did this without Rose. On Mondays, Rose's proxy would either make the forty-five minute drive to Franklin or meet Peters somewhere in between, where the money would be exchanged. Most weeks Rose lost, but in this one, late in 1985, he had won, which was perhaps one reason why he had chosen to come along.

According to Peters, the Cincinnati contingent had traveled in separate Porsches—Rose in one, Fry and Gioiosa in the other. Rose's winnings were $36,000 or $37,000. They sat down at a table, Rose autographed a bat "To Jonathan's Cafe," and then Gioiosa and Peters adjourned to a private spot. "I'm not sure exactly where," Peters said. "Maybe back in the restrooms or back in the kitchen or somewhere. It was not out in front in the open."

At that point, Peters handed over the money to Gioiosa. "He stuck it in his sock," Peters recalled.

In Rose's version of the trip to Franklin, Gioiosa said he had some business to transact, so Rose hopped in the car and went along with him without ever asking him what the business was. "I rode with Tommy. He said he had to do something—had to deliver something to somebody."

Not long after they got there, Gioiosa and Peters excused themselves and disappeared for a few minutes. Rose didn't ask then what that was about, nor did he raise the question with Gioiosa during the ride back to Cincinnati.

"They went in the back and talked about something," Rose said. "And it wasn't any of my damn business. And they came back out and sat down and we finished and we left."

No one who knows Rose would believe that he would take a ninety-minute round-trip with Gioiosa, his lackey, and never ask him what it was about. And that he would then watch him go into a back room to conduct some business and not inquire about that either. (The dealings in the back room, in particular, had the smell of criminal activity, which would have been sure to get Rose interested.)

Rose says that he did not know Peters was a bookmaker, and that he never asked the names of the people Gioiosa booked his bets with—"He knew I didn't want to be around bookmakers."

In any court proceeding, a witness's overall credibility is used in weighing his testimony on the key points. Although baseball's probe was an administrative proceeding and not a trial in a court of law, Rose did not fare well by this standard. His testimony on numerous questions was not credible, which made his denial that he bet baseball, in the face of the credible testimony of others, all the more difficult to believe.

At his deposition, Dowd showed Rose the betting slips and told him the handwriting expert had judged them to be in his hand. "I couldn't tell you if it's my handwriting," Rose said. "I don't recognize it as my handwriting."

Dowd also played Rose the tapes in which Bertolini and Chevashore spoke of the debts he owed to bookies. Rose said he didn't understand them.

"An amusing tape," Rose commented after listening to the April 4, 1988, conversation between Bertolini and Janszen in which they both lamented the money Rose owed to them as well as to bookmakers. Janszen had taped the conversation for federal agents. Rose conjectured that Bertolini was making things up because he suspected Janszen was taping.

"Making up negative information about you, his friend? The guy he'd die for?" Dowd interjects.

"He'd die for me but he knows I hate that guy he's talking to," Rose replies.

And if Bertolini wasn't making things up to throw Janszen off the track, then he was simply lying. Rose adds, growing impatient over the questions about his alleged debts. "I'm going to say this one more time," he tells Dowd. "I don't owe anybody a dime. New York; New England; New Mexico. A dime. Nothing."

In denying that he booked his bets through anyone but Gioiosa, Rose counted on his former housemate's loyalty. The strategy backfired.

Gioiosa did refuse to give a deposition to Dowd. But just before he was sentenced in February 1990 to five years in jail on cocaine trafficking and tax charges, he told WKRC-TV in Cincinnati that Rose had indeed bet on baseball.

Gioiosa's statement bolstered the already overwhelming case that Rose bet baseball. Not only had he lived with Rose and been a frequent companion for a decade, but Gioiosa was the only person Rose acknowledged involving in his gambling. Gioiosa, like Peters, had no reason to want to help Janszen. At his trial, Janszen was one of the key witnesses for the prosecution. He helped put Gioiosa in jail, just as he had Peters.

One of the charges Gioiosa was convicted on was a conspiracy count for a crime that he committed on Rose's behalf, which was claiming all of a $47,646 Pik Six ticket at Turfway. The prosecution said that Rose owned most of that winning ticket, and put on seven witnesses who said he had asked Gioiosa to claim it because Gioiosa was in a lower tax bracket.

The day after Gioiosa broke his silence, Rose held a press conference before delivering a speech at the University of Florida. He once again denied betting on baseball, and said of Gioiosa, "I feel sorry for him, but if you break the law, bad things are going to happen to you."

That was more of Rose's typical disloyalty and ingratitude to friends, perhaps one of the most outrageous examples: Gioiosa signed the ticket because Rose asked him to, then Rose wrote him off as just another one of his friends who had gone bad.

A. Bartlett Giamatti, Renaissance scholar, former Yale president, and baseball junkie, liked to talk about society's "moral purchase." It was his fancy way of referring to an individual's duty to do what was right, no matter how unpleasant or unpopular.

Giamatti also had a famously lofty way of expressing his love for baseball. In his introduction to the second volume of *The Armchair Book of Baseball*, he wrote of the game's post–Civil War origins, its beginnings in "the surge toward fraternalism" and its continuing hold in the nation:

> Genteel in its American origins, proletarian in its development, egalitarian in its demands and appeal, effortless in its adaptation to nature, raucous, hard-nosed, and glamorous as a

profession, expanding with the country like fingers unfolding from a fist, image of a lost past, evergreen reminder of America's best promises, baseball fitted and still fits America. It fits so well because it embodies the interplay of individual and group that we so love and because it conserves our longing for the rule of law while licensing our resentment of lawgivers.

. . . Law—defined as a complex of formal rules, agreed-upon boundaries, authoritative arbiters, custom, and a set of symmetrical opportunities and demands—is enshrined in baseball. Indeed, the layout of the field shows baseball's essential passion for and reliance on precise proportions and clearly defined limits, all the better to give shape to energy and provide an arena for equality and expression.

Lurking in this thicket of metaphor and literary and historical allusion is an essential truth about baseball's troubled summer of 1989: Pete Rose and Bart Giamatti were fatally mismatched.

Giamatti loved the rules. Rose loved to break them—whether that meant sliding headfirst when others went in feetfirst, getting more hits than was supposed to be possible, playing into his midforties, cheating on his wife at home as well as on the road, or ignoring the large-print sign at the entrance of every major-league clubhouse that warned against betting on baseball.

Giamatti valued the association of individuals, and said upon leaving Yale: "My goal has been to encourage jointness, to push people to think of affiliations rather than to operate as solo entrepreneurs."

Rose was the ultimate clubhouse free agent, who, when it was suggested that the money players earned from postgame radio appearances be pooled for team parties, said he'd just as soon keep his for himself.

Confronted with Janszen's allegations, his documentation and his impressive memory of events, it's difficult to imagine any baseball commissioner who would *not* have moved against Rose. But it's also difficult to imagine one who would have done so with Giamatti's fervor and unyielding conviction in the rightness of his cause.

Rose was no mere lawbreaker. He was an affront to Giamatti's unique vision of the game.

*   *   *

Dowd's prediction that Rose's legal team would challenge Giamatti became a self-fulfilling prophecy when Dowd unintentionally gave Rose the ammunition he needed—a letter to Ron Peters's sentencing judge, written by Dowd and signed by Giamatti, attesting to Peters's "truthful cooperation."

Federal judge Carl Rubin received the letter on April 18, 1989, and instantly recognized it for what it was—a strategic blunder on baseball's part.

The letter should never have been signed by Giamatti, who by the rules of baseball's disciplinary process would sit in judgment of Rose. John Dowd, baseball's special counsel in the Rose probe, had actually written the letter and he rather than Giamatti should have signed it.

The other serious mistake was to say that Peters had been "truthful," rather than simply cooperative in giving his testimony. Trying to defend the letter, Giamatti gave it a legalistic reading and tried to claim that it meant Dowd—and not the commissioner—had found Peters truthful. But since Giamatti had been the one to sign the letter, his argument made little sense, no matter how ardently or eloquently he tried to make it.

The letter was something Rose's legal team could use to great advantage, and what Rubin did next assured that they would.

After receiving it, he called Reuven Katz and left a message on his answering machine at home.

"My wife and I got home late that night, and there was a message from Judge Rubin, saying that, I believe he said that he had received something that he thought I ought to know about, and would I call him the first thing in the morning," Katz would later remember.

The Cincinnati connection was at work. Pete Rose's hometown was about to close ranks behind him.

Reuven Katz, Harvard Law class of 1950, is a dapper little man with the bearing of a European count. He practices in areas of the law that do not generally make attorneys famous—estate planning, banking, corporate work. But because of his representation of Pete Rose, he's probably the best-known lawyer in Cincinnati, which cannot have hurt the rest of his practice.

Few people think of Katz as a "sports agent." He represents only a handful of athletes—Johnny Bench is another—and makes sure that the public knows he charges them by the hour, rather than by taking a percentage of their contracts as most agents do.

Katz was a sort of father figure to Rose. He watched his bank accounts, cosigned his checks, advised him on his investments, and told him how much he should spend each month. Rose often told people that Katz had him on an "allowance." According to Janszen, Rose used to tell people that if he ever got in any sort of legal trouble in Cincinnati, he was sure Katz could take care of it before it became public.

When the scope of Rose's gambling became public, the reaction of many Cincinnatians was that Rose must have somehow broken from Katz's leash—that Katz either did not know what Rose was doing or had tried to control him but could not.

But if Katz was naive about Rose's gambling and his gambling debts, he remained so partly because of questions he apparently chose not to ask. In 1987, he authorized and signed a $34,000 check, which Rose needed to pay off a gambling debt. The check was made payable to Tommy Gioiosa. According to Rose's testimony to John Dowd, he asked Katz to authorize the check after Gioiosa hed told him that bookies were threatening to burn his house down.

Rose said he told Katz he needed the money to pay Gioiosa, but he could not remember if he specified to his lawyer that the money was needed to pay off a gambling debt. "Did you tell him it was for a gambling debt?" Dowd asked Rose. "No, I don't believe I did, " Rose replied.

Katz was asked about signing the check in a depostion he gave to baseball's lawyers. As Katz described it, he sometimes authorized checks from Rose's account without inquiring about why the money was needed. "Sometimes Pete would call and say, 'I want—' he would call and say, 'Reuv, do me a favor. Will you'— it's always, do me a favor . . ."

Dowd asked Katz: "So, Pete Rose called you up said, 'Reuven, can you do me a favor? Can you write a check for $34,000 to Tommy Gioiosa?' "

"Yes," Katz replied.

"Did you ask him what it was for?"

"No sir."

"Did he tell you?"

"No sir."

Most people who know Katz hold him in the highest esteem.

"He's the most ethical and moral person I know," says Reds broadcaster Marty Brennaman, who is also Katz's client. "Whatever Reuven says, you can take to the bank."

(Katz declined to be interviewed for this book. His quotes are taken from a deposition he gave in connection with Rose's 1989 lawsuit against baseball, which sought to block Giamatti from sitting in judgment on him. Judge Rubin also declined to be interviewed. An aide in his office said that his talking about the Rose case would be a violation of "the canons of judicial ethics.")

After getting the intriguing message on his recording machine, Katz, as instructed, called Rubin first thing the next morning.

"I was put through to the judge, and the judge says, 'I have a communication here I think you ought to see,'" Katz recalled.

"And I said, 'When would you like for me to see that?'

"And he said, 'Why don't you come right over?'"

Katz and Rubin were boyhood friends, "friends for 60 years," Rubin told *The Cincinnati Post*. They had once belonged to an informal club of young lawyers who met once a week over breakfast to talk about cases and careers. As a corporate lawyer, Katz didn't spend much time in court, so he had to ask his old friend where his office was. He found out that Rubin's chambers in the federal courthouse were right across the street from him.

"I hurried over, and I waited for a moment or so, and then I was brought into his chambers," Katz recalled. "At that point, he showed me the letter. . . . He said, I think you ought to read this."

The letter related to the criminal case brought against Peters by the U.S. attorney's office. Neither Rose nor Katz had anything to do with Peters's case; they had no legal standing in it. And Judge Rubin had nothing to do with baseball's investigation of Rose.

In other words, there was no reason for them to be talking about Giamatti's letter—except that Judge Rubin had discovered a way to help Pete Rose, and wanted to share it with Katz. Rubin was already on record as a big admirer of Rose's. He was the jurist who spoke so glowingly of Rose while Rose was in his courtroom as a plaintiff in the 1981 Jeep giveaway case against the IRS.

Katz read the five-paragraph letter in front of Rubin, and then they discussed it. "I commented upon my immediate dismay over the letter," said Katz. "And he commented about his surprise at the letter.

". . . He said to me that morning, 'Do you have any suggestions as to what I should do with the letter,' or something like that. Did

I want to recommend something or suggest something to him?

"And I said to him, it was of such a serious nature, that I would really like to think about it, if that was all right with him, and that I would. And would it be all right if I came back to see him the following morning. I told him I wanted to discuss it with my associates, as well.

"And he said, 'That's fine. I'm in no hurry. Call me tomorrow and we'll pick a time.' "

Although they had agreed that Rubin would not make any moves without first consulting Katz, the judge then plowed ahead without him, according to Katz. The result could hardly have been more pleasing to Katz and his legal team.

On April 21, he placed the Giamatti letter into the court file, and at the same time called in Peters's lawyer and the assistant U.S. attorney who prosecuted Peters. He had a court stenographer attend the session and her transcription was then placed in the court file. Two days later, the Giamatti letter, and Rubin's angry reaction to it, ended up in the newspapers.

Just like Jerry Springer and so many other Cincinnatians, federal judge Rubin thought Rose was getting a raw deal.

"I don't want to get into an imbroglio involving Pete Rose," the papers quoted the judge as saying in the conference. "Now, it is conceivable—I guess the odds are 1 in 3—that if you indict him [on tax charges], that I may draw that indictment. . . . There is evidence here, in my opinion, of a vendetta against Pete Rose.

"Again, I don't care, but it seems to me that whatever cooperation Mr. Peters gave them on their investigation is totally and thoroughly irrelevant to any charges against Peters, and the idea of confusing the two of them, I just find very offensive."

Rubin, of course, could have simply disregarded the Giamatti letter in determining what sentence to give Peters. Judges get such letters all the time. They can take them into account or not; they rarely make a public issue of them.

A few days after speaking out, Rubin said he wished he hadn't, and he at the same time recused himself from sentencing Peters. "I should have kept my mouth shut," he told a reporter, adding that the Rose investigation "is really none of my business."

But if Rubin's intention was to score one for the home team, to help Rose, he had already achieved that.

Katz, in his deposition, said Rubin's actions—entering the letter in the public record, calling the conference, then holding a mini–press conference in his office—had come "as a complete surprise to me."

Only later did Rubin call Katz in to tell him all of what he'd done. "He said, 'Would you like a copy, a transcript of the proceedings?' And I said, 'I would very much like a transcript of that proceeding.' "

Armed with the letter and the comments of his longtime friend, the irate federal judge, Katz knew just what to do. He told the press that the letter proved what Rose's side had suspected all along: Giamatti was not open-minded; he had prejudged Rose. He should not be allowed to be "the judge, jury, and appellate court."

For the next four months, with a case that consisted almost entirely of that one letter—the strategic blunder—Rose's lawyers were able to keep Giamatti at bay. Rose was able to stay in baseball and draw his half-million-a-year salary. And pay his lawyers, too.

Rose and his lawyers hammered away at Giamatti, saying the letter was proof that he had prejudged the case. If Peters said Rose had bet on baseball, and Giamatti considered his testimony to have been "truthful," then how could he sit in judgment of Rose?

On June 19, a week before Rose was scheduled to have his hearing in front of Giamatti, Rose's lawyers filed suit against the commissioner, major-league baseball, and the Reds. They sought to have Giamatti replaced by "an impartial decision-maker" because of his "displayed bias and outrageous conduct."

It's possible that nothing in the whole Rose affair cast Cincinnati in a harsher light than the decision issued later that month by Judge Norbert Nadel. In an extraordinary, nationally televised Sunday court session, Nadel restrained major-league baseball from moving against Rose—and the Reds from firing him. (By having his job guaranteed by court order, Rose was for a short time the most secure manager since Connie Mack, who was also his club's owner.)

In issuing his ruling, Nadel said, "It therefore appears to this court at this point that the commissioner of baseball has prejudged Peter Edward Rose. We further find that the hearing set for tomorrow in New York before the commissioner of baseball would be futile and illusory and the outcome a foregone conclusion."

Numerous legal experts said the decision had no basis in law. Courts do occasionally overturn the outcome of administrative proceedings, like baseball's probe of Rose, but they almost never intervene, as Nadel did, before the process has run its course. The judge himself spoke of entering "uncharted" legal territory.

Newspaper columnists, including those in Cincinnati, lambasted it as a shameless hometown call issued by a judge facing reelection. Even one of Nadel's colleagues on the bench indicated as much: Judge William Matthews told *The Cincinnati Post* that Nadel had "a tough decision to make with the hometown crowd watching."

Rose's lawsuit was a direct challenge to the historic authority of the baseball commissioner, and a more direct challenge to Giamatti personally, who had only held the job two months. And that's exactly how Giamatti responded to it. Not just Rose's but also Giamatti's future in baseball was at stake. The commissioner was no athlete, but he was competitive. He dug in. He was determined not to lose.

According to Dowd, throughout the summer of legal maneuvering between Rose's lawyers and baseball's lawyers, "Bart would role-play. Constantly. He would say, 'OK, what does his lawyer do next? And if this happens, *then* what does he do?' He would never have given up his role. If it had gone all the way up to the U.S. Supreme Court, and they said that only someone else could convene a hearing, then there would have been no hearing. That's how firm he was on that point."

After Nadel's unfavorable ruling, Giamatti told the press, "I have absolutely no prejudgment nor prejudice regarding Pete Rose. We will contest this matter tooth and nail."

As so often happens, the central issue in the Rose case—whether or not he bet on baseball—became fuzzed once the case entered the courts.

The questions pondered first by Nadel, and then by a federal judge, were: Could Giamatti judge Rose fairly in light of the Peters letter? (Even while he was alive, the answer to that question was unknowable.) Had the investigation been fair? At what point, if any, should the judiciary intervene in major-league baseball's internal disciplinary process?

As the summer wore on, the public may have asked another question: If given the opportunity to convene a hearing, could Giamatti shed his tooth-and-nail attitude and become a fair-minded arbiter?

Rose was perfectly within his rights to raise the questions and to pursue his case in court, although the sports press criticized him because his case detracted from the games on the field. It was said that Charlie Hustle, with his livelihood and good name in peril, was fighting too hard and too long. His struggle was holding an entire season hostage.

Rose's lawyers succeeded in postponing his banishment. What they could not do, through their legal wrangling, was make the evidence against him disappear—the testimony from his former close associates, the canceled checks, betting slips, betting notebooks, and telephone toll records.

Could Giamatti have held a fair hearing?

Did Rose bet baseball?

The questions, ultimately, were unrelated.

Any fair-minded person would have found that Rose wagered on the game.

So did Giamatti, whatever his state of mind was. If the commissioner prejudged Rose, if he made up his mind before all the evidence was in—which Dowd and others insist he did not—it did not make Rose's baseball betting any less of a fact.

While Rose's lawyers fought his legal battle, he continued to manage his baseball team. All the while, he was trailed by dozens of print and broadcast reporters and dogged by the same unpleasant questions in every town he visited.

A CBS television crew (producer, cameraman, sound technician) kept a camera and microphone trained on him before and after every game, from early March through August 24. Sometimes they would shoot him as he walked through an airport. Rose periodically asked, "Don't you have enough pictures of me yet?" At another point he mused, "How much money do you think that's costing CBS?"

Some of the veteran sports journalists talked of being on their third "Rose watch," the first two being the 44-game hit streak and the Cobb chase. This one, of course, was different. It was a deathwatch—staying by Rose's side, checking his pulse each time his situation worsened.

Parts of Pete Rose had already died. Parts of the myth.

His boyish enthusiasm, celebrated for so long, had now been flipped onto its less attractive side, and was now being cast as the immaturity of a forty-eight-year-old man who had never learned to obey the rules.

Even his doggedness, his unwillingness to give up, the *hustle* in Charlie Hustle, was being turned against him. Why didn't he just leave the stage and let everyone enjoy the pennant races?

The myth of Rose's popularity within baseball was also shattered. Few players spoke out in his defense, and those who did offered only lukewarm support. Johnny Bench said Rose should resign, and that if he bet on baseball he didn't deserve to be in the Hall of Fame. "The winner has to be baseball," Rose's former teammate said. "The winner can't be any individual."

You had to empathize with Rose in the spring and summer of 1989. It was as if Richard Nixon, at the height of Watergate, had to hold court on the White House lawn for several hours a day while reporters peppered him with questions. Eventually, even the reporters might have felt sorry for him.

In the ballpark, Rose had nowhere to hide. Except for the forty-five minutes leading up to the game, a manager's office is a public place, open to the media.

Rose got a lot of credit, deserved, for the grace and sense of humor he showed while his career disintegrated. Numerous columnists harked back to Rose's response in 1979 to the filing of divorce papers against him—how that had set him off on one of the greatest hitting tears of his career.

Yes, this was the part of Charlie Hustle that still lived in 1989: the manly resistance to inner turmoil. He could not be rocked.

Before a Reds-Phillies game on April 30, a writer, his voice filled with admiration, asked Rose about his superhuman composure: "You know, Pete, you just don't look like this troubles you."

Rose's answer was a rare admission. "I'm acting," he said.

The more perceptive people around Rose already knew that. One of them was Larry Starr, the trainer.

"I'm a big fan of Elvis," Starr said early in July, "and I'm reading this book on him right now called *Are You Lonesome Tonight?* And it's scaring the hell out of me. People who reflect back on Elvis Presley now say, 'Who were his friends? Where were they when he was taking all these drugs? Where were they when he was not sleeping?'

"So much of it reminds me of Pete Rose. The more powerful men are, the more difficult they are to reach. They dominate you. If you try to help them, they fend you off."

In early May, Starr sent Rose home from a Reds road trip—the team was about to move on from Montreal to New York—for the announced reason that he had bronchitis. And Rose did have a severe upper respiratory infection. But what caused Starr to insist that Rose go home was that his blood pressure had risen to dangerous levels. "We were getting readings of one eighty, one ninety over one ten," Starr said.

Throughout the summer, Starr was also laying the groundwork to do an "intervention" on Rose—to prevail upon him, if necessary, to check into a mental health care unit. He and the Reds' team physician, Dr. Warren Harding III, had talked at length about it, and Starr had also discussed the possibility with Murray Cook, the team's general manager.

Starr had been involved in interventions with his mother, who was an alcoholic, and also with a player who had a drug problem. "In the long run, it did not succeed," Starr says of the treatment his mother received. "She still succumbed to the disease. But at least I had the peace of mind to know we tried.

"What you do in an intervention is confront somebody and tell them they need help. With Pete, it wouldn't just be me. It would be me and Dr. Harding and [Reds owner] Marge Schott and Reuven Katz and Murray Cook and his best friend and whoever. You tell the person, 'We're doing this because it's in your best interests and because we love you and think you need help.'

"Right now," Starr said in July 1989, "I don't yet feel that sense of urgency. At least outwardly his mental state is still confident. But if it has to be done, I'll have no fear of doing it, because I love Pete, and I feel very highly for what he has achieved and what input he could have in baseball for the rest of his life."

There were others who feared Rose to be in an even more precarious mental state.

"He had become self-delusionary," says Marty Brennaman. "When my name surfaced in the report as someone who knew about his [football and basketball] gambling, he said to me, 'What do you know about my gambling activities?'

"I said to him, 'Pete, need I remind you? About all the football games we had discussions on about the [betting] line, and what I thought about the line? And the betting sheets you showed me?'

"He said, "Oh, shit, Marty, it don't matter, does it?' But he had deluded himself into thinking that I didn't know."

Brennaman believed that Rose in midsummer was despondent, dangerously so. Brennaman said on July 4, "Some people have talked about the ultimate—suicide. I think that's possible."

On August 21, 1989, a Monday, the Reds beat the Cubs 6–5 at Wrigley Field. The last out came at 10:10 P.M., Chicago time.

Pete Rose bounded out of the Reds dugout and shook hands with relief pitcher John Franco, then stood along the first-base line and greeted the other eight players as they left the field. This would be his last moment in major-league baseball.

Early the next morning, he left the team and returned to Cincinnati to be with his wife, Carol, for the birth of their second child, daughter Cara Shea.

On August 23, Rose did not return to Chicago to manage his ballclub. The boy who had wanted nothing more than to play baseball, who had pounded the ball against the wall at Schultes Fish House and played catch in Geneva, New York, when his minor-league team was not practicing or playing, passed up a last chance to pull on a major-league uniform.

Late that afternoon, just as the Reds were finishing their game in Chicago, lawyers for Rose and for baseball completed an agreement that they had been negotiating on and off for most of the spring and summer.

The final terms amounted to Rose's unconditional surrender.

He accepted the ultimate penalty allowed under the bylaws of major-league baseball—a lifetime suspension, with the right to apply for reinstatement after one year. That right is spelled out in baseball's bylaws for all cases calling for lifetime suspensions. But of the fourteen previous individuals issued such suspensions, none had ever been reinstated. There had even been several posthumous applications filed by kin of banished players, including one from relatives of Shoeless Joe Jackson. All were rejected.

Rose got no guarantee from Giamatti that he would be the exception, only a promise that he would be considered. It was, however, in Rose's personality to believe deeply that he would be the exception—to *anything*.

The agreement even took something away from Rose that he had started with: an option to fight the commissioner's decision in a court of law.

"Peter Edward Rose acknowledges that the Commissioner has a factual basis to impose the penalty provided herein, and hereby accepts the penalty imposed on him by the Commissioner and agrees not to challenge that penalty in court or otherwise," the document reads.

The agreement gave major-league baseball everything it wanted and needed. The agreement removed a known gambler, a perceived *baseball* gambler, from its ranks, probably permanently, and it reaffirmed the authority of the commissioner.

The five-page document signed by Rose and Giamatti did give Rose one concession. It was this sentence: "Nothing in this agreement shall be deemed either an admission or a denial by Peter Edward Rose of the allegation that he bet on any major-league baseball game."

But the penalty he accepted was no more lenient than if there *had* been a finding of baseball betting. Viewed as a plea bargain, the Rose-Giamatti agreement was analogous to an accused murderer bargaining his charge down to manslaughter but at the same time accepting the death penalty.

Why, after battling Giamatti for six months, would Rose accept this deal? There were several reasons.

The first was that Rose had no defense to the charge of baseball betting. In addition, what he had admitted to in his sworn testimony, the illegal gambling on other sports and consorting with gamblers and other undesirables, was by baseball precedent enough to earn him a year's suspension and quite possibly more.

Rose's lawyers had hoped to be able to impeach the testimony of Dowd's key witnesses but could not. In fact, one of their efforts in this direction turned out to be laughable.

They had obtained a jailhouse interview with a man named Scott Estes, who had served time with Michael Fry in a federal prison in Terre Haute, Indiana. Estes told an investigator for Rose's legal team that Fry had bragged to him that he and Janszen had framed Pete Rose.

In *Pete Rose: My Story*, Roger Kahn cites Estes's statement as evidence of the shoddiness of the Dowd Report. "One Scott Estes has provided a sworn statement that he personally heard Michael

Fry, a convicted felon and former Janszen associate, state that he and Janszen conspired to frame Pete Rose," Kahn writes.

Fry was not one of the witnesses who said Rose bet baseball. He said he had only known Rose to bet on other sports, and it was his personal opinion that Rose would not wager on his own game.

Dowd's investigators did some research of their own on Estes. He had pleaded guilty in 1987 to a federal indictment charging him with making a false report of consumer tampering. The charge arose from a television interview Estes had given in which he claimed to have swallowed a straight pin inside a Hostess Ding Dong cake.

Estes was frank about his propensity to lie. In a 1988 letter to federal judge Sarah Evans Barker, who sentenced him on the consumer fraud rap, he wrote, "I'm sure there are a lot of people who are still wondering why I swallowed a straight pin and why I lied on TV about it. It's simple, I got attention and later thought I could get some money out of the deal. I was a liar, and it was just another lie."

This was to be one of Rose's witnesses to shoot down the Dowd Report.

Another reason Rose folded was the specter of his own encroaching criminal problems.

His battle with Giamatti was largely one of public relations—an effort to make the baseball fans of America believe that he, "a modern-day legend," as his lawsuit described him, was being railroaded by the bearded former college president and the testimony of convicted felons.

Rose carped to Dowd about the convicted criminals who were ratting on him. "And you know as well as I, those guys could have a quintet the last three months," he said. "Because they're all singing. They're all singing a lot. They have to sing or they'll be in Sing Sing."

Rose's lawyers and supporters pointed out at every turn that many of his accusers were convicted felons. Dope dealers, no less. Of course, in a bookmaking or narcotics case, the key witnesses are rarely upstanding citizens. They're usually people involved in the same activities. Every day, in criminal courts all over America, defense lawyers make the argument: *How can you believe this convicted felon, this thief, this drug dealer?* The argument does not usually work, unless the lawyer can impeach the witness's credibility and not just his character.

But in Rose's case, it was a persuasive argument with the public. No one wanted to see an American hero sold down the river by the likes of the Gold's Gym crowd. Even *Sports Illustrated,* which broke the first details of the Rose investigation, said as much in the "Scorecard" section of its April 17, 1989 issue.

"Has Janszen been telling the truth?" the magazine asked. "Rose denies betting on baseball—or indeed engaging in any illicit gambling and it would be hard to accept the word of a felon over that of one of baseball's greatest heroes, even one as tainted as Rose." In that same piece, the magazine did quote an unnamed federal agent as saying that Janszen's credibility was "ten on a scale of ten."

Another problem with the how-can-you-believe-a-convicted-felon approach was that by midsummer Rose's lawyers knew full well that their client was well on his way himself to being a convicted felon. A grand jury was already hearing the evidence of Rose's failure to report cash from card shows and winning tickets at racetracks.

If Rose continued to push his case against Giamatti, there was the possibility that he would be called on to testify and the danger that questioning could move into areas related to his criminality. Rose's lawyers obviously did not want him to have to answer those sorts of questions. Nor did they want him to have to invoke his Fifth Amendment rights against self-incrimination, a spectacle that would have hardly helped his case with the public.

"This was the best deal we could get," says Robert Stachler, the Cincinnati lawyer who argued Rose's case against baseball. "Believe me, we were not looking at a lot of options."

To Rose, what sealed the deal was that there was no official finding that he had wagered on baseball—even though he had been penalized exactly as if there had been such a finding.

Haggling over the wording of that part of the agreement was what held it up for most of the summer. Baseball would not accept a document to which Rose denied betting on baseball. Giamatti would not accept a "not guilty" plea.

The final wording—"Nothing in this agreement shall be

deemed either an admission or a denial by Peter Edward Rose . . ."—was the equivalent of a nolo contendere plea.

In Rose's mind, no admitted baseball bettor was ever going to be readmitted to baseball. Equally important, or perhaps more so, no baseball bettor was going to be voted into the Hall of Fame.

Back in Ueberroth's office in February, he had teased the baseball executives about the pictures of the immortals on the wall. Why wasn't Pete Rose up there?

Rose believed the wording of that one paragraph saved his spot on the wall, a theory that will be tested when he first becomes eligible for the Hall of Fame in 1992.

On the night that Rose agreed to accept the lifetime banishment, consented to walk away from baseball after twenty-six seasons, he left his wife and day-old baby and flew to Minneapolis to appear on the Cable Value Network's "Sporting Collections Show." Sitting beside the studio host, who wore a cheap-looking imitation Reds jersey, Rose hawked autographed balls for $39, bats for $229, and jerseys for $399.

The next morning, he and Giamatti held back-to-back press conferences. Giamatti, at the New York Hilton, went first. He wore the look of a winner, and some found him much too smug.

"The matter of Mr. Rose is now closed," Giamatti intoned. "It will be debated and discussed. Let no one think it did not hurt baseball. That hurt will pass, however, as the great glory of the game asserts itself and a resilient institution goes forward. Let it also be clear that no individual is superior to the game."

Giamatti said that he had imposed baseball's ultimate penalty on Rose because he believed that Rose had committed its ultimate crime—wagering on the games of his own team. Rose's decision to bypass a hearing, he said, had forced him to come to a personal decision—apart from the neutral wording of the agreement—on whether Rose had bet on baseball.

"In the absence of a hearing and therefore in the absence of any evidence to the contrary, I am confronted by the factual record of the Dowd Report, and on the basis of that, yes, I have concluded that he bet on baseball," he said in response to a question.

And on the Reds?

"Yes."

Having come to that decision, he said, the rules of baseball required that he impose the lifetime ban. "This whole episode," Giamatti said, "is about whether you live by rules or not."

August 24 was a soupy, funereal day in Cincinnati. Gray. The news on Pete Rose had broken the night before. Spread across the top of the morning *Cincinnati Enquirer* was a one-word headline in three-inch-high red type. "SUSPENDED." A smaller headline explained: "Cornered Rose Strikes a Deal."

As Giamatti closed out his New York press conference, Rose began his in an undersized room on the lower level of Riverfront Stadium.

Standing at the podium, Pete Rose looked as he always did when he wore a business suit—like an imposter. Flecks of gray showed in his porcupine-quill hair. He was forty-eight years old, just three years and ten days younger than Giamatti.

Thirty years earlier he had walked into professional baseball, announcing, "Hey, mister, I'm Pete Rose." Now he looked beaten, sapped of his bluster.

He said he still loved the game. He used his famous love for the game as a defense—an alibi.

How could anyone believe he would break baseball's ultimate rule? Even though he bet on just about everything else, Pete Rose said he did not wager on baseball, because "I have too much love and respect for the game."

Through a tunnel leading to the field, not a hundred steps from where Rose stood, was home plate, where just four years earlier he had uncoiled from his left-handed crouch and slapped the line drive that put him past Cobb.

Base knock number 4,192.

The pinnacle.

Pee-Wee from Anderson Ferry. Too small. Too slow. More hits than Cobb, Aaron, Musial, Speaker.

On this dark morning, nothing above Riverfront Stadium's upper deck was visible. Not Harry Francis Rose, not Cobb, not Kenesaw Mountain Landis. A hard rain pounded the plastic tarpaulin that covered home plate.

The only vision was an unfathomable one: Pete Rose without baseball. A boy without his game. Charlie Hustle at home, an old man and his young family.

Afterword

Banished from baseball, facing federal criminal charges, his life a shambles, Pete Rose hired a publicist before he hired a psychiatrist. His new mission was to gain the sympathy and support of the American public—and the votes of the baseball writers who cast Hall of Fame ballots.

This repackaged Pete Rose was a better husband, a more caring father, a charity-minded citizen. Newspaper stories said that he awoke early each morning to pour cereal and milk for five-year-old Tyler before driving him to La Petite Preschool in Plant City, Florida. A magazine photographer snapped a picture of him holding his new baby, Cara, in his lap while also clutching one of her dolls, which she was still too young to take much of an interest in. He posed for a photo with a March of Dimes poster child. Publicist Barbara Pinzka said she was seeking to line up more charity involvement for her client, who previously had excelled only at raising money for himself.

On November 8, 1989, Rose admitted publicly for the first time to being a compulsive gambler. The forum he chose was the *Donahue* show, in a appearance intended to promote his book (which did not contain this revelation). The show opened with Phil Donahue reading a statement from Rose: "After I was suspended from baseball on August 24, I decided to see a psychiatrist because of the many accusations made in recent months that I have a gambling problem," it said. "Since then, I have come to learn and accept the fact that I do have a problem related to gambling—what my doctor, James Randolph Hillard of the University of Cincinnati Medical School, calls a gambling disorder—and I am getting help."

The statement went on to say that Rose had not recognized his problem sooner because he had been so unlike the average compulsive gambler. (Rose still could not let go of the notion that he was utterly unique.) "If you know me, you know I'm not typical about anything I do," the statement said. In a letter released the same day by Dr. Hillard, through Pinzka, Rose's psychiatrist said: "Pete has not been a typical baseball player and he has not been a typical problem gambler either."

This was part of a new Pete Rose myth, closely related to the old one: Yes, he was a compulsive gambler, one of millions of Americans, celebrities as well as just plain folks, who had owned up to an addiction. But he still wasn't run-of-the-mill. Charlie Hustle could never be that. Among compulsive gamblers, he was one of a kind, just as he had been as a ballplayer.

As a celebrity delivering a personal confession, Rose had hit the daytime-television equivalent of a grand slam. When Donahue finished reading his statement, Rose bounded down the aisle from the back of the studio and toward the stage, acknowledging a standing ovation with a smile and a half-wave. But one of the first questions from this generally sympathetic audience riled Rose— so much so that it melted his new wrapping.

The question came from a young woman who wondered how he could have exercised the self-control not to wager on major-league baseball games. Wouldn't a normal compulsive gambler have given in to the temptation to bet on what he knew best? "I have a problem with that," she said, meaning she found Rose's denial hard to believe.

"She has a problem with that," Donahue repeated.

Rose leered at the young woman. "We'll take care of that problem after the show, honey," he responded.

Donahue cut for a commercial.

Barbara Pinzka winced.

Exiled from baseball, Pete Rose vacillated between contrition and bitterness, acceptance and defiance. Some of the essential lessons of his downfall still seemed to elude him.

For instance, he continued to blame others for his problems, referring at one point to the members of his former entourage as "so-called friends [who] didn't care about my gambling or me." Given his shoddy treatment of them, why *would* any of his associates have cared about him? The remarkable thing was that some of them did.

Rose also seemed unwilling to accept that his troubles had hurt other people. In the statements he put out through Pinzka, he apologized all around—to his wife, his children, the baseball fans of America, the Reds, the city of Cincinnati, the game itself. He said he knew he had sullied an entire baseball season, caused pain, let people down.

But when he spoke for himself and not through his publicist, he protested that he had been the only one hurt. "I made mistakes and I'm very sorry for them," Rose was quoted by Peter Pascarelli of *The National* on February 21, 1990. "But I'm paying for those mistakes every day. Hell, I lost a $750,000-a-year job. I'm the one that is the target for all these lies. But there are too many guys who are either writers or criminals with something to gain who won't leave me alone. And sometimes I can't understand that."

In an interview published in *USA Weekend* on April 6, 1990, Rose said, "I was waiting for it to come out of the [1989] World Series that I caused the earthquake. No one got hurt but me. Let me alone."

In the same article, Rose attacked the Dowd Report and questioned the evenhandedness of baseball's probe. He complained that just about everyone quoted in the Dowd Report had something unkind or damaging to say about him. Why hadn't they talked to more people who liked him, who would have said nice things about him?

That wasn't the point, of course. The commissioner's office did not spend upwards of $1 million to hire a former federal prosecutor, and a couple dozen other lawyers and investigators, in order to assemble a testimonial to Pete Rose. And once the investigation began, all of Rose's records and accomplishments could not protect him against the consequences of his gambling. Rose couldn't accept that. In his mind, he was still a special case and he deserved special treatment.

"Here's a guy who, for two and a half decades, loved the game, breathed the game and sold baseball," he told *USA Weekend*. "And I got the most lopsided investigation ever."

On April 20, 1990, Pete Rose pleaded guilty to two felony charges of concealing income on federal tax returns in 1985 and 1987. The next day, as quoted in newspapers across the nation, Rose sounded genuinely contrite. "I am truly sorry for what has happened, and not just because I have had to leave baseball, the sport I love, and face still more punishment because of my mistakes," he said. "My family and friends have suffered as well, and I regret the pain I have caused them. I mean that from the bottom of my heart. I also realize that millions of baseball fans may have been disappointed because I didn't live up to the respect and admiration they gave me during my career. I am not a bad person, but I did some bad things.

"I just hope that you will understand that I have a sickness. I first realized last October that I had a gambling problem and made that public in November. I have been able to stop gambling since then—but I will need help for the rest of my life."

Although widely quoted, Rose himself actually had nothing to say that day. His quotes were taken from a photocopied sheet handed to reporters by Pinzka as her client hustled out of the courtroom to a waiting car.

Rose spent most of his first year away from baseball at his winter home in Plant City, in large part because it served his new obsession, golf, which he had taken up after his banishment from baseball. Rose approached golf with his customary single-mindedness; he played nearly every day, usually starting off at the practice tee, where he routinely hit six hundred balls before walking onto the course.

He could play year-round at the Walden Lake Polo and Country Club, where he qualified for membership because he owned a house in the adjacent community. In Cincinnati, even in good weather, he had to wait for invitations to play. According to Pinzka, Rose had experienced a chilly reception at his hometown country clubs. Polite society in the Queen City, which adopted Rose when he was riding high, now had cooled toward him. "Pete's not been able to get into any of the country clubs here," Pinzka said. "Nobody's told him no, but nobody has invited him to join, either. That's one of the reasons he stayed in Florida. It's easier for him to play down there."

The extended golf holiday presented one problem: Rose's psychiatrist was back in Cincinnati. In the first six months of his therapy, Rose said he saw Dr. Hillard, the chairman of the psychiatry department at the University of Cincinnati Medical School, twelve to fifteen times. Most of the sessions—"the vast majority," Pinzka says—took place at Hillard's office in Cincinnati, but some occurred over the telephone.

Rose claimed never to think about gambling unless he was asked about it, and he felt secure enough about his recovery that he contemplated going to the Kentucky Derby in May 1990. He finally decided against it for reasons unrelated to his gambling addiction. "I don't want to tick anybody off in the commissioner's office by going to the Derby," he told *USA Weekend*.

Comments like those raised eyebrows among people involved in treating compulsive gamblers. "That shows you where he's at," said Arnold Wexler, the executive director of the New Jersey Council on Compulsive Gambling. "Nobody, less than a year after seeking help, is strong enough to go to the track. I wouldn't recommend that any recovering compulsive gambler *ever* go to the track. When you've got the disease, you've got to be clean as a whistle. You can't buy a lottery ticket. You can't flip a coin. I think Pete Rose understands he has a problem, but I don't think he understands how to deal with it."

Wexler, himself a onetime compulsive gambler, thinks Rose should join Gamblers Anonymous or some other self-help group. "It's good to have a therapist, but you also need the support of people who have been through this. That's how you arrest this disease. I've never seen it happen any other way. Never. If he's an exception, he'll be the first I've seen."

A psychiatrist I interviewed questioned the usefulness of Rose's telephone sessions. "If the relationship between the doctor and patient is well established, then it can be maintained, to some extent, by phone," he said. "It's like a love affair. You can keep one going by phone, but it's tough to get one started."

Barbara Pinzka brushes off criticism about Rose's therapy as sour grapes emanating from clinics that didn't get his business. "We've gotten people calling us from the high-dollar clinics, trying to get Pete to check into there, so they can brag about having him like the Betty Ford center does about the people who go there. They're unhappy because he hasn't done what they wanted him to do."

The true measure of Rose's therapy will be if he stops gambling. As late as June 1990, there were rumblings in Cincinnati that he had not—that he continued to bet on horses and professional sporting events through associates who placed the wagers for him.

"I've had people tell me that he's still having bets placed for him at the track," one of the investigators involved in the federal criminal probe of Rose told me. "I tend to believe it. From everything I learned about Pete, I find it hard to believe the gambling does not persist."

Pinzka said she heard the rumors and took them seriously enough that she asked Rose if he was still gambling. "I confronted him, and he denied it," she said. "I believe him, because I think he understands what gambling has done to his life, and he knows a return to gambling would destroy what little he has left."

A large part of what Pete Rose has left is the hope of being elected to the Baseball Hall of Fame. If Rose is to make it, voters will have to shed the notion that there is some relationship between being a good person and being a good ballplayer. Rose's former Phillies teammate, the loquacious Larry Christenson, chuckles when he considers whether Rose belongs in the Hall of Fame.

"Look at all those guys in Cooperstown," he says. "How many drugs do you think some of them have done? Or drinks they've had? Or how many women have they knocked up? How many abortions have they caused? How many wives have they had? How many of their kids have they beaten up? How many kids have they molested?

"Everybody's got their own thing. Pete's got his thing, I've got mine, and all these people who have the votes in their hands have their thing, too. They're not preachers. And by the way, some of the preachers ain't so great either."

The Hall of Fame is aware of no convicted felons among its 206 honorees. Pete Rose would be the first. Nor is it aware of any saints.

Ty Cobb was among the first group of five players to be selected for the Hall of Fame in 1936, along with Babe Ruth, Honus Wagner, Christy Mathewson, and Walter Johnson. He was elected even though voters were well aware of his beating of a handicapped fan, his various other brushes with the law for his violent eruptions, and his involvement in the gambling scandal with Tris Speaker and Joe Wood. Apparently, most voters only considered Cobb the player when casting their ballots: Cobb was named on 222 of the 226 ballots, giving him the most votes among that first group of inductees, even more than Ruth.

In more recent years, however, the voters (members of the Baseball Writers Association of America with ten years' experience covering the game) have put candidates to a test of morality and citizenship.

Leo Durocher, sixth among managers in career wins, has been denied his place in the Hall of Fame because of a 1947 suspension for associating with known gamblers. Pitcher Ferguson Jenkins, with 284 career wins and six straight seasons of 20 or more victories at Wrigley Field, has so far been kept out, almost certainly because of a 1980 drug arrest for possessing small amounts of cocaine, hashish, and marijuana. Juan Marichal, with 101 more wins than losses (243–142) and a career earned run average of 2.89, had first-ballot credentials, but he was made to wait two years before being elected; his blemish was an ugly incident in which he attacked Dodgers catcher Johnny Roseboro with a bat during the course of a game.

The writers who take off-field considerations into account find justification in Paragraph 5 of the Rules of Voting, which reads: "Voting shall be based upon the player's record, playing ability, integrity, sportsmanship, character, contribution to the team or teams on which the player played and not on what he may have done otherwise in baseball."

The provision is ambiguous, and there is no general agreement on how or even if it should be applied. What if Jenkins had been convicted of drunken driving, a more palatable offense to many of the older writers? Would he have been voted in earlier? Are overwhelming playing credentials, as Rose has, a counterbalance to problems in the area of integrity, sportsmanship, or character? Is there some sort of equation: the better the player, the greater the character flaws overlooked? Should the barring of Durocher be a precedent in considering Rose? Must Durocher, who was a lesser violator of baseball's gambling rules, be voted in before Rose?

One of Pete Rose's ambitions had been to be the first unanimous selection to the Hall of Fame, a possibility before his gambling scandal but not now. Rose has since lowered his ambitions and just wants to be voted in, by however slim a margin. He even made a plea for admission to the Hall of Fame on the day he submitted his guilty plea in federal court on tax charges.

"I'm asked a lot about the Hall of Fame," his written statement said. "There's no question that my baseball records earned me a place but I understand that the Hall of Fame means more than 4,256 hits. In a year and a half, the baseball writers will have to make the decision about whether or not I'm worthy of the Hall and I hope they'll understand that the mistakes I made off the field were caused by my gambling disorder. In November 1991, I hope they'll see that I came clean about my problem, got help and stayed out of trouble. "

I asked nearly everyone I interviewed for this book what had happened to Pete Rose. What caused him to self-destruct?

"My own theory is Pete really needed a friend," John Dowd answered. "A friend is someone who grabs you by the collar and tells it to you straight."

Pete Rose's mother, LaVerne Noeth, thought that what her son needed most was his father, who had died in 1970. "None of this would have happened if Big Pete was still alive," she said.

A surprising number of people commented that the real turning point in Rose's life was when he split with his first wife, a decade after his father's death. "Karolyn wasn't afraid of Pete," explained Danny Gumz, owner of the Gay 90s restaurant. "Maybe Pete didn't always listen to her, but she'd tell him whatever it was she thought. She didn't hold back. After Karolyn, I don't know who could tell Pete anything."

Tommy Helms thought his old friend simply fell in with the wrong crowd. "Me and the coaches and the writers would go have a beer after games and talk baseball, but Pete never did like to come along," he said. "I wish now that we would have dragged him with us."

Dave Rose believed his brother got caught up in "the big-league life-style. He saw other guys getting away with things, drugs or whatever, so he thought that he could do the thing he enjoyed, gambling, and nobody would do anything. And then at the end he started hanging out with this crowd from the gym, and they weren't good people, and that's when it all fell apart."

None of the answers satisfied me because they implied that someone else could have saved Pete Rose—his father, his first wife, a good friend, his old baseball buddies. The sad fact is that no one could have helped him because he had a way of silencing those few friends who ever tried. The rule was, if you wanted to remain his friend, or part of his entourage of lackeys and gofers, you didn't question him. Anyone who persisted he pushed out of his life. If Harry Rose had lived and challenged too strongly his son's gambling or any other aspect of his life, I believe he would have received the same treatment.

What happened to Rose?

Tom House, the Texas Rangers pitching coach and psychology Ph.D., speaks of all professional athletes as being in a state of "terminal adolescence." Coddled in high school for excelling in sports, honored and enriched as adults for playing a children's game, waited on at home by their wives and at the ballpark by all manner of attendants, shielded from real-world problems and responsibilities—Rose was among many athletes who lived on an "allowance" from his financial advisers—they do not mature emotionally because they never have to.

Rose was an exaggerated example of this. He was raised by parents who made him an icon in his own home just for being born a boy, and therefore a ballplayer, and nothing else was ever expected of him except that he excel on the field of play.

He entered adulthood with one admirable value, his estimable work ethic toward his job: baseball. He gave his employer and the fans their money's worth.

Other than that, Pete Rose was utterly without values. He was not a loyal friend, a faithful husband, a loving father, a giving person. He had no regard for rules that others had to live by, and no regard for telling the truth.

Pete Rose did not gamble—or begin to gamble more heavily—because he lost any of the better influences in his life. He gambled because it was the only thing that interested him besides baseball and his own fame.

Rose continues to rail against the Dowd Report and major-league baseball's treatment of him because he truly believes he was treated unfairly. He wasn't. He was treated, for the first time, like an adult, which was so unfamiliar to him that he mistook it for unfairness.

It says a lot about Rose's skewed priorities that, with all his other problems, he still places such a high priority on gaining the votes of the four hundred baseball writers who cast Hall of Fame ballots. But even if Rose himself learns no lessons from his own downfall, the rest of us can.

As sports fans, we should grow up.

We should expect great athletes to be just as flawed as the rest of society. (To be realistic, we should probably expect them to be *more* flawed.)

We should honor and admire great athletes for what they do, not what they are. We really don't know what they are, do we?

Rose earned his banishment from major-league baseball by flagrantly violating its rules against gambling.

And he earned his place in baseball's Hall of Fame.

What Pete Rose leaves to the game he loved, his legacy, is not romance but a disquieting reality: A man can belong both in the Hall of Fame and in federal prison.

Pete Rose, habitually the first player at the ballpark, showed up for his sentencing fifteen minutes early. He took a seat in the front of the courtroom at the table reserved for criminal defendants and passed the time before the judge came in looking straight down at that table. Not once did he look back into the gallery, which was filled to capacity with two hundred reporters. Before he entered, the reporters were talking among themselves; now they sat silently, staring at Rose as he stared down at the table.

Rose's three lawyers, Roger Makley, Reuven Katz, and Robert Pitcairn, sat with him in the front of the high-ceilinged turn-of-the-century courtroom. His wife, Carol, was one row behind them.

Rose has said that one reason he likes making so much money is that he can outfit his wife in leather, and, he has noted, she looks real good in leather. In the courtroom, Carol wore a black suit, conservatively cut. It was cotton, not leather, and the hem of the skirt came to just above her knee. She looked as if she could have been attending her husband's funeral.

Two other people accompanied Rose to court. One was his publicist, Barbara Pinzka. The other was Jeff Ruby, the Cincinnati restaurant owner who credited Rose with having helped pull him out of a deep depression in 1987. Ruby told me some months earlier that Rose had been a "true friend" to him, which was the only time during a year of research that I heard anyone praise Rose's qualities as a friend.

I saw no other friends of Rose's in the courtroom—no former teammates, no one connected with the Reds, none of his old buddies from Cincinnati's West Side.

At the government's table in the front of the courtroom sat William Hunt, the assistant U.S. attorney who put together the

case against Rose and would have prosecuted him if it had come
to trial. Hunt is a Cincinnati native and a longtime Reds season
ticket holder, and part of him still mourns for Pete Rose the
ballplayer. The day before the sentencing Hunt had talked of
wearing his "4,192" T-shirt under his suit—the shirt commem-
orating Rose's record-breaking hit—but he didn't go through with
it. Rose's image on the T-shirt might have shown through Hunt's
starched white shirt, which wouldn't have looked lawyerly.

At precisely 10:00 A.M., the court crier called out, "All rise!
God save the United States of America and this honorable court!"
and U.S. District Court judge S. Arthur Spiegel, square-jawed with
thinning gray hair and wire-rimmed glasses, took his seat on the
bench. Spiegel is by all accounts a straight arrow with a passion
for fairness: equal justice for all, rich or poor, famous or not.

The judge began by asking Rose, "Do you wish to make any
statement on your own behalf in mitigation of punishment?"
Rose did. He spoke for ninety seconds, without notes. Twice his
voice cracked, and it seemed that he might break down and cry.
This was his entire statement:

> Your honor, I would like to say that I am very sorry. I am very
> shameful to be here today in front of you.
> I think I'm perceived as a very aggressive, arrogant type of
> individual, but I want people to know that I do have emotion, I
> do have feelings, and I can hurt like everybody else, and I hope
> no one has to go through what I went through the last year and
> a half. I lost my dignity. I lost my self-respect. I lost a lot of dear
> fans and almost lost some very dear friends.
> I have to take this opportunity to thank my wife for giving me
> so much moral support during this ordeal. It had to be tough on
> her when your five-year-old son comes home from school and
> tells her that his daddy is a jailbird.
> I really have no excuses because it's all my fault. All I can say
> is, I hope somewhere, somehow in the future I'm going to try to
> make it up to everybody that I disappointed and let down. Thank
> you very much.

A sentencing is the final act of a real-life tragedy, the end result
of a human failure. I've never been to one that did not make me
profoundly sad. I don't grieve for the length of the sentence, not
even always for the defendant, but for the whole chain of events
that leads to the terrible moment when one human being decrees

that another must be removed from society and locked away. At the sentencing, it all seems so preventable.

For all those years, Pete Rose had angrily brushed off even the mildest suggestions or criticisms. He replaced his friends with sycophants and yes-men. Now, a stranger held ultimate power over him.

Judge Spiegel's remarks were brief and eloquent. "We must recognize that there are two people here," he said before imposing his sentence: "Pete Rose, the living legend, the all-time hit leader, and the idol of millions; and Pete Rose, the individual, who appears today convicted of two counts of cheating on his taxes.

"Today, we are *not* dealing with the legend. History and the tincture of time will decide his place among the all-time greats of baseball. With regard to Pete Rose, the individual, he has broken the law, admitted his guilt, and stands ready to pay the penalty. Under our system of law and sense of fairness, when he has completed his sentence, he will have paid his debt to society and should be accepted by society as rehabilitated. Only time will tell whether he is to be restored to his position of honor for his accomplishments on the ballfields of America."

Spiegel gave Rose five months in a federal minimum-security prison, to be followed by three months in a halfway house or community treatment center. The sentence fell squarely within the federal sentencing guidelines for offenses of Rose's level.

Rose will serve the first five months in the minimum-security prison at Marion, Illinois. The town happens to be the birthplace of Ray Fosse, the catcher whom Rose steamrollered in the 1970 All-Star Game. The Ray Fosse Softball Field is about a mile from the federal prison. (The prison has its own softball field, as well as tennis and racquetball courts, and patio furniture with sun umbrellas.)

In prison, Rose, who so cherished playing by his own rules, will play by someone else's. He will not be able to sleep in his own bed with his wife, be a father to his two young children or his older ones, eat food of his own choosing, play golf, or pick out his own clothes.

On hot days, he will dress in prison-issue khaki shorts and khaki shirt; on cooler days, in olive-green pants and shirt. He will be issued an eight-hour-a-day job, mowing grass or doing laundry or cooking food. He'll have a roommate. As many as seven times a day, his presence will be noted by guards conducting a count to make sure that no one has skipped from the facility, which has no wall or fence.

One thing Rose will not be without is admirers, which should be a comfort to him. "A lot of the guys here are from Ohio and Indiana," Marion inmate Howard Jungels told me over the telephone a few days before Rose's arrival. "They say their lifelong dream was to meet Pete Rose and shake his hand, but they're sorry it'll be under these circumstances."

I can imagine Pete Rose busying himself with his prison job, haunting the weight room and the racquetball court in his off-hours, and finding no time for introspection. I can imagine him enjoying his status as a celebrity inmate and greedily taking whatever special privileges come with it. I can imagine him, with his remarkable ability to close himself off from unpleasant thoughts and experiences, emerging from prison unchanged.

I sense that Judge Spiegel has allowed for that same possibility, and that is why he tacked on to Rose's sentence one thousand hours of community service—twenty hours a week for one year—to be performed at five Cincinnati elementary schools and a boys' club. All are in impoverished neighborhoods where, even in Cincinnati, Pete Rose is no particular hero.

In imposing this part of the sentence, Spiegel said, "The sentence will also require Mr. Rose to return to his roots in the inner city during his supervised release in order to help children there make something of themselves and to encourage them to work to succeed in their goals with the same determination and dedication that he did in his own life."

If the community service is to have any effect on Rose—and I think he stands to benefit from it more than the children do—he'll have to return to something more than his geographic roots. He grew up without money, but after he got rich he adopted an attitude of utter disdain for people who weren't.

"That person doesn't matter," Rose would often say of someone he thought was hassling him. "He don't have no brains and he don't have no money." In his deposition to John Dowd, Rose said he preferred the company of people with money. It didn't matter to Rose how they made it, which is why he didn't mind hanging out with drug dealers.

I asked Charles Anderson, the plant manager at one of the schools designated by Spiegel, what Rose can do to help.

"Just come here and be a person," Anderson said.

That may be more difficult for Pete Rose than being in jail.

The judge gave Pete Rose three weeks to report to prison. The next day he said he didn't need it. He wanted to go as soon as possible. Get it over with. Move on. He is Charlie Hustle to the end, charging off to do his time.

Index